WORKING WITH 'DENIED' CHILD ABUSE: THE RESOLUTIONS APPROACH

WORKING WITH 'DENIED' CHILD ABUSE: THE RESOLUTIONS APPROACH

Andrew Turnell and Susie Essex

Open University Press

Open University Press
McGraw-Hill Education
McGraw-Hill House
Shoppenhangers Road
Maidenhead
Berkshire
England
SL6 2QL

email: enquiries@openup.co.uk
world wide web: www.openup.co.uk

and
Two Penn Plaza,
New York, NY 10121-2289, USA

A catalogue record of this book is available from the British Library.
ISBN-10: 0335 216 560 (pb) 0335 216 579 (hb)
ISBN-13: 978 0335 216 567 (pb) 978 0335 216 574 (hb)

Library of Congress Cataloging-in-Publication Data
CIP data applied for

Typeset by BookEns Ltd, Royston, Herts

Printed and bound by CPI Group (UK) Ltd, Croydon, CR0 4YY

This book is dedicated to Andrew's mentor,
M.C. (Mary Caroline) Richards, and
Susie's children, Sam, Ned and Seren,
and her mother, Shelia Alice Essex.

CONTENTS

ACKNOWLEDGEMENTS

The journey of creating the resolutions approach to working with situations of serious 'denied' child abuse has involved many people over 15 years. At the outset, the model was created by Susie and her colleagues Colin Luger and John Gumbleton. Colin and John continue to use the approach in their own practice and have undertaken significant research into the efficacy of the model. Colleagues George Walker, Harry Proctor, Jan White, Margaret Hiles, Andy Lusk, Rudi Dallos, Steve Edwards, Kay Benham and Alison Hay have collaborated with us and contributed important ideas and inspiration along the way. Susie wants to thank Jack and Mel for their support, Robert Meller for his love and encouragement, and in particular Sam, Ned and Seren for keeping her laughing as she has been practising, teaching and writing this work.

Andrew, with Susie's English colleagues, wants to honour the fact that it has been Susie's willingness to try something different that has been the energizing force behind the creation of the resolutions model. As Susie has observed, creating and practising this model has frequently led her to feel something like a flying squirrel, in that she regularly demonstrates the courage or perhaps madness (or both) to leap out into space while trusting she will land on her feet. For Andrew, it has been one of the greatest pleasures of his professional career to learn from Susie and then develop and write this model with her. Andrew wants also to thank his partner Sonja Parker for her support and love throughout the challenges of writing this book and for reviewing the manuscript.

The resolutions ideas are illustrated throughout this book by practice applications undertaken by frontline child protection workers in three different countries. We want to thank English social services practitioners Sharon Elliot, Kath O'Leary and their supervisor Viv

Hogg; Swedish social workers Anna Svensson, Christine Witt and their team leader Ann Gardeström; and US child protection practitioners Cindy Finch, Sue Lohrbach, Rob Sawyer, Linda Billman and Donna Smyrk for their contributions to this work. The examples they have contributed have been altered to ensure anonymity and are published here with permission of the relevant organizations.

The light globe illustration in Chapter 3 was prepared by Kim Prendegaste. The children's drawings for the injured baby words and pictures document in Chapter 5 were provided by Daniel Glamorgan. The pictures for the family safety guidelines in Chapter 7 were drawn by Ruby Simms-Cumbers, and the illustrations for the final safety plan in Chapter 9 were contributed by Keayn deVries-Turnell. We thank these children for their artwork, which provides a visual reminder within the text that, at the end of the day, this work is all about the children.

Chapter **One**

IMAGINING 'DENIAL' DIFFERENTLY

The world will change when we can imagine it differently, and, like artists, do the work of creating new social forms.

M.C. Richards

Anatomy of a 'denial' dispute

Imagine you are Jasmina, a social worker on a long-term social services team, and you are presently working with a family comprising Jack, a 42-year-old real estate agent, Janice, a 39-year-old part-time child care assistant, and their daughter Rosemary, who is currently 17 and a half. Rosemary also has an 8-month-old baby, Robert. (This scenario is not an actual case, but rather has been created as a typical composite example of a 'denial' case based on the authors' experience of a number of similar cases.)

This case first came to social services' attention four years ago, when Rosemary was 13 years old. Rosemary's teacher and deputy-principal had become increasingly concerned about their student, since she was often very withdrawn and achieving poor grades relative to her obvious intelligence. The teacher and deputy-principal called a meeting with Jack and Janice to discuss their concerns. As a result of this meeting, it was agreed that Janice would work to help Rosemary with her homework and the school nurse would meet regularly with Rosemary to try and help draw her out of herself.

Thus Rosemary began to see Trisha, the school nurse, on a weekly basis. Over the next two months, they built what Trisha felt to be a good relationship, and Trisha would often say to other school staff that Rosemary was a 'quiet and sad girl'. During this period, Trisha came to wonder whether Rosemary might have been sexually abused. Trisha's suspicions had first crystallized during an interview with Rosemary's best friend, Sue. Meeting with Sue about a different matter entirely, Sue and Trisha had talked about the two girls being friends and what they did together. During this conversation, Sue had commented that she didn't like going to Rosemary's home because she thought Jack was a 'dirty old man'.

Trisha's suspicions heightened when she put Sue's comment together with her own observation that Rosemary seemed to become tense whenever the nurse tried to get Rosemary to talk about her father. Following this, Trisha thought she would approach the matter from a different direction, and in their next meeting she spent almost an entire session asking Rosemary to tell her about things she enjoyed in her life. It took a little while to get started, but to Trisha's surprise Rosemary first began to describe things she liked at school. Talking about her science classes, Rosemary explained that she really liked her teacher in this subject. She also stated that she liked coming to school because that was where she spent most time with Sue, her closest and pretty much only friend. Trisha then moved the conversation on to Rosemary's life at home and the 13-year-old described things she enjoyed doing with her mother and with several of her mother's cousins. When Trisha asked Rosemary what she liked about her father and what she liked doing with her father, Rosemary again seemed to become tense and was unable to give any answer.

After this session, Trisha decided that she wanted to ask Rosemary directly about her concerns. It took two more sessions before Trisha found the courage, the right words and the right time to ask Rosemary, but when she did, Rosemary's response was something the nurse will always remember. Following the inquiry, Rosemary's eyes widened and for what seemed like an interminable moment, the nurse and the teenager's eyes held each other. Trisha felt she saw fear written all over Rosemary's face. Finally, Rosemary rose from her seat, 'looking white as a ghost' (as Trisha was later to tell social services) and, without saying a word, she rushed out of the room.

Immediately after this session, Trisha contacted the local social services office. In the resultant interview between Rosemary and an investigative social services social worker, at which Trisha was also present, Rosemary disclosed that her father had been sexually abusing her for the past three years. At this point – as required by joint investigative protocols – the police became involved in the matter. A second interview was arranged for later that day involving Rosemary, the investigative social worker, and a policewoman who specialized in interviewing sexually abused children, with Trisha there to support

Rosemary. This interview proceeded very slowly and carefully, with the social worker and police officer focusing on obtaining evidence on which to lay charges against Jack.

That evening, Rosemary's parents were both interviewed in their home. Jack aggressively denied the allegations, repeatedly complaining: 'that school nurse has put these crazy ideas into Rosemary's head'. Janice was interviewed and had very little to say. Appearing very confused, Janice constantly said she 'couldn't believe that my Jack could do such a thing'. Rosemary was placed in temporary foster care that evening.

The following day, the investigative social worker and a colleague returned to speak further with Jack and Janice. Jack was even more vehement in refuting the allegations at this meeting. He also angrily refused to move out of the home in response to the social services worker's suggestion this would enable Rosemary to return home. Speaking to Janice again on her own, the social workers tried to persuade Janice to leave Jack. Janice became very distressed at this suggestion, saying that she was a Christian and it was against her faith to do such a thing. As a consequence of this, the investigative social worker made application for, and gained, an immediate court-ratified care order for Rosemary. Thus Rosemary was found a long-term foster placement within the week and a social worker named Cheryl was appointed as the ongoing case manager. Based on Rosemary's statements given during the interviews, the police laid charges against Jack.

Not surprisingly, Rosemary was often very upset and anxious. She often wanted to talk about whether she had done the right thing and what would happen to herself and her parents. Cheryl, Trisha and the foster parents worked very hard to support Rosemary. Rosemary and Janice had contact once a week. Their time together was supervised, since Cheryl and her supervisor were concerned Janice might try and influence Rosemary to retract her allegations. Rosemary's foster mother reported to Cheryl that Rosemary would not eat her dinner after the Friday afternoon contact with Janice and would then usually cry herself to sleep and often would not eat anything for most of the next day. Cheryl arranged for Rosemary to see a specialist psychologist and to join a group for young women who had been sexually abused.

After eight months and shortly before the case was to come to trial, the foster parents privately asked Cheryl whether Rosemary could be moved since they felt they were unable to deal with Rosemary's moods any longer. They also believed Rosemary was having a negative influence on their own children. Cheryl persuaded the foster parents to keep Rosemary with them until the court case was over. In the subsequent court case, Jack maintained his innocence. Rosemary gave her evidence to camera and, although there was argument about some of what she said – particularly relating to times and dates of specific allegations – the jury found Jack guilty. The judge sentenced Jack to five and half years' imprisonment – with good behaviour he would be released after three years.

Rosemary held herself together very well through the court hearing, with constant support from Trisha, Cheryl and the psychologist. However, Rosemary completely isolated herself at her foster home because one of the family's children had told her they were 'going to get rid of her'. Once the court case was over, Rosemary was moved into a group home, from which she very quickly started to run away, sometimes getting involved with a group of young teenagers who were involved in petty crime, drinking and drug use. On several occasions, Rosemary was brought back to the home from her mother's house. Cheryl worked as quickly as she could to organize a new foster home, but this new placement made little difference to Rosemary's behaviour. It was at this point that Jasmina became involved as the new case manager; the case was handed over to her when Cheryl changed jobs.

At the beginning of their first meeting, Rosemary confronted Jasmina with a list of complaints and demands. Rosemary said flatly that she wasn't going to any more sessions with the psychologist or to the group programme. Rosemary also complained about her new foster family, saying that she hated them and that she wasn't going to stay with them any longer. Following this, Rosemary quickly escalated her running away behaviour, often being found at her mother's home. When Rosemary was at her foster home, she was constantly rude and insulting to the family. Within a month the placement had broken down. Jasmina was worried about the situation and she and her supervisor met for almost two hours to discuss the situation and try to decide on the best home for Rosemary. The supervisor excluded the possibility of any further foster placements because they were unlikely to succeed and, since Rosemary refused point blank to go back to the group home, it was agreed – despite reservations – to ask first Rosemary and then Janice whether they wanted to live together again. Both Rosemary and Janice were excited at the prospect and in this way they were reunited.

At this point, Jasmina decided it was important to work very hard at building a relationship with Janice. This turned out to be easier than Jasmina was expecting, since Janice viewed Jasmina as 'the social worker who returned my Rosemary'. Jasmina was also able to provide Janice with practical and emotional support. With Jack in prison, Janice had struggled financially and Jasmina helped Janice think through her financial position. As a result of these discussions, Janice sold the family home and purchased a small unit into which she and Rosemary moved.

Up until Jasmina came on the scene, Janice had been largely unable to talk to anyone, other than Jack, about her problems. Janice's family – her sister and cousins – who previously were Janice's primary support, had stopped having any contact with her shortly after Rosemary's allegations. They were angry at Janice for siding with Jack. Janice continued her church attendance and participation, but was ashamed to talk about her problems there, in part because she knew other parishioners were already gossiping about her. So once Jasmina began making home visits, Janice would talk for hours at a time about how distressing and confusing the whole experience was for her. Jasmina tried in many ways to convince Janice that Jack had abused Rosemary; however, Janice would never say she believed her daughter. On one occasion, Jasmina was talking to Janice about how important it was for girls who had been abused to be believed by their mothers. Jasmina thought she might be on the verge of making a breakthrough, but was shocked when Janice said 'Whatever happened, I have to forgive him because I am Christian and whatever you say I won't leave my Jack. He's lost everything now – his job, his house, everything – and *he* has looked after me for years.' Rosemary told Jasmina that Jack was sending three or four letters to Janice each week and that he was ringing daily. Jasmina felt she did achieve some important progress, however, when she persuaded Janice to get Jack to ring while Rosemary was in school and also not to read the letters to, or in front of, her daughter.

During this period, things seemed to stabilize somewhat. Rosemary was attending school and starting to focus on her education again, even though there was a lot for her to catch up on. At times Rosemary would concentrate quite well on her studies, but her moods continued to fluctuate dramatically. Jasmina tried to encourage her to recommence therapy and to start attending the groups again. Rosemary would have nothing to do with these suggestions, saying that the psychologist and the groups hadn't helped her before and that she didn't want to talk about it anymore. However, had she been asked, Rosemary could have said that she rarely experienced a waking hour when she did not think about the abuse and the events that followed her disclosure. Rosemary did continue to have contact with, and receive counselling from, Trisha up until the nurse accepted a position at another school. At this point, Jasmina tried to spend extra time with Rosemary, focusing particularly on helping her with issues at the school, where she continued to have periodic problems at times when her mood deteriorated.

The next development occurred when Janice and Jasmina discovered that Rosemary had a boyfriend called Nick. Nick was part of the group of young people Rosemary had met when she was running away from the group home. Both Janice and Jasmina were dismayed to discover Rosemary had still been spending time with this group. Janice tried unsuccessfully to stop Rosemary seeing Nick. Before very long, that concern was subsumed by the revelation that Rosemary was pregnant. This sparked a whole range of issues for and between

Rosemary and Janice, including arguments in which Rosemary said she would have an abortion, and long discussions about the possibility of adoption. Rosemary vacillated between wanting the baby when she was in good spirits, and not wanting it at all when she was depressed. Janice's position never varied; once she had got over the initial shock at learning of the pregnancy, Janice had determinedly sought to persuade Rosemary to keep the baby, arguing that they could raise the child together.

Following the birth, Jasmina was supporting Rosemary with plans to adopt baby Robert, while Janice was strongly opposed to the idea. In this process, the relationship between Jasmina and Janice became increasingly strained, Janice being upset that Jasmina had, in her view, been wrong to encourage Rosemary to consider the options of either abortion or adoption. By the time Robert was 4 months old, Rosemary told Jasmina that she was keeping the baby, that she didn't want to talk about adoption anymore, and that she wanted Jasmina to leave her alone.

A little while after this, Jack's parole social worker contacted Jasmina with concerns he had arising from Jack's recent letters to Janice, which the prison were monitoring. In these letters, Jack had asked Janice to persuade Rosemary to 'tell the truth', to retract the allegations, and said that if she did this they could all get on with their lives. Jack had also suggested to Janice that the two of them should adopt Robert and then Rosemary could start her life afresh and so could they.

This information alarmed Jasmina and she made a time to talk with Janice and Rosemary about these issues. Their discussions at a home visit went very badly; Janice became angry with Jasmina and asked her to leave. Both Janice and Rosemary told Jasmina that they wanted Jack to come home and live with them when he got out in just over a year, and that neither of them wanted to see Jasmina again. Janice concluded the conversation, saying that she and Jack had been talking about rehiring their lawyer to get social services out of their lives.

In talking to her supervisor about these developments, Jasmina was hoping he would help her to find a new approach to the situation. Instead, Jasmina was shocked when her manager told her that she had spent too much time working with this particular family already and that she would need to close the case. The supervisor asserted that there was no point in keeping the case open since Jack wasn't due for release until after Rosemary's 18th birthday. Seeing how upset Jasmina was about this, the supervisor added that 'if we need to be worried about Robert's safety we can reopen it again next year. However, until then there's nothing more we can do.'

Jasmina did not see Rosemary or Janice for more than two months but neither had she closed the case, telling her supervisor that she'd been too busy to do the paperwork. When she thought about the case, Jasmina would always feel ashamed and guilty, believing that she had let Rosemary down. Jasmina's workmates had been sympathetic and listened to her talk about the case several times; one of her colleagues summed up the views of the others when he said, 'Don't worry about it anymore, it's not your fault. You've done your best, just think how much time you've spent on the case. Anyway, this happens all the time in these sorts of cases. It just shows you how well Jack groomed Rosemary and Janice.'

Despite this, Jasmina did not stop thinking about the case. In fact, on a number of nights she lost a lot of sleep going over how she had responded and trying to think if there was more she could have done. Jasmina was particularly disappointed because at one time she felt very pleased with the relationships she had built with both Janice and Rosemary. Jasmina started to wonder whether she was really suited to child protection work and began looking for other job opportunities in the newspaper.

Reflections

In Rosemary's case, as with most 'denial' cases, the usual professional imagination about progress revolves around Jack admitting that he has sexually abused his daughter. If Jack does not do this, then it is seen as essential that Janice openly accepts what Rosemary has said has happened. Given this way of imagining what needed to happen, the professionals quickly removed Rosemary from home when both Jack and Janice refuted the allegations. Rosemary was placed in a stable foster home and given very good support to give evidence that resulted in the conviction. Most probably the professionals involved assumed that once the conviction was achieved, Janice would relent, concede the abuse and separate from Jack. If this had been the case, Janice and Rosemary would probably have been assisted to reunite and to rebuild a life supporting each other. Unfortunately, this was not how things proceeded.

An old social work adage suggests that *blood is thicker than social services* and so it proved to be in this case. For all sorts of reasons and motivations, Janice and Rosemary reunited, focused in this instance on the new baby, Robert, and on their shared view that social services had made their individual and collective lives more problematic.

Jasmina's colleague is right when he says 'this happens all the time in these sorts of cases'. We have considerable experience of working with child protection systems in the UK, continental Europe, the USA, Canada, Japan, New Zealand and Australia. In working with 'denial' cases in these locations, we have found that some aspects of the situation vary between countries and jurisdictions, but usually only in the style and timing details of the professional response and services. We have found that essentially the same scenario of professional frustration and helplessness, and the entrenched nature of the professional-family dispute are re-enacted time and again with 'denial' cases in all these places. In our experience, child protection professionals in all these countries readily identify with the difficulties of dealing with the likes of Rosemary's case and resonate with Jasmina's sense of frustration.

Almost every experienced child protection professional can describe 'denial' cases they have been involved with that became stuck in a similar manner, where what we would call a 'denial dispute' results in a stand-off between the professionals and family. In a 'denial' dispute, the professionals try to convince family members – usually the parents – of the 'truth' they believe has happened. Counter to this, key family members, including the alleged perpetrator, argue that the professionals are wrong, or they simply resist conceding the professionals' position. Cases caught in a 'denial' dispute can often escalate to a point where enormous amounts of professional time, resources and energy are poured into them. Such situations are often the most difficult cases that child protection professionals work with, not because the abuse itself is necessarily the worst they might see, but because professionals become locked into an ongoing and escalating fight with the families. These sorts of cases often also evolve into protracted legal struggles, involving not only social services but also many other professionals.

The logic of the professional side of the dispute is based on the foundational assumption of Western psychology, that an individual who is seen to be responsible for a problem must admit responsibility, and gain insight into their problematic behaviour, as the means by which change can occur. Our view, which we will extrapolate more fully throughout this book, is that this view of change constricts the professional imagination for responding to 'denial' cases, and that this traditional and individualized way of thinking contributes significantly to these cases becoming more problematic. From our perspective, this usual way of thinking means professionals become over-organized by their framing of the problem and their framing of the nature of denial. This usual way of thinking means that admission becomes the only portal by which safety can be achieved, and when the parents maintain a position of 'denial' the professional imagination about what to do becomes exhausted.

Imagining the problem and its resolution differently

This book will describe a radically different approach for responding to the problem of 'denial', and is based on the developmental work undertaken by Susie Essex, John Gumbleton and Colin Luger. In 1990,

Susie, John and Colin found themselves working together at a large children's charity in Bristol, England, where they began to develop the resolutions family therapy model for responding to situations of 'denied' child abuse (see Essex, Gumbleton and Luger 1996; 1999; Essex, Gumbleton, Luger and Lusk 1997; Essex and Gumbleton 1999; Gumbleton and Luger 1999).

The resolutions approach came about because all three had worked, in different contexts, with situations of child abuse since the late 1970s. Susie, John and Colin all had experiences, particularly involving situations in which infants had suffered serious injuries and in sexual abuse cases, where they found themselves caught in the middle of 'denial' disputes of the sort facing Jasmina. Susie, John and Colin became increasingly dissatisfied and disturbed with their professional efforts to help children in these situations. Their experience of what professionals usually achieved is well captured in the words of a poem written by a 12-year-old girl, for the professionals who were 'supporting' her through the disclosure of sexual abuse. This poem was read by the then New South Wales Assistant Commissioner of Police, aired on the Australian Broadcasting Commission's Radio National 'AM Programme' in February 1994, following an inquiry into police, court and child protection responses to children who made disclosures of sexual abuse.

> I asked you to believe me,
> and you said you did.
> Then you took me to court,
> where lawyers put *me* on trial,
> like I was a liar.
> I can't help it,
> if I can't remember times or dates,
> or explain why I couldn't tell my Mum.
> Your questions confused me.
> My confusion got you suspicious.
> I asked you to put an end to the abuse.
> *You put an end to my family.*

The experience of this child is not isolated, rather it reflects the experiences of many children who have been caught up in the child protection system. This is confirmed by a growing body of research that describes the views of children involved with child protection services. (See, for example, Butler and Williamson 1994; Farmer and Owen 1995; Thoburn et al. 1995; Westcott 1995; Westcott and Davies 1996; Farmer and Pollock 1998; Gilligan 2000; Cashmore 2002.) In summary, children consistently tell researchers that they feel they are like pawns in an adult game that is going on above their heads, driven by professionals who rarely ask them what they want. This widely expressed view is a key reason that children and young people will rarely, of their own volition, contact social services when they feel their safety or well-being is threatened, but will more readily contact child-help telephone services where they can retain their anonymity (MacLeod 1996). Interestingly, Aldgate and Statham (2001) observe that when young people feel that out-of-home placement decisions have been imposed upon them, it is not uncommon that they will seek to undermine the placement in a manner similar to Rosemary's behaviour in her second foster care arrangement.

Research focusing on the child's experience of child protection services began to be published from the mid-1990s. However, Susie, John and Colin's earlier practice experience echoed the findings this research would later confirm: namely that professional responses were letting children down, particularly in situations where the abuse they alleged was denied. As the 12-year-old's poem suggests, professionals' actions frequently 'put an end to the family'. Not only does this outcome cut across children's commonly expressed desire to '*stop the abuse, not my family,*' but when the family is ended, a likely child abuse perpetrator typically moves off into the community to very probably join a new family and thereby place other children at risk.

Alternatively, the family engages in a long fight with the professionals until the professionals give up, usually because of the pressure of other work and the management view that scarce resources are being excessively and unproductively focused on the case in question. In such circumstances, the family will usually end up reuniting. In both scenarios, Susie, John and Colin felt dissatisfied. Whether the family separated or managed to reunite, it was easy to think that the likely perpetrator had become much wiser about how to avoid the professional system if they chose to abuse children in the future. In both scenarios, the Bristol team felt that children were left more vulnerable following professional intervention than when the professionals first became involved. Exploring similar territory, Bagley (1997: 272) frames such professional responses to child abuse as 'iatrogenic assessment and intervention', meaning that in such instances intervention is 'more harmful than the disease it purports to cure'.

In 1991, Susie, John and Colin found themselves working together on a case very similar to Rosemary's, and they began their efforts to create a different approach, based on a different framing of the problem and its resolution. Their thinking was particularly informed by social constructionist ideas that were increasingly influential in the family and brief therapy fields by the late 1980s. (See, for example, Watzlawick, Weakland and Fisch 1974; Procter 1981; Boscolo et al. 1987; Anderson and Goolishan 1988; Procter and Walker 1988; Aderman and Russell 1990; Jenkins 1990; Masson and O'Byrne 1990; de Shazer 1991; White and Epston1990; Checcin et al. 1992; Lipchik 1993; White et al. 1993; de Shazer and Berg 1995).

In a nutshell, Susie, John, Colin and their colleagues came to see 'denial' not simply as something inherent in the makeup of the alleged perpetrator, or even the family system, but as at least in part a construct that was interactionally created and reified by the professional system in its dealings with the family. Framing the problem differently allowed the Bristol team to create a model of practice that was organized around future safety rather than the past dispute. This model bypassed the 'denial' dispute, not by endeavouring to obtain a confession from the likely perpetrator, but rather seeking to enlist the family to create a future life that would demonstrate to all the concerned professionals that nothing like what was alleged (or convicted) could happen in the future. A focus on the seriousness of the allegations/convictions could be maintained because this approach always referenced future safety around the concerns held by the statutory authorities.

In bypassing the attempt to get the likely perpetrator to admit to the allegations, the resolutions approach challenges conventional professional thinking about how to respond to situations of child abuse. Susie, John and Colin were well aware that their approach was outside of mainstream thinking and were therefore careful to evaluate the outcomes of their approach. The Bristol team found that re-abuse rates of up to 7 per cent (depending on how the calculation is made) for families involved in the resolutions programme compared very favourably with re-abuse rates of between 16 and 43 per cent from other studies (Jones 1987; Department of Health 1995; Farmer and Owen 1995).

On the other side of the world in Perth, Australia, in a somewhat parallel process during the 1990s, Andrew Turnell was working with Steve Edwards and over 140 Western Australian child protection practitioners in creating the signs of safety approach to frontline practice (see Turnell and Edwards 1997 and 1999). This approach, like the resolutions model, also sees most child protection practice as excessively 'problem saturated' (White and Epston 1991). The signs of safety model proposes a relationship-grounded, strengths-based to statutory practice that maintains a rigorous focus on the seriousness of the problems/concerns, but is fundamentally organized around future safety. There is significant overlap between the orientation and aspirations of each approach; the main difference being that the signs of safety model is primarily designed for statutory practitioners, while the resolutions model was created as a treatment approach to respond to families after the statutory investigation and court processes had taken their course. In August 1996, Andrew met with Susie, John and Colin in Bristol and was able to observe (from behind a one-way glass screen) the Bristol team using the resolutions model with three different families. Andrew was immediately struck by the team's approach, most particularly because one case he observed was almost identical to a case he had been involved with the previous year in which he felt his professional endeavours had made things worse. Inspired by what he had seen, Andrew, with Steve Edwards, Kay Benham and later Alison Hay, formed their own family therapy team back in Perth to use the resolutions approach. The Perth team videotaped each session, often sending copies to Bristol, and consulted closely by phone and email with the Bristol team about their practice. By this process, an Australian incarnation of the resolutions model evolved. More than this, through Andrew's ongoing development of the signs of safety approach with colleagues and agencies in Australia, Japan, the USA, Sweden and the UK, the ways in which the ideas of the resolutions model might be applied to frontline statutory work were further explored.

This book

This book will lay out and explore the resolutions approach with two parallel foci. The first will be to present a comprehensive description of the entire family therapy treatment model as developed by the Bristol team. However, we are well aware that it is not possible to offer this complete treatment response in every case of 'denied' child abuse. Whilst it is possible to undertake the complete model in some cases, especially the most worrying, professional systems do not have sufficient time or resources to offer all aspects of the resolutions approach in every 'denial' case. Hence it is important for us to describe how different aspects and elements of the approach can, and have been, productively utilized in a more limited manner, in particular by frontline social services professionals. This then will be the second focus of the book. This second focus on the more general application of the resolutions approach will also enable us to explore the issue of 'denial' in less serious cases, for example in a situation in which a social services worker is of the view that a father who has several times physically abused his son has problems with his drinking while the father denies he has any such problem.

Throughout the book we will provide examples from frontline social services professionals who have made use of resolutions ideas and practices in their work. To highlight these examples, they will be presented in shaded boxes within the text. All of these examples, many of which identify the worker involved to honour them for their practice, have been altered to remove any identifying information about the original case and are presented here with the permission of the worker and their organization.

This book examines the treatment and social services foci throughout. Chapter 2 offers a summary of the entire treatment model to provide the reader with a full map of the territory, before diving into the particularities of the approach in subsequent chapters. Chapter 3 provides a detailed exploration of the thinking and practice principles that inform the resolutions approach. Chapters 4 through 9 will successively describe the various stages and elements of the resolutions approach and consider the use of the approach in relation to numerous composite, anonymous case examples. The final chapter offers some thoughts about the complexity inherent in such practice.

Chapter **Two**

AN OVERVIEW OF THE
RESOLUTIONS MODEL

This chapter is designed to provide a synopsis of the resolutions treatment model. An understanding of the whole picture should provide a context in which the reader can more fully understand each stage of the resolutions process that will be explored in more detail in the subsequent chapters. We will draw again on the case example of Rosemary, Janice and Jack and further illustrate each stage by briefly describing how we would envisage using the approach with this case.

The resolutions programme is designed to be offered to families who want to reunite where there is serious alleged or substantiated abuse and the parents or caregivers deny responsibility for that abuse. The programme provides the family with the opportunity to demonstrate to the statutory agency and court that it can take the concerns seriously by creating future safety commensurate with the allegations and/or convictions. The resolutions approach can be divided into seven stages and each will be described in turn. These stages are:

1   Preparatory
2   Engagement
3   Words and pictures
4   Interim family safety guidelines
5   Similar-but-different role-play
6   Final family safety plan
7   Follow-up

The table towards the end of the chapter diagrammatically summarizes the approach and includes a typical implementation timeline with guidance about how the family's successful completion of each stage is linked to a social services-monitored, incremental family reunification process. Generally, a full implementation of the resolutions approach involves 16 to 20 hour to hour-and-a-half sessions. To allow time for the development and implementation of a meaningful safety plan and to allow time for the family's implementation of that plan to be monitored by social services, stages 2, through 6, are usually spread out over a period of at least six months. We have found that this approach transfers well across different cultures and religions because the model does not prescribe a definitive account of the problem and because we involve the naturally occurring community around the family in ensuring the child's future safety.

At the end of the chapter we will also summarize research results regarding the outcomes and effectiveness of the resolutions approach.

Stage 1: Preparation

The preparatory process is a two-step process, the first being to brief the professionals involved with the case, the second being to brief the family.

Briefing the professionals

The first item of business before the resolutions approach can be offered to the family involves ensuring that the key professionals working with the case have a thorough understanding of the resolutions approach and are committed to being involved in the programme's implementation with the family. Most importantly, any statutory authority involved in the case, such as the courts and social services, must endorse the use of the resolutions approach, since their authority and leverage is essential to motivating the family to engage in the safety-building process. Once professional endorsement is in place, the family can be approached.

To utilize the resolutions approach in Rosemary's situation requires that Jasmina, her supervisor and Jack's parole social worker are committed to the process. In the first instance, we would want to brief Jasmina and her supervisor about the process so they fully understand the resolutions approach. The supervisor's support is necessary to bring the authority of the child protection agency in behind the resolutions work and so that Jasmina can be given organizational endorsement to be fully involved in the process. The exact nature of Jasmina's involvement needs to be clearly negotiated at this point. To further maximize the leverage available to the resolutions practitioner, we would also be approaching the parole social worker to see if it were possible to have Jack's participation in the resolutions process set as part of his parole conditions, including the requirement that Jack live separately from the family until significant progress is made in the programme. We would also explore with social services what authority they would feel able to place behind the requirement of initial separate living arrangements after Jack is released from prison.

While it may seem unlikely that Jasmina's supervisor would shift from wanting to close the case to making a renewed commitment to it, our experience is that when the supervisor understands that the resolutions approach will offer a different, more directly safety-organized response to the problem, they will often embrace the option. In fact, it is often the case that statutory authorities need to feel they have exhausted more usual treatment avenues before they will engage with the resolutions process. For statutory authority professionals to embrace the approach, the resolutions practitioner must engage them with a vision that the process can offer a productive way out of the 'denial' dispute.

Briefing the family

With the professional collaborators endorsing the approach, it is then possible to brief the family. We do this by briefly summarizing each stage of the process to the family so that they know exactly what the programme involves if they decide to go ahead. Throughout the briefing we emphasize the opportunity the resolutions process provides to satisfy social services and the courts that the alleged abuse cannot happen in the future, and that this not only shows that the children are safe but will also protect the accused perpetrator from future allegations or misunderstandings. If the family has engaged a legal representative, we always ask that the lawyer be present at the briefing. Lawyers are usually invaluable in promoting the resolutions approach to the family, since they generally quickly grasp the opportunity the programme offers to protect the accused client, while also engaging the family in a productive process of demonstrating that the children will be safe in the future. Conversely, if the family's lawyer is not involved in the briefing process they will more typically oppose the approach as another professional intrusion into their client's life. The resolutions work proper can only commence once the family makes the decision to participate.

In Rosemary's situation we would endeavour to undertake the briefing with all of the family together, most likely this would need to be done at the prison. We would want Jack's parole social worker to be present and would also encourage the family to have a lawyer with them, or someone else they felt they could trust to advise them. Choosing our words carefully, we would explain that the resolutions approach is not about getting Jack or Janice to say that the events Jack was convicted of had happened, rather it is about demonstrating to social services and the parole agency that nothing like this could happen in the future.

It is very likely that Jack would protest that he didn't abuse Rosemary so there is nothing to worry about. This sort of protestation of innocence is to be expected, and it is important that the resolutions practitioner does not oppose but instead utilizes the energy of the protest. To this end, we would utilize this sort of statement as an opportunity to explore with everyone present whether Jack's assertion of innocence is something that would leave the authorities more or less worried about him. We would then most likely explore the fact that there will be ongoing professional concern about Jack being associated with children for the rest of his life. In this light, we would offer the resolutions option as a way in which the family could demonstrate that the behaviour Jack was convicted of could not happen in the future and thereby protect him from future difficulties.

We would also ask for time in which we could speak with Rosemary separately, either with or without her mother, to answer any questions she might have and ascertain her position about the resolutions process. We would want this to occur before the family provides us with a decision about their involvement. We always ask the family and their advisors to take several days following the briefing to deliberate about whether they want to participate in the process.

In briefing the family we are promoting a context in which the family, and particularly Rosemary and Janice, can step outside of the dispute with social services and the usual polarized dynamic of arguing for or against Jack's innocence and instead step into a process of actively creating future safety. In Jack's situation it is hard to argue against undertaking a process that will enable him to demonstrate future safety for his grandchild and protect himself and the family from further professional intervention. Our experience of working with families like Rosemary's is that everyone excepting Jack will be keen to go ahead, though he will also usually agree to participate. It is not uncommon for a person in Jack's circumstances to say something like 'I really don't have an option, I have to do it to get social services and parole off my back'. We always accept this sort of rationale for participation without comment or challenge.

Stage 2: Engagement

The first one or two sessions of the resolutions approach are given over to building a solid working relationship between the resolutions practitioner and the parents. We do this by allowing the parents to tell their story of the events in their own way and own words, with the aim of building the parents' sense that we understand how they see the situation. This will usually take up most of the first session, but can take longer. Once they have told their story and we have demonstrated to them we understand their experience, we start to explore the events from other perspectives. We usually begin by exploring the perspectives of members of their immediate and extended family, friends and others in their network, and then move on to the perspectives of the statutory agency, the court and other professionals who might be involved. This process of opening up different perspectives allows us to move towards the story we develop with the parents to explain the allegations and the subsequent events to the family's children.

In Rosemary's family we would follow the process as we have just described with one extra dimension. We would also seek to meet with Rosemary separately on a regular basis, accompanied, if possible, by her own independent support person. Throughout the resolutions programme we would focus on Jack and Janice, but would see Rosemary separately to make sure she understood and supported everything we were doing with her parents. Only occasionally would we seek to have Rosemary involved in sessions together with Janice and Jack.

Stage 3: Words and pictures

Tillman Furniss (1991) observed that child abuse is a syndrome of secrecy. For children, including both the victim and any siblings, the stories that surround situations of 'denied' child abuse can become very confusing, and it is not uncommon for children to blame themselves or make up their own explanations to fit what they know of the facts (Berliner 1991). The 'words and pictures' process is designed to address this problem and create an explanation, agreed upon by the parents, that captures the seriousness of the allegations or convictions in words that are appropriate for the family's children.

Once the resolutions therapist and the parents have agreed upon the words, this explanation is presented to the children, who then together with the resolutions practitioner create 'pictures' or drawings that relate to the explanation. Through this child-centred process, the 'words and pictures' document is produced. The 'words and pictures' are then presented to a family-chosen, child protection agency-approved network of extended family and friends that creates a network of informed adults around the immediate family.

The heart of the words and pictures explanation provides a straightforward statement regarding the alleged abuse, and for this to be acceptable to the alleged abuser it also includes a statement that the accused says s/he didn't do these things. Thus, a typical words and pictures explanation involving 'denied' sexual abuse includes a statement that reads something like this:

> The judge and the social worker are worried about Shari and Mary. They are worried because last year Shari said that Daddy touched her on her private parts and that Daddy got Shari to touch him on his private parts. Daddy said he didn't do these things but the judge was still worried and can't decide what to think. The judge wants to make sure nothing like that happens to Shari and Mary in the future and that they stay safe.

In Rosemary's situation, we would be presenting the whole process as a means of the family demonstrating to social services that Robert will be safe in the future and to avoid circumstances where Jack might come under suspicion regarding his grandson and/or social services might consider removing Robert into care. In this case, we would be seeking to write the words and pictures story for Robert as the primary audience. We would work with Janice, Jack and Rosemary to develop the explanation, as the story the family will provide to Robert when he is old enough. We would ask the adults to create drawings with us that would help the explanation make sense to Robert when the time came to provide it to him.

In this case, the description of the worries would include a paragraph that would read:

> When your mummy was 13 she told the police and a judge that
> grandpa had touched on her private parts and that grandpa had
> got your mummy to touch him on his private parts. The judge
> was very worried and listened very carefully to lots of people.
> After this the judge said what grandpa had done was very wrong
> and the judge sent him to prison.

Stage 4: Interim family safety guidelines and involving a network

Once the family has completed the words and pictures stage, the first
significant changes can begin to be made in the family's contact
arrangements in the process of moving towards reunification. Presenting the words and pictures to a group of adults involved with the family
is an important step in creating a naturally occurring network of safety
for the children. To advance the reunification and safety-building
process, we then draw upon these people to supervise contact between
the alleged or convicted perpetrator and the children when they have
contact. A set of safety guidelines is created that provides the ground
rules to demonstrate that the children will be safe during the contact.

The primary purpose of developing the safety guidelines in this way is
to begin the process of getting the possible non-abusing caregiver and
the network to think through the issues around enacting demonstrable
future safety relative to the concerns. As contact increases, the safety
guidelines are developed and modified to match the changes in the
contact arrangements. This process sets the scene for the later stage of
creating a final safety plan that will guide the family's living
arrangements as they reunify. The guidelines themselves, like the safety
plan that will come later, are only words on paper, the real work occurs
in the process of creating the rules and then in their implementation. To
deepen the process of getting the family and network to organize
themselves around future safety requires the involvement of the social
services worker following up on each contact visit to monitor and help
strengthen the implementation of the guidelines. Lessons learned and
difficulties that arise in the implementation of the safety plan are then
explored in subsequent resolutions sessions.

> As indicated earlier, in Rosemary's case we would endeavour to
> have in place parole arrangements that would requiré Jack to live
> outside the family home while the resolutions process was
> undertaken and a safety plan set in place. Having completed

the words and pictures process we would increase the contact between Jack and Robert and have them supervised by people from the family's own safety network. In this process, we would look to reconnect Janice to her sister and cousins and enlist them in the network, as well as involving people from Jack's side of the family. At some point during the next stage, in which Jack and Janice undertake the similar-but-different role-play process, we would look to undertake the first overnight stays with a safety network person being present.

Stage 5: Similar-but-different role-play

During this stage, usually undertaken over four sessions, the parents role-play a hypothetical couple from a family that is facing similar abuse issues but in this similar-but-different scenario one of the parents is admitting that they are the perpetrator. This process is designed to enable the parents/caregivers to discuss issues they are usually unwilling or unable to overtly discuss in their own situation. The similar-but-different role-play gives the couple the opportunity to demonstrate to the child protection authorities they can understand and explore issues that professionals would typically associate with child abuse, such as victim awareness, grooming processes, power inequities and cycles of violence.

In Rosemary's situation we would want Jack and Janice to undertake the similar-but-different role-play. The idea of creating the hypothetical process arose from Susie's experience of chairing child protection case conferences in England in the late 1980s. In cases exactly like that of Rosemary, Janice and Jack, Susie became very concerned that professionals gathered at the conference were expecting someone like Janice to be protective, understand the seriousness of the concerns, and see Jack as a future risk, in a very short space of time and with no training or preparation. The primary purpose of involving Janice and Jack in the similar-but-different process is to create a context in which together they can explore issues associated with the sort of abuse that Rosemary alleged, a context that is safe for Janice and in which she is supported to become more robust in her thinking about the issues.

Stage 6: Final family safety plan

Building on the already created interim safety guidelines, the last major step in the resolutions process involves the development and implementation of a rigorous and detailed final safety plan, which becomes the basis for demonstrably safe living arrangements as the family reunifies. The plan is designed to ensure and demonstrate that contact between the alleged or convicted perpetrator and the children is transparently safe and to protect the alleged or convicted perpetrator from future allegations or misunderstandings. The safety plan strengthens the roles and responsibilities of the likely safer caregiver and a network of adults around the family.

The safety plan is first drafted through a collaborative process involving the likely or possible non-abusing parent supported by one or two other key people. Following this, the safety plan is finalized together with the alleged abuser. Once the rules of the plan are finalized and the statutory authorities ratify them, the safety plan is presented to the children. The children are again involved in drawing pictures that relate to each rule in a similar manner to the creation of the words and pictures document. With the safety plan document completed in this way, it is then presented to as wide a group as possible of people from the family's normal extended kin and friendship network.

In Rosemary's situation, our aim would be to draft the final safety plan together with Janice and Rosemary plus one or two other people they felt could help them in this task. One of our major aims in involving other people in this way is to break down the secrecy, shame and isolation that tend to surround situations of serious abuse. Given the isolation Janice and Rosemary have experienced following the allegations, it would probably be challenging for them to consider and then find people to help them with this work. Many professionals have suggested to us that people like Janice and Rosemary are too isolated to identify or involve others, but our experience is that if we are persistent and supportive even very isolated individuals are able to find people to support them in the resolutions work.

As with all safety plans involving alleged sexual abuse, the key rule of the plan in Rosemary's situation would stipulate that Jack is never to be alone with children and probably a second rule stipulating he is never to be alone with Rosemary. In this case, since Rosemary's child, Robert, is too young to be involved we would again ask the adults to be involved in drawing pictures for the safety plan that would help him understand the rules when they are explained to him when he is older. There will be many challenges from and for Jack, Janice and Rosemary in creating and implementing such a safety plan. Our approach to such challenges always is to see each difficulty not as resistance but as an additional opportunity to explore the issues facing this family in making sure Rosemary and Robert are safe and Jack is protected from any further allegations.

Our experience would suggest to us that if the resolutions approach was used in Rosemary's case the process would create a context in which Rosemary could securely elect to live separately from Janice and Jack but still maintain involvement with her family. This would include Jack having contact with Robert but based around the rules of the safety plan, which would provide security and protection to all the members of the family.

Stage 7: Follow-up

By this stage the work of the resolutions practitioner is mostly complete, but it is important that social services maintain involvement to monitor the implementation of the plan. Ideally we would want this monitoring process to continue for at least three to six months following reunification. After the completion of the programme we usually conduct two follow-up sessions, one at three months and the second at twelve months, to review with the family their implementation of the safety plan.

In Rosemary's family such reviews would be important to ensure Robert's safety and protect Jack, and we would want the parole officer as well as the social services social worker to be involved in monitoring the implementation of the safety plan during the follow-up stage.

Resolutions programme: An overview

The session numbers described overleaf are not prescriptive but are offered as a guide. LPA refers to likely or possible abuser, LNAC refers to likely non-abusing caregiver.

Stage	Purpose	Involving	Sessions	Contact Arrangements
PREPARATORY	Reach agreement regarding participation with all parties fully understanding programme. To proceed both professionals and parents must make commitments to participate.	All professionals involved with the case. Parents, their advisors and key network people.	1 1	At this stage LPA or children will ideally be out of the home.
ENGAGEMENT	Engage with parents through understanding their experience, whilst continually exploring other perspectives. The resolutions practitioner positions themselves with maximum flexibility regarding the issues, whilst at all times focusing on the seriousness of these issues.	Parents Social services worker to observe as agreed in stage 1.	2	Professionally supervised contact between LPA and children. *Following successful completion of each stage, the resolutions practitioner recommends increased contact, the statutory agency or court must decide on the changes.*
WORDS AND PICTURES	Create agreed-upon, age-appropriate explanation regarding the allegations and/or convictions with the parents. Present to the children, then to the network.	Developed with parents. Presented to children with help of parents. Presented to network with help of family.	1 or 2 1 1	Increase professionally Supervised contact. Contact supervised by network begins.
INTERIM FAMILY SAFETY GUIDELINES	Identify in detail how family life will be arranged to demonstrate future safety for children and avoid further allegations/misunderstandings directed at suspected abuser. Initially created for contact arrangements but successively evolves as each step towards reunification is taken.	Developed with likely LNAC, children and key support people.	1	Increase contact supervised by network.
SIMILAR-BUT-DIFFERENT ROLE-PLAY	Allows couple to overtly speak about the previously unspeakable as they role-play a couple where abuse is admitted. Aims to strengthen and educate LNAC, and focuses successively on perspectives of perpetrator, non-abusing caregiver, victim, other siblings and family members and the consequences as future grandparents. Educates re	Parents/caregivers	4	First overnight stay.

Stage	Purpose	Involving	Sessions	Contact Arrangements
	power dynamics, grooming cycles, perpetrator behaviours/tactics. This is NOT a process designed to gain an admission by stealth.			Increase overnight stays.
FINAL FAMILY SAFETY PLAN	Final plan, which documents future living arrangements to allow reunification. Plan includes consideration of future difficulties and a family safety object.	Developed with likely LNAC, children and key support people.	2	
		Presented to LPA and network.	2	Family reunification.
FOLLOW-UP	Monitor and refine implementation of family safety plan.	Everyone possible	2	

Outcomes

As mentioned in the introduction, there have been a number of research studies that have evaluated outcomes of the resolutions approach. Gumbleton (1997, also summarized in Essex and Gumbleton 1999) studied re-abuse rates for children in families that had undertaken the resolutions programme and also explored services users' views of the programme, as did a study undertaken by Hiles (2002). Luger (2003) interviewed referring professionals to gather feedback about whether their hopes and expectations of the resolutions service were met.

Re-abuse rates

Gumbleton (1997) studied outcomes for 38 children from the first 17 families that had undertaken the resolutions programme in the UK. The follow-up data were derived from child protection registers and social services files. The families involved in the study had completed the programme between 8 and 45 months prior to participating in the study, with an average time since completion of 27 months. The study found that the resolutions programme had been successful in helping protect the vast majority of the children in the sample, with only one child known to have experienced further abuse. Depending on whether the re-abuse calculation is made relative to the number of families or number of children in the study, this equates to a re-abuse rate of 3 or 7 per cent.

There are many methodological issues involved in interpreting and comparing child maltreatment re-abuse rates derived from different studies (see Fluke and Hollinshead 2003 for discussion on this matter), however a wide range of studies suggest re-abuse rates for families involved in the child protection system generally fall in a range between 20 to 40 per cent (see, for example, Browne 1986; Cohn and Daro 1987; Corby 1987; Bentovim et al. 1988; Alexander et al. 1990; Faller 1991; Farmer and Parker 1991; Murphy et al. 1992; Bools 1993; Cleaver and Freeman 1995; Farmer and Owen 1995; Gibbons et al. 1995; Levy et al. 1995; Thorburn et al. 1995; Sharland et al. 1996; DePanfilis and Zuravis 1999; English et al. 1999; Haapasalo and Aaltone 1999; Fluke et al. 2001; Fluke and Hollinshead 2003; Ellaway et al. 2004). In general and not surprisingly, studies that have a longer follow-up period show higher re-abuse rates. Most of the studies cited above have gathered their data around the two-year mark, which makes them comparable to Gumbleton's research.

Referrers and parents' experiences

Between them, Gumbleton, Luger and Hiles interviewed parents or caregivers and professionals involved in 32 cases in which families had completed the resolutions programme. The qualitative data from each study show that both professionals and parents were consistently appreciative of the resolutions approach, offering a productive way forward out of the professional-family dispute that had bogged down each case. A typical expression of this sentiment is captured in one parent's words, 'they were someone to help you overcome the barriers between yourself and social services' (Hiles 2004: 28).

Parents consistently valued the openness they experienced from the resolutions practitioner. One parent described the approach 'as a breath of fresh air', another stated 'if there's anywhere people can relax it's there' (Gumbleton 1997: 62). To Hiles (2004: 23) one parent stated that the resolutions work was like a 'light at the end of the tunnel, you've got a chance of being back living together, whereas before you feel you've got no chance'. Of the 27 caregivers interviewed by Gumbleton, 23 felt the resolutions programme had made a positive difference to their family, with most talking about improved communication and relationships. Seven respondents specifically described the increased awareness the programme gave them regarding the seriousness of the concerns and child safety. One father stated that 'it made us feel we have to do things within the family to satisfy other agencies to allow me to get home. The way the resolutions team made it, allowed us to accept we had to do that' (Gumbleton 1997: 56).

Luger (2003: 23) interviewed referring professionals, several of whom made comments such as the following:

Your work is very open and inclusive of professionals. I think that is quite healthy because it also gets the message across to the actual families that we've got to be open about this, that we have to have professionals involved and build trust with professionals because in this case, and another case since, there was an absolute polarization with the local authority and nobody trusted anybody. So the way in which you work does build up trust.

One of the big things is about including professionals. I think that's important because all the social workers involved have found it a very interesting experience. It broadened them, educated them and anything that does that is to be encouraged.

As we proceed through the following chapters, we will draw further upon comments from parents and referrers who participated in these studies.

The studies described above have limitations. All are small in scale and have been conducted by people who have developed the approach or are close to the developers of the approach. Having said this, it is worth noting that each of the studies has been conducted within university contexts, with independent advisors and examiners guiding the methodologies. These studies were undertaken because as Susie Essex, John Gumbleton and Colin Luger worked to develop the resolutions model, they felt that it was imperative to research the outcomes and impact of the approach before it would be appropriate to promote it more widely. We would certainly like to see further inquiry into the model's use and efficacy, but the research that has been conducted seems to suggest that the resolutions programme is a productive intervention strategy and has significant merit in circumstances of 'denial', in which there are generally few treatment options.

Chapter **Three**

PRINCIPLES AND PRACTICES INFORMING THE RESOLUTIONS APPROACH

Constructive working relationships between professionals and family members, and between professionals themselves, are the heart and soul of effective practice in situations in which children suffer abuse. A significant body of thinking and research tells us that best outcomes for vulnerable children arise when constructive relationships exist in both these arenas (see Reder et al. 1993; Department of Health 1995; MacKinnon 1998; Walsh 1998; Cashmore 2002; Trotter 2002). Unfortunately, in situations of serious 'denied' child abuse the task of building purposive working relationships tends often to be over- whelmed by disagreements and tensions regarding what occurred and what should be done. These tensions not only surface between professionals and the family but also arise between professionals themselves. In our view, one of the primary reasons for the poor outcomes in situations of 'denial' comes about not necessarily because the suspected abuser refutes what the professionals believe they have done, but because of the level of disputation and polarization that builds up in these circumstances.

The resolutions approach aspires to build constructive working relationships amongst the professionals, and between the family members and the professionals, by focusing on the creation of future safety as a way of moving beyond the disputation about the past. To implement the resolutions approach requires a shift in both the thinking and practices of professionals approaching situations of 'denial'. In this chapter we will articulate some of the key principles that underpin the approach alongside practices that flow from these concepts.

Principle 1: 'Denial' as an interactional process

Professionals and lay people most commonly speak about denial as if there is an independent, evident and certain truth (that is, that a particular person has abused a particular child) that is being refuted by the person or people deemed to be 'in denial'. This is both an essentialist (the truth is out there) and an individualistic way of framing the problem of denial.

Anyone who has worked with serious child abuse, and particularly sexual abuse, has experienced the frustration of individuals who appear to be lying, or who give explanations that seem outrageous, and that seem to dismiss or minimize the allegations of the victim. Sometimes it also seems that the accused person is continually repeating explanations so that they and others become convinced that what they are saying is the truth. All of these behaviours are part of what professionals commonly speak of as denial, and we tend to ascribe these attributes solely to the individual. There are clearly individual and psychological defence mechanisms that propel individuals to be more or less truthful; however, in working with situations of alleged child abuse it is crucial to maintain awareness of interactional processes that sustain and feed denial-type responses.

There are very few benefits to be accrued by an alleged perpetrator in admitting to abusing a child. A person who takes responsibility for seriously abusing a child may garner a clearer conscience but they may also very likely face criminal charges, job loss, exclusion from their family and community, as well as other major negative repercussions. This highlights the inappropriateness and injustice of framing denial solely as an individual psychological distortion of an evident truth, when there are so many strong social and interactional pressures that make denial a compelling response.

Several examples can further illustrate the interactional nature of denial. We have worked with a number of cases in which infants had been injured where parents have stated quite clearly they did not tell what they knew because they felt they had been treated pejoratively by investigative and medical professionals, and also because they quickly realized that if they spoke openly they were very likely to face prosecution.

In a sexual abuse case Andrew was involved with, social services removed the young children late at night from the family while tactical response police officers held the father on the ground at gunpoint, in front of his house. This process angered both parents considerably and was very distressing for the children. This event occurred despite the fact that the mother had taken the youngest to the doctor earlier the same day and had openly discussed with the doctor the possibility the child was being sexual abused. Almost three years later, when Andrew became involved with the case, the mother was still very angry and related the story of that night with tears. She wanted to know why the police and social services had acted so aggressively. She was also very clear that her subsequent lack of cooperation (which was regularly described in social services files as a demonstration of her denial) had its genesis in the events of that night. The mother also made the point that while she was the first person to raise the concerns by taking her daughter to the doctor regarding vaginal secretions and soreness, no professional had ever acknowledged or recognized this. It seemed to us the forceful removal brought the parents together to fight against the professionals in a manner that distracted from addressing the issue of possible abuse. While this is an extreme case in terms of the force used in the childrens' removal, it is very common for parents to feel alienated by the way professionals deal with them in such cases (Farmer and Owen 1995; Teoh et al. 2003; Trotter 2003; Turnell in press). This in turn tends to escalate parental behaviours that are then interpreted as forms of denial.

Unrealistic professional expectations and/or a lack of compassion can also contribute to practitioners seeing behaviour as denial that might, at least in part, be better understood as a family in crisis. Smith (1989: 31) observes: 'Often we expect too much, we expect that the mother will align with the child, believe them and provide support. With no training and little power we expect her not to crumple herself and to act as if none of this had a major impact on her personally.'

There are other, broader issues that increase the likelihood of denial in child abuse cases, one of which almost always is the fear of authority, of sanction and prosecution. Child abuse is a subject that carries considerable taboo and shame in most Western countries, which contribute significantly to restraining open discussion of the issue. More broadly, moral and ethical thinking in the West has developed primarily from Judaeo-Christian origins, which draw heavily on the idea of sinfulness. In this tradition forgiveness and salvation can only come about through individual acknowledgement of sin. The process of confession within Catholicism serves as an exemplar of the Christian approach to human atonement. This orientation to human transformation has undoubtedly influenced Western psychology, for example Foucault (1986) suggested that as the power of the Church waned, the confessional came to be replaced by the therapist's couch. Within psychoanalytic, behavioural and humanistic psychology, awareness and acknowledgement are seen as the cornerstone of change and denial is seen to be damaging. In psychoanalytic terms, sustained denial can lead to splitting of the ego (Freud 1966). These religious and psychological antecedents mean that most helping professionals' antennae are acutely tuned towards signs of denial which are seen to interrupt the primary mechanism for bringing about individual transformation. This is a context in which signs of denial can readily be constructed as a cardinal sin, and in this way professionals make their own interactional contribution to reifying and escalating the problem of denial.

To avoid simply blaming the problem on the alleged perpetrator and those close to them, it is important that professionals are continually mindful of the interactional and societal factors that contribute to the creation and manifestation of denial-type behaviours. Sensitivity to these factors will enable the professional to more skilfully and thoughtfully build working relationships with individuals and families deemed to be 'in denial'.

Practising with sensitivity to the interactional dynamics surrounding 'denial'

By highlighting some of the interactional dynamics that generate alleged denial, we are hoping to encourage professionals to maintain an acute sensitivity to how they intervene and respond to families facing problems of child abuse, since professional behaviour can significantly impact the extent and level of denial-type behaviour that family members display.

> At about the same time that Andrew was involved with the sexual abuse scenario mentioned above, he was also consulting on another sexual abuse case involving a social services worker, Caroline Sullivan. In this case Caroline worked very carefully, respectfully and sensitively with everyone involved. As a result, the mother stepped into and sustained a robust level of protectiveness, the teenage daughter was supported and protected, and the stepfather admitted to the sexual abuse he had committed, though the step-uncle continued to deny that he had raped the young woman. Caroline also worked closely with the police so that charges were ultimately laid, but this did not occur until the mother and daughter were ready to go through the legal process. This case is documented fully elsewhere (Turnell and Edwards 1999: 158–63). What struck Andrew from being involved in both these cases almost simultaneously was the extent to which careful and sensitive practice could indeed influence the way in which family members respond and the way safety is created for the child.

In studies with non-abusing parents, Smith (1989) and Humphreys (1992) confirm that the way in which professionals such as social workers, doctors and police approach parents in situations of alleged incest has a significant bearing on their subsequent reactions and the actions parents take to deal with the issue.

Principle 2: 'Denial' as a continuum of behaviours

The concept of 'denial' is usually framed in common language and much professional discourse in all or nothing terms. This tendency is reflected in the usual way of speaking about the problem in which a person is said to be 'in denial'. This expression identifies the problem as something akin to an illness, framing denial as if a person either has the problem of denial or they don't. This way of thinking tends to identify any denial-type behaviours as complete denial and erase statements of partial acknowledgement and other possibly useful behaviour that people seen to be 'in denial' or those around them often make.

A mother whose partner has been accused of sexually abusing her child will very typically vacillate in her thinking. Sometimes she will tend to believe her child while at others she will tend to lean toward her partner's assertions that he did not abuse the youngster (Faller 1991). This simple example points to the idea that it is possible, assuming the allegations are correct, to think of 'denial' as a continuum from complete denial to full acknowledgement. In her research with mothers of children who say they have been sexually abused, Kathleen Faller (1991) also found that some mothers, though they never overtly stated that they believed their children's statements of abuse, none the less took actions to safeguard their offspring. In a typical example this might involve a mother restricting the possibilities for the child to be alone with the alleged perpetrator. Again, this suggests a continuum of responses to allegations of abuse rather than a simple denial–acknowledgement disjunction. Likewise, in cases in which an infant is injured, parents who refuse to enter any conversation about how the injuries may have happened are a very different proposition to another couple who will talk about possibilities even when the ideas they suggest do not seem to correlate with the seriousness of the injuries. However, there is a tendency to speak about both sets of parents as if they are both equally 'in denial'.

Practising continuum thinking

Approaching the problem of denial in this more fluid way opens up many practice possibilities adopting a response-based stance (Todd and

Wade 2004) towards the events surrounding alleged child abuse. An example of this sort of approach might involve talking to a likely non-abusing partner about their response to the child's allegations, suggesting that it is common for a parent in their position to feel overwhelmed and to vacillate sometimes towards believing the child, at others towards the partner.

Sharon Elliot, an English social services practitioner, worked with a case involving a mother we will call Mieke, her current partner Dirk, their 5-year-old son Walter, and Tineke, Mieke's teenage daughter from a previous relationship. This case involved separate allegations by both children alleging that Dirk had sexually abused them. When Walter made his allegations, his statements were somewhat ambiguous and inconclusive. As a result, the police were unable to prosecute because of lack of evidence and social services were also unable to take the matter further. At this point in time, Mieke provided no acknowledgement that she believed her son, as a result of which the police formed the view that she was colluding with Dirk's abuse of their son.

Fourteen months later, Tineke alleged that her stepfather had sexually and physically abused her, which Dirk also denied. Based on Tineke's statements the police and social services required Dirk to move out while the investigation proceeded. Despite Dirk being out of the home, the police were adamant that Mieke was unprotective, based on her response of the previous year, and put a lot of pressure on Sharon and her team leader that both children should be removed into care. Sharon resisted this pressure, aiming to build a working relationship with Mieke and to explore her experience of the previous and current situations. As part of this process, Sharon talked with Mieke about how hard it must be for her to be placed in a situation where she had to decide about conflicting statements from two people she loved. Following this, Sharon asked Mieke the extent to which she believed what Tineke had said on a zero to ten scale. Rather than answer on a ten-point scale, Mieke responded that she was 95 per cent certain of what Tineke said. Later, Sharon asked Mieke whether Walter's statements of the year previous had had any lasting effect or made any difference to her. Mieke described that she had spoken to both Dirk and Walter about what Walter had said and, although at the time she didn't want to face the possibility of Dirk sexually abusing their son, none the less Walter's statements had left her with a niggling doubt. As a result, from that time on, Mieke had done everything she could to ensure that Walter was never alone with his father.

By Sharon thinking more flexibly and openly about what Mieke's 'denial' of the previous year might have meant, she broadened her own capacity to hear and utilize the mother's current and previous experience. We will look further at how this case unfolded when we come to principle 4.

Principle 3: 'Never believe without doubt'

In the contested and anxious environment of child protection casework (Morrison 1996) there is, as we have already begun to explore, a constant impulse to want to establish the truth of a given situation. As Baistow and her colleagues suggest:

> Whether or not we think there are absolute perpetrators and absolute victims in child abuse cases, and whether or not we believe in a single uncontaminated 'truth' about 'what happened', powerful forces pull us towards enacting a script, which offers us these parts and these endings. (Baistow et al. 1995: vi)

These powerful forces frequently centre around the process of professional assessment, as the following example demonstrates. This case involved a pre-school aged girl who had made statements that indicated she had been sexually abused by her father. The father quickly alleged that his ex-wife had scripted his daughter to make these statements. While social services substantiated the allegations, the court was not willing to accept this judgement and appointed a professional expert witness to ascertain the veracity of the child's statements. In working with the child, the expert witness used male and female anatomical dolls to make her assessment. She then prepared a report to the court that stated definitively that the abuse did not happen, since the child was unable to demonstrate the abuse on the dolls. The judge in this case accepted the expert's report and reinstated shared care arrangements for both parents.

In this situation, social services, on the one hand, adopted as truth the position that the child was abused, while the expert witness adopted the reverse position. This scenario is typical and illustrative of the pre-eminence professional systems tend to place on the idea that it is possible to be certain, which as a consequence casts the professional in the role of above all having to establish the truth of what occurred. This example is a clear demonstration of how professionals can end up in conflict because of the certainty imperative. Although not writing about child protection practice, psychoanalyst and social psychologist Erich Fromm (1968: 63) stated it well when he wrote, 'man has an intense need for certainty and he wants to believe that there is no need to doubt the method by which he makes his decision is right'. A mother of a baby who had suffered injuries deemed by a medical practitioner to be non-accidental and caused by the parents, put it more bluntly when she observed to Andrew 'the doctor was black and white. While the rest of us were in the grey area, the real world, we were obsolete from her point of view.'

The insights and knowledges of experienced professionals drawing on research, assessment procedures and professional wisdom are important, but they are never definitive and certain. Dalgleish (1998), Parton (1998), Munro (2002), Parton and O'Byrne (2002) and Fergurson (2005) each point to the 'irreducible uncertainty' (Hammond 1996) that adheres to the highly complex situations in which children are vulnerable and at-risk. Despite the intense desire that naturally arises to ascertain 'the truth' in situations where children are vulnerable, our experience tells us that to work effectively with situations of denial, professionals need to create processes that loosen this need for certainty.

The stance that informs the resolutions approach to working with denied child abuse is probably best articulated for us in the words of Danish physicist Nils Bohr: 'never believe without doubt'. The extent to which the professional acts as if they either know or can become certain of 'the truth' will undermine their capacity to think themselves into and through the complex terrain of denied abuse and constrain their capacity to work with the varied and varying positions of family members and other professionals. Eileen Munro, who has spent a considerable amount of her professional energy exploring typical child protection errors of practice and reasoning, makes a similar point forcefully when she writes 'the single most important factor in minimizing error is to admit that you may be wrong' (Munro 2002: 141).

In 1986, Dale, Davies, Morrison and Waters published a defining and influential book on the treatment of severe child abuse called *Dangerous Families*. This book framed denial as a process of secrecy arising within the family system. The authors stated that 'it is a fundamental premise of change that the perpetrator should become able, through the assessment work, to *take responsibility* for the abuse' (authors' italics). Thus, in situations of severe abuse, where the family has not engaged with the professionals and where acknowledgement was not forthcoming, the family was assessed authoritatively and with little or no room for uncertainty as a 'dangerous' family and permanent separation was deemed necessary (Dale et al. 1986: 157).

The first author of this influential publication, Peter Dale, has continued to work with situations of child abuse deemed to involve denial, focusing particularly on situations in which infants have suffered serious physical injuries. Traditionally, these cases have been described as 'shaken' or 'battered' baby cases, a professional designation that captures very clearly the idea that the expert knows the truth that the harmed baby was injured by its parents or caregivers. However, in many, if not most, instances in which young infants suffer severe, seemingly non-accidental, physical injuries, parents offer explanations that do not fit medical understandings of the severity and cause of the injuries. Anyone who has worked with such cases will recognize the impulse to assert the truth of what professionals think they know, namely that one of the parents caused the injuries. As with most denial-type situations, this will tend to escalate the denial dispute and fracture the relationship between professionals and family members. With new colleagues Richard Green and Ron Fellows, Dale writes in 2005 that 'the concept of "denial" in investigation and assessments of serious suspicious physical injuries to infants is biased toward an assumption that parents are deliberately concealing conscious awareness of maltreatment, and that their refusal to confess is confirmatory evidence of this.' They go on to point out that the range of 'scenarios that are conceptually included within the term "denial" are in fact very varied', including those where it is a credible possibility that the parents are truthfully denying responsibility. This leads the authors to conclude that 'the time has come to abandon the use of the term "denial" in professional discussions and legal proceedings concerned with serious suspicious injuries to infants' (Dale et al. 2005: 140).

Thinking in this way has led Dale and his colleagues (2002; 2005) to propose a different name for situations in which professionals and parents have conflicting explanations regarding an injured infant. They have proposed describing such cases using the acronym 'SIDE', referring to situations involving serious injuries and discrepant explanations. This descriptor is a very useful proposal since it avoids the automatic assumption of abuse and the pejorative connotations of the 'battered' and 'shaken' appellations, and brings a pause to professionals' impulse to believe they can know with certainty the truth of a given situation.

Taking Dale and his colleagues' ideas further, it is evident that the concept of 'denial' tends to propel professionals toward the assumption that parents or caregivers are concealing awareness of the maltreatment not just in instances where infants are injured but in all cases of serious alleged child abuse. When professionals describe a situation as a 'denial' case, this implies the truth of the situation is being denied and thereby erases the possibility of any other explanations. We want therefore to take Dale, Green and Fellow's logic a step further by proposing an alternative descriptor for all child abuse situations that are typically labelled as 'denial' cases, by suggesting the alternative designation 'ACADE', standing for cases that involve alleged child abuse and disputed explanations. The ACADE descriptor is less presumptive, allows room for doubt and the possibility the professionals may be wrong. Focusing on the dispute about explanations through using the ACADE label is also more accurate to both the facts and the central dilemma of these cases and can potentially assist professionals in avoiding the offence that the family often feels based on the assumption of denial.

Utilizing the ACADE descriptor can serve as an implementation of Bohr's maxim, but adopting a stance of uncertainty and doubt is unsettling and can seem anathema to what being a professional is supposed to be all about. Adopting the SIDE label in relation to disputes regarding the cause of injuries to an infant is less confronting than using the term ACADE to describe a situation in which an adult refutes allegations of child sexual abuse. Some professionals may feel that to describe these as ACADE cases is a minimization of the seriousness of situations in which children make allegations of sexual abuse. However, for us, the major difficulty of responding to situations of serious alleged child sexual abuse lies in the fact that even after treatment, 75 per cent of likely perpetrators maintain their stance of denying the allegations (Hyde et al. 1995; Bentovim 2003). This usually renders impotent professional intervention with the likely denying perpetrator. When a child discloses that they have been sexually abused, we accept that reality, but to believe that the sole solution to this problem lies in the likely perpetrator acknowledging the allegations seems to us to be a professional means of collectively turning away from the complexity of the terrain. The resolutions approach is above all about creating space for allegations of child abuse to be taken seriously by professionals and families and to enlist everyone in the task of building future safety rather than being mired in a dispute about the truth of the allegations. In our experience, it is far more important for the professional to be expert in the process of how future safety can be brought about, than to try and colonize an expert position about whether one scenario is true or not.

In practice: Working with multiple perspectives

The professional who builds their capacity to tolerate doubt and uncertainty simultaneously also builds their capacity to work and engage with the multiple viewpoints that they will hear from both professionals and family members in ACADE cases. The following is a very good example of a social services practitioner working with multiple perspectives to make headway in a situation in which a father was charged with possessing child pornography.

An English social services worker was dealing with a situation in which a father of an 8-year-old girl had been charged with possessing child pornography downloaded from internet websites. The worker had received some other, inconclusive information that suggested that the man had also shown his daughter some of the material. The man was pleading not guilty to the criminal charges, arguing he had visited sites 'as research', and was asserting that his daughter knew nothing and was completely unaffected by what he had done. At the same time, some of the worker's colleagues were strongly of the view that not only did he have a large collection of child pornography on computer, the father was very likely also sexually abusing his daughter. There was, however, no evidence to confirm the latter.

The worker had initially found herself very frustrated with the case since she seemed to be repeatedly arguing with the man about the significance of what he had done. This situation changed when the worker began to talk to the man about multiple possibilities and perspectives. The worker began to reflect back to the father that she understood that his position was that he had only visited the websites as research and that he had not realized that he had downloaded material from them. She then asked did he understand how this explanation might sound to herself and her supervisor? In the course of the following conversations, the worker talked to the father about it being her job to consider the worst scenarios as well as make sure she understood his position. In this way, she talked about having to consider the possibility that perhaps what the father was saying was true, but that she had also to consider other possibilities. For example, the possibility that he was addicted to internet child pornography, the possibility that his daughter had seen the material and also the possibility that the man was sexually attracted to his daughter and actively sexually abusing her. In response, the man acknowledged that in the worker's position he would regard what he was saying as suspicious, at one point going even further, saying in her position he would probably remove his daughter into care.

Susie likes to describe the idea of working with multiple perspectives as the ability of the practitioner to hold at least five different stories in their head at one time. This is probably the core skill of utilizing the resolutions thinking and approach.

Principle 4: Viewing the likely non-abusing parent and other people around the family as protective resources

Within the child protection field, there has been a strong tradition of identifying child maltreatment, and particularly sexual abuse, as arising from family dysfunction and pathology. In the case of sexual abuse, when the abuser is most often male, this analysis has often promoted the idea that the mother is complicit or even pivotal in allowing the abuse to occur. This perspective can be found in a considerable amount of professional literature between the 1960s and early 1990s (see, for example, Giaretto 1982; Sgroi et al. 1985; Bentovim et al. 1988; Tinling 1990). Henry Kempe, widely credited with the 'rediscovery' of child abuse in the 1960s was instrumental in promoting this view. Articulating views typical of the family dysfunction perspective, Kempe wrote of 'long standing active or passive maternal collusion and support of child abuse' (Kempe and Kempe 1978: 62). On the subject of familial sexual abuse, Kempe stated that 'incestuous behaviour is given an extra push by a wife who arranges situations that allow privacy between father and daughter' and describes 'mothers as playing an important role in facilitating incest between father and daughter' (Kempe and Kempe 1978: 66).

Researchers have found that the tendency to implicate and blame the mother has been widely accepted among child protection professionals. Kelley (1990) undertook research with social workers, police and nurses involved with child protection matters and found that 84 per cent of her respondents believed that the non-offending mother was at least partly to blame for sexual abuse of her children. Dietz and Craft (1980) found similar results, as did Kalichman et al. (1990). The latter also described that 'when the father admitted the abuse he was blamed more; when he denied the abuse the mother was blamed more' (Kalichman et al. 1990: 74).

This sort of mother-blaming located within many family systems perspectives to situations of child abuse has been strongly challenged by feminist thinkers and practitioners (Faller 1988; MacKinnon and Miller 1988; Elbow and Mayfield 1991; Hooper 1992; Davies and Krane 1996; Hooper and Humphreys 1998; Featherstone 1999). Research supporting the feminist challenge found that far from being collusive, the majority of mothers actually respond, at least to some extent, in protective ways after disclosure of sexual abuse (Berliner 1991; Humphreys 1992). Examples of mothers' protective responses include communicating their belief to the victim, offering support, contacting professional services and confronting the alleged perpetrator. At the same time, women in this situation are often faced with a myriad of confusing, painful and disjointed thoughts and are not certain where to turn for help. Hill (2005: 360) quotes a mother who described being caught between social services and the alleged perpetrator as being 'like a rat trapped in a corner'. Humphreys (1992: 30) writes that mothers consistently 'felt alone and vulnerable in their effort to support and protect their child. It is not a social context which encourages sustained belief in the disclosure of child sexual assault.'

While mother-blaming is now less pervasive and extreme, especially in the literature following the feminist critique of the 1980s and 1990s, the logic of implicating the non-abusing parent (particularly when that is the mother), as well as others in the family system, still holds considerable currency among helping professionals involved with child protection issues (Scourfield 2001 and 2003; Allan 2004). This was demonstrated in a case Andrew was involved with regarding alleged sustained sexual abuse by a father of two primary school-aged children. The father denied the allegations that arose from police and social services interviews with the children and a couple who had stayed with the family. When the allegations against the father first came to light, the children went to live with their aunt (the father's sister) and her partner for eight months. Unfortunately, because the aunt was unwilling to acknowledge that her brother had sexually abused the children, she was deemed to be collusive with her son and the children were removed and placed in foster care. This view served to erase the commitment the aunt had made in taking the children in, despite the fact that she and her partner would not allow the children to be alone with their father when he visited and that the children's health, school results and emotional outlook improved markedly in the period they had stayed with her.

The resolutions approach challenges this perspective and from the outset of involvement with the families we endeavour to be alert to ways family members have sought to be protective, even if these actions are undertaken quietly (as was demonstrated in Sharon Elliot's case, mentioned above, in which Mieke endeavoured to keep Tineke from being alone with Dirk after her son's allegations). From the outset we are also looking to identify and strengthen the likely safer parent or caregiver and identify others in and around the immediate family who can support future safety, even when they are not willing to openly admit they believe the allegations. The professional who subscribes to the view that a family caught in an ACADE scenario is a dysfunctional unit will tend to find the idea of identifying a safer parent and other protective adults within the network as at least somewhat anathema.

In practice: openness toward the likely non-abusing parent and other family

Protective actions by family members often get hidden under the chaos of the crisis that envelops the family after disclosure. These past actions and the potential for future safety are likely to be further overlooked if the professional is not acutely sensitive to the possibility of protective-ness within the family. The primary practice outcome we are looking to promote from this principle is for child protection professionals to sustain and build a greater openness towards likely non-abusing caregivers and other members of the extended family. This is vital to the resolutions approach since we are not, like most treatment responses, aiming to achieve acknowledgement from the likely perpetrator. The object of the resolutions response is to build an extensive group of people from the naturally occurring network within and around the family to commit to ensuring the children's future safety.

In training professionals in the resolutions approach, we developed a 'before and after' illustration that utilizes the humour of 'light globe jokes' to demonstrate this different way of practising with ACADE cases. The 'before' drawing shows a light globe that seems faulty, representing a person who is deemed to be 'in denial'. The 'after' drawing shows the same seemingly faulty light globe, but visually demonstrates the resolutions purpose is not to try and fix that light globe but rather to install a whole new lighting system.

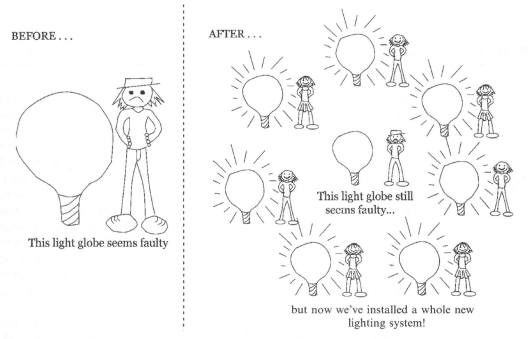

BEFORE...

This light globe seems faulty

AFTER...

This light globe still seems faulty...

but now we've installed a whole new lighting system!

Figure 3.1 Resolutions and the faulty light globe

Returning to Sharon Elliot's case described above. Sharon had been open to the possibility that Mieke had been protective in the past and this gave her confidence to ask the mother for her ideas regarding what needed to happen for the children to be protected in the future. Mieke was able to offer numerous ideas around allowing Dirk to see the children only on her and the children's terms and never allowing him to be alone with them in the future. Sharon then asked Mieke what support she needed to do this. Mieke spoke about the support Dirk's parents had offered her in the past and that she wanted to involve the paternal grandparents in protecting the children. Sharon met with the grandparents, focusing initially on how important they were to Mieke and the children and that Mieke wanted their support. Though Sharon had wondered where Dirk's parents' allegiances would lie, the upshot of Sharon's openness, first to Mieke and then to the grandparents, was that they provided rigorous support and committed themselves to making sure Mieke was able to keep the safety rules she had established. If Sharon had adopted the same pessimistic view that the police held about Mieke and assumed Dirk's parents would be collusive, it would have been unlikely that she could have involved them in this safety-building work.

Principle 5: Organizing practice around future safety rather than past denial

In the introductory chapter we argued that the child protection field tends to be over-organized by the problem of denial. This comes about because of the overarching prominence helping professionals tend to confer on acknowledgement as the primary vehicle for change. This viewpoint commonly results in very high levels of risk being ascribed to situations seen to involve denial, to such an extent that many such cases come to be regarded as untreatable (as well as Dale et al. 1986, see, for example, Gelles 2000). We have no argument with the assertion that denial is an indicator of increased risk of re-abuse. Our argument is that the level of risk commonly ascribed to the problem of denial is over-inflated. To our eyes, at least some of the dangerousness ascribed to ACADE cases comes about because of the powerlessness professionals experience about how to build meaningful safety in the face of behaviour they view as denial.

Our view, put simply, is that the denial is not the core of the problem; rather the alleged abuse is the main problem. Acknowledgement is certainly one path towards future safety, but it is only one means and, as already noted, tends to be the exception rather than the rule in ACADE cases. Further, the dominant 'acknowledgement-is-essential' paradigm obscures the reality that it is possible to create safety in ACADE cases even without acknowledgement and that even with a full acknowledgement children can still be, and are, re-abused. The resolutions way of thinking about child abuse aims to organize all practice around directly targeting and building future safety whether acknowledgement is forthcoming or not. This is the heart of the resolutions approach to denied abuse and is represented diagrammatically in Figure 3.2.

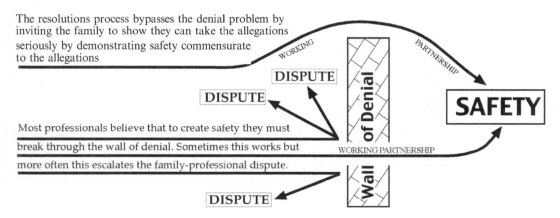

Figure 3.2 The resolutions approach and the problem of 'denial'

Focusing on safety creates a shift from the narrow emphasis on changing the alleged perpetrator, to broader aims including strengthening the likely safer parent, building a network of safe adults around the family, and making public the concerns and allegations to as many people as possible in and around the family. This is a shift away from a dispute about the past towards taking positive action that will satisfy the courts and the statutory agencies. Focusing on future safety is also usually a more energizing context in which to build partnership and collaboration.

Safety-organized practice

The whole of the resolutions process is designed to enable the professionals, the family and their network to collaborate together within a constructive, future-focused context, concentrating on creating a rigorous, family-enacted safety plan that addresses the seriousness of the allegations. This is the primary practice outcome of the resolutions work. In Chapters 7 and 9 we will describe in considerable detail our ideas for creating meaningful safety plans with the family and their kin and friendship networks.

While the idea of organizing practice to create future safety rather than organizing it in reaction to the alleged denial is a concept that is relatively easy to understand, it can be challenging to enact given the power the concept of denial holds in the consciousness of the helping professions. To demonstrate the challenge that safety-organized practice can pose, we want to return to the example described earlier of the family in which the father had denied the allegations of sexually abusing his two primary school-aged children. In this case, Andrew had worked with the children's aunt, who understood clearly that social services had substantiated that her brother had perpetrated the abuse. Arising from the work with Andrew, the aunt and her partner had committed themselves to demonstrating to social services that the children were safe and protecting the father from any possible future allegations by ensuring he was never alone with the children when he visited them. Since they lived in an isolated location and social services could not provide supervisors, the aunt ensured friends of hers who understood the sexual abuse concerns were always present when the father visited so they could provide independent verification that the children were safe. The aunt and her partner continued to do these things for the eight months the children were with them. During this period, the children, both of whom suffered severe learning difficulties, stabilized and made progress in ways they had not achieved previously in their lives. All of this was done with the approval of the relevant social services professionals. During the final month of the placement, however, the social services professionals involved with the case changed and the new team leader was not comfortable with the safety-organized logic of the case practice. The new team leader decided to remove the children from the aunt's care based on the fact that she refused to openly acknowledge the father had sexually abused the children.

From our perspective, the aunt had done everything asked of her to demonstrate the children were safe, but without this woman acknowledging that she believed her brother had sexually abused his children this was not enough for the new team leader. This demonstrates well the challenge that the safety-organized logic of the resolutions approach can present, as well as the need to maintain a common agreement about the direction of the casework among all the key professionals.

Principle 6: Skilful use of authority and leverage

Helping professionals have a strong proclivity to want to see change arise out of the one-to-one relationship they have with their client. Clark calls this the social work professions' 'characteristic myopia' (2000: 92). Eileen Munro, looking specifically at child protection practice, believes that child protection professionals' preference for the personal and private is a major obstacle for 'changing their use of theory and evaluating practice' (1998: 89). Within the therapy arena most theory and training is constructed around working with voluntary clients or patients. It is not surprising, then, that many therapists are wary of working with child protection cases. In the family therapy field, leading figures like Haley (1980) and Boscolo et al. (1987) have argued that social control has no place in the therapy room.

These sorts of perspectives often make it difficult for helping professionals to work with situations of severe child abuse, since involuntary clients will often only engage in a working relationship through skilful use of statutory authority and leverage. While not a common topic in the helping literature, there is an increasing body of written material on the subject (Winn 1996; Jeffreys and Stevenson 1997; Turnell and Edwards 1997 and 1999; MacKinnon 1998; Trotter 1999 and 2002; DePanfilis 2000; Healy 2000; Rooney 2000; Turnell 2004;).

The skilful use of authority is absolutely central to using the resolutions approach throughout each stage of the process. As MacKinnon and James (1992: 175–6) observe:

> The exercise of coercion by those mandated to intervene in family violence appears to be a necessary aspect of protecting the vulnerable and creating leverage for change. Unless coercion is used in a considered and skilful fashion, however, it is likely to reinforce the very beliefs that allow an abusive parent to maintain violence as an option.

Leverage and the capacity to use authority arise in the first instance in child abuse cases from the involvement of the statutory child protection agency and/or the court. It is then the role of the resolutions therapist to utilize this leverage skilfully to engage the family in the process of change. Figure 3.3 demonstrates how the resolutions professionals locate themselves to construct the leverage needed to implement the resolutions approach.

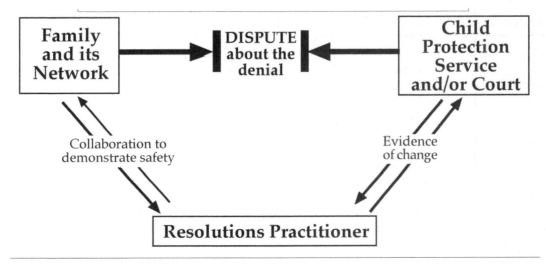

Figure 3.3   The position of the resolutions professional

As MacKinnon observes, 'leverage can be constructed or elicited when the therapist has some influence over a situation, event or relationship that is valued by the parent' (1998: 164). The primary leverage in the resolutions approach arises from offering the family the opportunity to demonstrate to social services and the court (when involved) that they can provide a safe environment for their children in the future so that they can reunify. In this way the resolutions practitioner offers the family and the statutory agency a way out of the dispute about the alleged denial. This is the value that the resolutions professional offers to both the family and the statutory agency, which creates a point of leverage and influence for the therapist in working with both the family and the other professionals. In the words of one parent whose family had been through the resolutions programme, the resolutions practitioner is 'someone to help you overcome the barriers between yourselves and social services' (Hiles 2002: 28).

Practising and learning to use leverage skilfully

Since the skilful use of leverage is often not part of the helping professionals' usual toolkit, most professionals need to spend time developing and practising this skill. This was certainly the case for Andrew when he first began to use the resolutions approach in 1996 under the supervision of Susie and her colleagues. At that time, Andrew's practice as a family therapist drew upon a more typical therapeutic agenda that prioritizes starting where the client is, listening carefully, understanding the client's experience, matching the client's language, and allowing the client to define both the problem and the desired solution. These therapeutic skills are still important in the resolutions process, but the therapist is also purposefully directive and influential in this approach.

The resolutions approach often involves responding firmly to many challenges from family members as well as questioning their language and thinking. The approach also involves asking them to think about and do things that are difficult and that they would probably otherwise avoid. These include eliciting and maintaining family members' involvement in creating a straightforward explanation for the children about the allegations; asking the parents to find people from the family's naturally occurring network and telling them about the allegations; involving the parents in a hypothetical exploration of what it would be like to be in a family in which equivalent abuse was acknowledged; and challenging the family and its network to consider the worst possibilities indicated by the allegations and building a safety plan to those contingencies.

As the last case example of the two siblings involved in alleged sexual abuse demonstrated, successful implementation of the resolutions process also requires constant negotiations with a range of professionals typically involved in these cases. This will often include advocating and defending the safety-organized focus and objectives of the resolutions approach, while at the same time sustaining and maintaining the ongoing involvement and commitment of those professionals in the process. For Andrew, it took a number of years before he felt confident and comfortable in integrating the more usual therapist's skill set alongside the influential role required by the resolutions approach. Andrew believes it would have been much more likely that the two siblings could have remained with their paternal aunt if he had been more alert to the arrival of the new supervisor and met with him quickly to argue for the safety of the placement. While it takes most professionals time to find their ease with this role, in every new case we undertake we continue to learn more about using leverage skilfully.

Principle 7: A 'dirty' solution to an 'ugly' problem

Writing and reflecting on his career in child protection services, Gerald de Montigny states that he came to realize that his practice and that of his colleagues 'did not conform to the idealizations of the texts. Yet we did our best inside the reality of the organization. It is this reality that must serve as the beginning for enquiry and theorizing and not the idealized fantasies of social work educators of what good social work should look like' (1995: 131). While de Montigny is focusing specifically on the social work profession, his words are a remarkably candid articulation of the unspoken experience of many other professionals who work with child abuse. Most professionals find themselves practising in the uncertain space between the idealizations of theory, their own best hopes of being able to improve the circumstances of maltreated children, and the day-to-day realities of the complexity and messiness of the interactions between the client family and the professional helping systems. Rather than frame his practice as 'ideal' in any sense, de Montigny goes on in his final chapter to speak about his best practice as 'dirty' practice. He writes 'real social workers get dirty week after week. Their lives and the lives of clients cannot be scrubbed clean' (1995: 223).

As de Montigny indicates, helping professions have a penchant to speak, write and act as if it is possible to achieve ideal solutions to problems of child abuse. This is probably in part a legacy of Enlightenment visions of the perfectability of the human condition, which not only inform Western culture generally but were also a central part of the underpinning logic that saw the emergence of helping professions within Western countries. This tendency is frequently demonstrated in the way child death inquiries are conducted. Such inquiries tend to start out with high ideals and strong public statements that suggest answers will be found so that the sort of tragedy the inquiry is considering will never happen again. However, these same inquiries have a tendency to conclude their activities with an extensive report focused primarily on organizational and procedural change. While the changes these reports propose often seem compelling, they also leave many feeling that the problems they are designed to solve have been made more, rather than, less complex (Parton 2004; Reder and Duncan 2004).

The search for ideal solutions is understandable since child protection work focuses on the needs of society's most vulnerable children. We would suggest, however, that aspiring to ideal solutions leads the professional towards exhaustion and pessimism because those ideals do not equate well with the complex and contested day-to-day realities of dealing with situations of severe child abuse. In like manner, we believe the helping professions' usual devotion to the ideal of perpetrator acknowledgement is a recipe for professional fatigue in many ACADE cases. Greater space is needed within the helping professions to speak openly about the uncertainty of practice in the face of the complexity of a case bogged down in a denial dispute. Following de Montigny's lead, we would suggest that it is more realistic and honest to adopt a pragmatic position that the best professional endeavours with situations of severe child abuse usually involve finding the least dirty solution conceivable to an ugly and complex problem. These are strong words, and some might feel they dishonour and diminish the efforts of committed professionals. On the contrary, however, we believe we are articulating a position that is closer to the realities of working in the child protection field, and one that offers a more grounded and sustainable position from which to practice.

The resolutions approach as our best 'dirty' solution to the complex problem of denied child abuse

For us, developing the resolutions approach has been the practice consequence of the pragmatism of seeking the best dirty solution we can conceive of to the complex problem of ACADE-type cases. The resolutions approach is not an ideal solution. In an ideal world, in situations of denied child maltreatment where abuse has occurred, we would certainly want the perpetrator to acknowledge responsibility, make an apology for the abuse, and undertake long-term therapy. We would also want to see substantial long-term professional and community support provided to all members of the family to enable them to deal with the problems flowing from the abuse. In reality, these sorts of outcomes will come about in very few ACADE cases. The resolutions approach is the best response we have been able to develop faced within the gap between the idealized solutions of the texts and our lived experience of the ways families and professional systems typically respond to each other when in dispute about alleged child abuse.

Chapter **Four**

BEGINNINGS: PREPARATIONS AND ENGAGEMENT

In this chapter we will explore how to begin the resolutions process. The opening section of the chapter focuses on the preparatory task of briefing first the professionals and then the family. The second section describes the process of engaging the crucial members of the family, once the decision to go ahead with the resolutions programme has been taken.

Section 1: Preparations

When the resolutions practitioner thinks about offering a resolutions-type service to a particular family, it is vital that they think systemically. Over the years of developing this model we have watched a number of experienced therapists who were excited to learn about the resolutions approach and in their excitement quickly offered the programme to a family with whom they had an existing relationship. Inevitably, this family had been caught up in a long struggle with social services regarding alleged abuse and the therapist wanted to find a way forward for the family. Usually, the family, because of their connection to the therapist, embraced the concept, but ultimately the resolutions process got nowhere because, while the family was on board, the statutory authorities saw little or no merit in the idea.

Briefing the professionals

First steps often define a journey. The first step the resolutions practitioner should take before proposing the programme to a family is to secure the endorsement of the statutory authorities. Social services and any court involved in the matter hold ultimate authority about how the case will progress and their leverage and influence are needed throughout the resolutions process. It is also crucial to brief all of the other key professionals who have significant ongoing involvement with the case. Once statutory endorsement is forthcoming and, at a minimum, the other professionals accept the use of the resolutions process, this opens the door for proposing the programme to the family.

Usually the initial inquiry about using the resolutions programme comes from a child protection worker or a court-appointed child representative who approaches the resolutions practitioner to explore the appropriateness of the approach for a particular case. In our experience, numerous exploratory conversations are required before the idea reaches some sort of critical mass so that a decision to use the approach is possible. Usually, the more professionals that are involved in a case, the longer this exploratory stage takes. However the first inquiry arises, our approach is always to provide a straightforward explanation of the resolutions process and offer a written summary, similar to that provided in Chapter 2, for the professional to take away and discuss with colleagues. As soon as an inquiry directly involves social services, we emphasize that use of the resolutions method requires the following three minimum commitments from the child protection agency:

1. The child protection worker allocated to the case must attend at least four of the resolutions sessions: the words and pictures session involving the children; the session where the words and pictures document is presented to the network; and two sessions involving the creation and presentation of the safety plan.
2. The child protection worker must be available for regular consultations with the resolutions practitioner throughout the life of the resolutions case.
3. The child protection worker must be actively involved in the co-creation of the safety plan and monitoring its implementation during the reunification process.

These expectations of social services need to be agreed upon from the outset, because the resolutions practitioner cannot afford to be in a position where they are working with a family and find that social services are unclear about their role. Sometimes social services do shy away from such time-intensive requirements, but more often social services engage with the resolutions service because the approach provides a productive way forward in worrying circumstances on which they have already expended considerable time and energy unproductively. Additionally, the caseworker is often keen to be involved because the resolutions programme gives them a safe environment to observe another professional working with a family they have struggled with. It is worth noting that we prefer if possible to have the social services worker attend and observe every session. Frequently, we are able to achieve this outcome.

The statutory child protection worker's active involvement in the resolutions approach is vital because:

- This enables the worker to gain increased insight into the family's perspective and to directly verify, on behalf of the statutory agency, the extent and nature of progress that is made during the resolutions process.
- The worker's presence underlines for the family that it must address the seriousness of the issues and implement future safety in ways that are convincing for the statutory agency.
- The worker's direct involvement enables the resolutions practitioner to stay focused on building working relationships with the family and professionals so that the issues can be seriously dealt with, separate from the dispute about responsibility for the alleged abuse.
- The worker's presence keeps the resolutions practitioner directly mindful of helping the family to deliver outcomes that will satisfy the statutory agency.

When the discussions among the professionals have advanced beyond exploratory conversations towards a more serious intent to utilize the programme, we ask social services to host a formal gathering so we can brief all the relevant professionals. At this stage we also ask to read the relevant written material so that we can go into that meeting with a good working knowledge of the particular case. At the briefing we explain the approach in detail, focusing particularly on how it might apply to the case in hand, and revisit our expectations regarding the involvement of all professional participants including social services. During the subsequent discussion we always clarify that all professionals are able to accept the resolutions objective of working towards safe reunification without an admission from the possible perpetrator. This matter needs to be dealt with overtly at the preparatory stage so that it does not become a sticking point later, after the programme has begun.

The importance of briefing and involving all the relevant professionals cannot be overemphasized. A considerable body of research suggests professional collaboration is a critical indicator of good outcomes for high-risk cases (Reder et al. 1993; Birchall and Hallett 1995; Department of Health 1995 and 2002; MacKinnon 1999). Further, our experience tells us that the resolutions cases in which we have experienced most difficulties are those where we did not take the time to fully brief or involve key professionals in the process at the outset.

Briefing the family

Once professional consensus regarding using the resolutions approach has been achieved, this clears the way to brief the family and their advisors about the programme. The steps involved in briefing the family include:

1. Verifying with the family that they are seeking reunification. In situations of alleged sexual abuse made by an older child or teenager, this also involves confirming separately with the young person that they are interested in reunification.
2. Providing written information regarding the programme to the family and their advisors.
3. Briefing the parents and their advisors in a similar manner to the professional meeting described above. We always encourage parents to involve legal representatives in the briefing process. (In one highly contested case in which Andrew was involved with separated parents, this meant the briefing was undertaken with 11 different lawyers!)

Throughout the briefing process we continually underline that we will bypass the dispute about whether the caregiver or parent against whom the allegations have been directed did or did not injure or abuse the child in question. We explain that whatever happened in the past, our job is to look forward and provide the family with an opportunity to reunify by demonstrating to social services and the court that whatever has been alleged cannot happen in the future. We emphasize that to do this means we will have to discuss difficult issues that will undoubtedly make them feel uncomfortable, but that our aim in this is to make sure we cover all the issues that the statutory authorities would want us to address.

In cases where a teenager or older child (for brevity we will mostly use the term 'young person' from here on) has made sexual abuse allegations, we usually meet separately with that young person in the company of the likely safer parent or someone the young person trusts. We explain each aspect of the programme very carefully to the young person and answer their questions, emphasizing throughout that we will involve them in each step of the resolutions process. Inevitably, the young person is particularly interested in the words and pictures explanation as a mechanism for getting the allegations out in the open in their family. We stress that we will ensure that they are comfortable with the explanation and the process before we present it to their siblings and extended family. We also ask the young person to meet regularly with an independent support person (perhaps a school counsellor, a youth worker, a residential care worker or the like) throughout the resolutions process. This provides the opportunity for the young person to explore independently the ramifications of the programme and whether it is working for them. The support person can also accompany the young person to all the resolutions sessions they are to be involved in. With the young person's permission, the support person can also act as the young person's advocate with the resolutions practitioner, which provides an independent avenue to keep the practitioner accountable to the young person's needs and perspectives. We ask the young person to take some time to think about whether they are willing to allow us to go ahead with the resolutions process.

Once the parents and their advisors have a good understanding of the programme, we similarly ask them to take time to consider their decision regarding involvement. Often, when parents advise us that they have decided to participate, the parent against whom the allegations have been directed will state that they really have no choice, the resolutions programme is their only way forward. Some professionals might want to argue that this is a poor motivation, but it is one that we will always accept since parents caught up in situations of alleged abuse frequently feel they have few options open to them. However they arrive at their decision, the resolutions programme does not begin until the parents, and where relevant the young person, have elected on their own terms to participate.

Section 2: Engaging the parents by creating space for multiple stories

Clients of helping services, of whatever type, first and foremost want the professional to understand them (Hubble et al. 1999; Trotter 2004). In ACADE cases, this basic element of the helping relationship often breaks down because the statutory professional has difficulty conceiving how to offer understanding, without feeling that they are condoning the alleged abuse. Ultimately, the success of the resolutions programme depends on the practitioner's ability to create professional understanding for the parents' stories, while also building their capacity to entertain the seriousness of the concerns that the statutory authorities have regarding the alleged abuse. In this section we will explore how we set about this task in the engagement stage. The chapter will conclude with an example of a child protection worker using these same skills during an initial child protection investigation in a case involving an injured infant of 4 months.

The first session: *starting with the parents' story*

As the family begins the resolutions programme, the first item of business involves asking the parents to tell their story about the events surrounding the allegations. Whether lay or professional, people who feel stuck in protracted disputes, such as those that arise in ACADE situations, tend to repeatedly tell the same story about their experience of the events, in the same particular way. This sort of storytelling is usually unproductive and unsatisfying, since it will tend to lead the tellers of the story, in this case the parents, back into a sense of disputation and powerlessness. So while we listen to the parents' story, we also endeavour to actively shape how this story is told, so that it does not further feed the frustration of the denial dispute.

In guiding how the story is told, we are seeking to introduce a sense of difference into the conversations (Watzlawick et al. 1974; Fisch et al. 1982; de Shazer 1991) through the questions we ask and the aspects we pay most attention to. To keep a sense of forward momentum to the parents' story, we seek to focus on:

1. What happened next?
2. Keeping out of the denial dispute
3. Crucial events
4. Meanings the parents ascribe to the events
5. Sticking points
6. Parents' insights into other perspectives
7. Mapping the terrain through the parents' eyes

1. What happened next?

Typically, we start to shape the storytelling by asking the parents to take us back to the beginning of the saga and talk us through the events chronologically. Throughout this conversation, we mostly listen while the parents talk and we keep our questions focused around simply asking 'what happened next?' Focusing on the sequence of events as the parents remember them is usually a straightforward mechanism to sustain a sense of forward momentum to the narrative and of intervening when the parents are caught up with one particular issue or incident. Throughout the parents' story we are also listening for small signs of safety or protectiveness that we may or may not comment upon, but will certainly make note of for future use. Examples we consider notable would include a parent taking the child to the doctor or hospital, extended family members involving themselves in the situation, or a mother going to the police interview with the child at the time of the allegation.

2. Keeping out of the denial dispute

When parents begin the resolutions programme they have generally been caught up in a denial dispute with social services for some time. In our experience this tends to mean that the parents have usually become habituated in talking about the problem to professionals in ways that seek to assert their innocence. It is therefore almost certain that the parents will seek to engage the resolutions practitioner in the same manner. It is important that the resolutions practitioner quickly demonstrates to the parents that they will stay out of the denial dispute, and to achieve this it is valuable to have strategies in mind for managing this situation. Our most usual strategy for achieving this is to paraphrase the parents' position and then (re)state that our role is to stay out of the argument about what exactly happened. This might proceed in something like the following manner:

Firstly, paraphrasing with statements like:

'Okay so it's clear to me that you are saying you didn't sexually abuse your stepdaughter.'

'So you are saying you have no idea how to explain how these injuries happened to your baby.'

Secondly, restating our role by saying something like:

Do you remember I said I was going to leave whether or not this did or didn't happen, or who did it, up on an imaginary shelf? If I side with your position that you didn't do it, I won't be able to help you at all and social services certainly won't want me to work with you. On the other hand, if I accept the social services' worry that you did do it as true, I'm sure I'll just end up in a fight with you and then I'll be no good to you either. My place in all this is to take the concerns social services have seriously and help you to show them that nothing like that can happen in the future so that you have the chance to get your family back together. So is it okay with you if we leave those issues on that shelf?

It is safe to say that the practitioner will have to repeat this sort of process numerous times in the first few sessions of the resolutions programme. It simply does take time for people caught up in a protracted denial dispute to engage with the resolutions approach of bypassing that dispute. Each time parents revisit the dispute we approach this as an additional opportunity to build the relational space between ourselves and the parents for the future-oriented, safety-organized process we are seeking to lead.

3. Crucial events

When parents relate their experience of a situation of alleged serious child abuse, there are usually events or aspects of the story that are particularly distressing or over which the parents believe they have been dealt with unjustly. Examples of such instances can include:

- Professionals telling one, or both, of the partners that they must separate.
- Professionals dismissing explanations parents were trying to offer for injuries to an infant.
- Parents feeling traumatized by professionals' descriptions of how they believe the injuries happened to an infant.
- A mother distressed about the fact that no professional acknowledged she acted immediately when her child made allegations of sexual abuse.
- Social services in concert with the police removing children from the parents' care with no opportunity for discussion.
- Parents not being told where their children were staying and/or given no input into where they were placed.
- Key professionals jumping to a particular judgement, without discussing their view with the parents.
- Professionals not considering the child's kinship network when placing the child outside the home.

In relating events like these, parents are inevitably emotional. In response we attempt to listen carefully, make sure they feel we understand their experience of the event and pay particular attention to the meanings they ascribe to it.

4. Meanings the parents ascribe to the events

One of the typical ways we keep the conversation moving forward and from becoming bogged down in particular events or positions is to move away from the specific issue by asking more meaning-focused questions such as:

- We could spend days talking and thinking about everything that has happened and I am pretty sure you have already done that, to help me better understand you and your experience – what was the worst aspect of it for you?

- What do you suppose is the worst of it for your partner?
- Perhaps this is a crazy question, but has there been anything good that has come out of all this for you?

In this way it is often possible to step back from being bogged down in any particular event while gaining greater insight into the parents' experience. Parents will often answer these sorts of questions by stating something like:

- They treated me like I was an idiot/an animal/a failure/like I couldn't understand/like I wasn't the child's mother/father at all.
- They judged me before they'd even talked to me.
- They weren't interested in my side of the question.
- We have learned to stand together.
- We have realized how important our family is to us.
- I wouldn't have thought before that I'd be strong enough to survive something like this.

5. Sticking points

If a parent is repeatedly going over the same ground, we will often ask questions like:

- I've heard you make these same sorts of statements several times now, is there something you feel I am not understanding?
- Is it useful to you to keep repeating this sort of position or story? How is it useful?
- Would it be okay with you to leave that issue up on the shelf today as I am aware of the time and if we aren't careful the programme will need to slow down. We can slow things down a bit and take more time here if you prefer. Do you think this is all happening a bit fast?
- Given that the social services worker is watching our discussions, do you think that when she hears you keep talking about this issue that she will feel we are building safety and moving forward or staying caught in the past?
- *(If the social services worker is not present:)* As you know I speak with the social services worker between sessions and he has the opportunity to see the video tape. What do you think they would make of the fact that you have raised this issue five times today?'

In asking these sorts of questions, as with all the ways we are attempting to direct the discussions, we are seeking to position ourselves within the conversations so that we can maximize our capacity to make the resolutions process useful to everyone involved. If we are successful, this is for us a demonstration of skilfully using the authority and leverage we have been given to assist the family to satisfy the statutory authorities through their efforts in the resolutions programme. A colleague of ours puts it another way when she tells us that to ask these sorts of questions, 'she has to put on her big girl's shoes'.

6. Parents' insights into other perspectives

By listening carefully to the parents' story we usually find opportunities within their account to explore other perspectives. For example, parents will often say things like:

- The social worker thought I did it, I guess that's fair enough, that's her job, but she needs to see I have another side of the story.
- She went to her aunt Jean because she trusts her. I think Jean tends to believe her more than me, but then she's never liked me, she never wanted me to marry her sister.
- The doctor was covering her arse I reckon. She had to say one of us injured the baby, it's the only way she could figure it out.
- My parents have been really helpful, they stuck by us and have helped out with the kids.
- I had to think about whether he'd done it, I wouldn't be a mother if I didn't. I had to run my own mental investigation, that's what social services don't realize.
- What the social worker doesn't get is that of course I can see her side of this, why else do you think I moved out?

In each of these instances, the parents are introducing other views about the events, which creates the possibility to ask further questions about the perceptions of the identified person. Sometimes we pick up that thread immediately, but more often we simply take note of other people the parents identify and return to discussing the perspective of that person in the next session, which gives us time between the sessions to reflect on what we have learned from the parents' story.

7. Mapping the terrain through the parents' eyes

In focusing on the parents' own chronology and story of the events, our aim is to map out the issues as the parents see them; to listen for their language, their perspectives, and identify people and issues that they see as important. It is worth remembering that very possibly this is the first time since the allegations came to light that the parents have experienced a helping professional paying careful attention to their story. Of itself this is inevitably a powerful intervention. For this reason, we usually dedicate a full session essentially to listening to the parents' account of events and would encourage the practitioner to tape the session so that this can be reviewed later. Taking time to listen or watch a recording of this first session always provides us with a fuller understanding of parents' viewpoint and we are then better able to engage them in the subsequent work.

Mapping the parents' language and perspectives in this way is vital if we are to fully involve them in co-creating the words and pictures explanation and in building a meaningful safety plan. Additionally, material from this first session always provides rich information for constructing the 'similar-but-different' scenarios so that they fit and are relevant to the parents' experiences. Finally, and not surprisingly, when the parents feel their story has been listened to and understood, inevitably they are more willing to open themselves to other perspectives, which we will seek to explore in the second session.

The second session: Utilizing the parents' story to explore other perspectives

In the second session our aim is to explore perspectives of others involved in the situation. Having reviewed our notes, or preferably a recording, from the previous session, we endeavour to link our questions about other perspectives with the parents' story as they have related it to us. The following are typical questions we seek to explore at this stage:

- What did the social worker/police/doctor etc., tell you about their thinking about the allegations/the injuries? What was the easiest part of that for you to hear? What was the hardest part of it for you to take in? What do you think is the most important thing about what they are thinking that you need to understand? Do you think it would surprise the social worker/judge that you can see that?
- When you made the decision to move out of home, what had you figured out about how social services saw things that led you to make that decision? How hard was it for you to see their perspective? How hard was it for you to make that decision to move out?
- It's a position no mother would want to be in – caught between their partner and their child. Most women in your situation that I have talked to say they vacillate between sometimes being more inclined to believe their partner and sometimes more inclined to believe their child. Is this your experience?
- If we create a scale from zero to ten, where zero is you don't believe what they said at all and ten is you believe it completely, what is the highest you have been in believing your husband? What is the highest you have been in believing your daughter?

- You told us last time that you conducted your own mental investigation. What sorts of questions were you asking yourself?
- For you ____ (*possible abuser*), what is it like to think your wife was making her own judgements about what you and your daughter were saying?
- You've said you've resigned from being a scout leader/Sunday school teacher/day care provider/sports instructor; can you explain to me what led you to that decision? What did you tell the church leaders/scout leaders/boss/coordinator about the situation? Have you thought that maybe this individual might be a really helpful person for us to involve later when we come to creating a safety network to show social services the kids are safe and protect you from any further allegations or misunderstandings?
- Who in your extended family and friendship network knows about the situation? What do they know? What have you told them? What have social services told them? What have you explained to them about why ____ (*partner or child*) are not living at home now?
- You said in the last session that your parents have been helpful, are there other people who have been helpful too? How have they been helpful to you through all this?
- Who would you say most agrees with your perspective? Who do you think isn't quite sure what to think?
- In terms of the people who most believe you and the people who perhaps aren't sure what to think, who do you think social services and the court would most want us to involve in the safety network? Wouldn't social services be more suspicious of the people who have been fighting your corner against them? Have you thought about the idea that the people in your family and your friends who are a bit more non-committal might actually be a real asset to you in getting back together? When you look at it this way, do you think it might be worth slowing down those who want to argue so strongly for your innocence?
- What do you think your mother/sister/father/brother/best friend/ priest makes of all this? What do you want to explain to them about what has happened?
- What do you think the doctor was thinking? What do you think they are most worried about? What do you think led them to write that in their evidence?

These questions need to be asked with sensitivity to the dynamics between the partners. Sometimes we will set the scene for a question by telling the likely abuser first that we want to ask their partner a particular question that they might find uncomfortable. Then we check with them whether it is okay to ask some difficult questions at that time. Often this provides a graceful means of raising challenging issues while acknowledging the pressure the couple may be feeling.

In situations in which infants have been hurt and medical experts believe the parents' explanations do not provide a reasonable account of the injuries, we usually explore different explanations in the following manner:

1. We review together the explanations the parents have given previously (some or all of this territory may have already been covered in the first session).
2. We ask about the explanations the doctors or other professionals may have offered (this is sensitive territory since sometimes the professional explanations parents have been given and the way they have been presented to them has left them angry or traumatized).
3. We ask if the parents would be willing to hear a range of explanations that other parents have told us when doctors have been worried about an injured child. At this point we typically make use of a baby-like stuffed toy and demonstrate some of the behaviour we are talking about while we offer the following explanations:

> One couple said that their baby woke in the middle of the night and wondered whether her ribs might have been broken when they were trying to burp her. They said they were going like this (*patting the soft toy's back reasonably gently*) and then ended up going like this (*now smacking the toy's back with increasing force*) when baby just wouldn't be quiet.

> Another couple said they got up in the middle of the night and the baby was just crying and crying ... they couldn't get him to stop ... the father said he ended up pleading with the baby (*while shaking the doll*), for God's sake please shut up, the neighbours will hear us!!

> Another mother said to me that her baby was crying and she was pleading with her baby to go to sleep ... in the end she'd just had enough and just dumped the baby (*throwing the soft toy into a seat*) in the cot and walked away thinking that was best.

In this way, the parents can perhaps hear a story that is not about caregivers who are monsters (which is often the message the parents have received in their discussions with professionals about the cause of the injuries), but rather of parents who are struggling to cope and at their wit's end. If used skilfully, these enacted explanations can open up more territory in talking with the parents about the injuries. The purpose here is not to get an admission but to:

- Provide some emotional release around the difficult issue of how the injuries might have occurred (often people are in tears during these explanations).
- Provide the parents with the chance to demonstrate to social services that they can consider broader, less innocent explanations.
- Set a context in which we can more fully revisit the causation issue later, in the similar-but-different stage.

Two processes beneficial for amplifying differing perspectives

To build a context with the parents where it is possible to explore alternative viewpoints, we focus on two processes:

1. Relationship questions

We constantly make use of a style of questioning that is variously referred to in the family therapy literature as 'relationship' (Berg and Kelly 2000), 'circular' (Boscolo, Ceccin, Hoffman and Penn 1987) or 'internalized-other' (Epston 1993) questioning. The essence of this sort of questioning is to ask the client for their insights regarding the perspective of another, for example asking a parent to describe the perspective of social services or another family member. These types of questions are a powerful mechanism for negotiating territory where the interpretation of particular events is contested and contentious. Relationship questions are a useful means of enabling the practitioner to resist the urge to 'tell' or preach at parents about alternative perspectives and also usually creates a context that allows parents to demonstrate that they are aware of the different positions of the other important players involved in their situation.

2. Weaving between difficult and easier topics

Negotiating and exploring differing views about events that have led to allegations in an ACADE case is a challenging process for everyone involved. For this reason we are very mindful of monitoring the extent to which the people we are working with are finding the subject distressing. We constantly seek to weave backwards and forwards between the parents' own perspectives and more challenging views, and between subjects that are experienced more positively and those that are more uncomfortable. Within this process we constantly seek to energize the discussions by complimenting or affirming the parents for being willing to engage in difficult conversations about distressing possibilities and viewpoints.

While working to open up space to explore differing and often difficult viewpoints, our aim is always to simultaneously sustain and deepen the working relationship with all members of the family and their network. The resolutions process hangs or falls on the capacity of the practitioner to achieve this. At times these conversations are tense but we are always looking to create a relationship in which the family members who have undertaken the resolutions process are able to say:

> Here I'm neither guilty or not-guilty. (A father in a sexual abuse case Susie worked with)

> He (*resolutions practitioner*) read the report and said to us, I don't know, I'll never know. He didn't just refer to the classic, 'Well seven doctors have said . . .' (Hiles 2002: 20).

> He actually spoke to me not at me. (Hiles 2002: 22).

> They made me look at it from other people's point of view. Helped me to know the seriousness of it all, of the situation that had arisen, how injuries can happen. Made me feel we did have to do a few things within our family to satisfy other agencies to allow me to go home. That way he (*resolutions practitioner*) made it, allowed us to accept that we had to do that. (Gumbleton 1997: 56)

Cases involving sexual abuse allegations made by a young person

As the scenario in the first chapter exemplifies, helping professionals often fail in their attempts to create long-term constructive outcomes in cases where young people make sexual abuse allegations against one of their caregivers. Professionals tend to build their interventions around a one-position response, such as the mother must leave the partner or the teenager must never again live in the family home. The problem is that the fluidity of family members' positions and responses throughout the period of dealing with such allegations tends to make such simple framings and solutions unworkable. Quite apart from the fluid and changing responses of parents, a teenager who has made allegations of sexual abuse is typically a very dynamic proposition. For example, it is not uncommon for a teenager in this situation to:

- Retract their allegations.
- Seek to return home because they miss their family or because they want to protect their younger siblings from abuse.
- Attempt suicide out of feelings of failure or self-blame.
- Find that life in the looked-after system is a distressing experience.
- Become angry or oppositional with professionals because they feel the helpers don't seem to be helping them very much.

In situations involving injured infants and sexual abuse allegations concerning younger children, the trajectory and outcomes of using the resolutions approach tend to be reasonably predictable, whether a family reunifies or not. Using the resolutions approach in situations of teenager-alleged but 'denied' sexual abuse is rather more of a 'work in progress'. Each stage of the process is often more challenging and involves more time and sessions because the work has consequences not only for the parents but also for a young person who is exercising at least some measure of independence. Additionally in these cases, the possibility of reunification is often constantly under review because the teenager may well run hot and cold about the idea.

Despite this, the resolutions approach is still particularly useful in these cases because the professional does not need to colonize a particular position or outcome but can use the process to explore the differing family and professional positions that unfold. At the same time, the approach creates a context in which the practitioner can engage the family members in purposive action; creating the words and pictures explanation of the allegations, involving an informed network around the family and young person, leading hypothetical discussions with the caregivers that explore worst case scenarios and creating a rigorous safety plan for the future. While these are all constructive interventions, and are usually seen as such by the young person, they can also, for a variety of reasons, still be distressing for them. Therefore it is crucial to proceed slowly and to weigh the impacts of the process with the young person at each stage. This is challenging, however, because working in this manner demands vulnerability on the part of the resolutions practitioner and a tolerance for uncertainty in a distressing and contested context.

When we meet with the young person at the engagement stage, we hope to see them together with their support person. If there has been some difficulty in establishing a connection with an appropriate support person we will slow the resolutions process until this relationship is in place. In meeting the young person and their support person we brief the support person about the resolutions approach, focusing particularly on the role we hope they can play. While this covers ground the young person has been over before, it provides another opportunity to deepen the young person's understanding about the resolutions process. Very often, the young person has given considerable thought to what we explained to them in the preparatory briefing session and often they have many questions. After exploring any questions or issues they have, we focus on preparing the young person for the words and pictures process.

To do this, we re-describe the words and pictures process and typically ask the young person how, and whether, an agreed-on, out-in-the-open explanation will make a difference for them. In our experience, the young person will very much still want the words and pictures process to go ahead but is often also worried that the younger children might blame them for making the allegations and upsetting the family. This would be typical of the sort of issue that teenagers and young people raise during the course of the resolutions process, and it is important to win their confidence by exploring and responding to their concerns. To this particular issue we usually propose that we will explore the draft of the words and pictures explanation with them and their support person before the explanation is finalized. We explain that in our experience in other cases younger children do not blame the older sibling, but that if this situation does unfold we will be active in dealing with the problem. We also let the young person know that we want them to witness the children's words and pictures session for themselves and offer them the options of being in the room or observing from behind a one-way screen or through a video link. In this, or like manner, we seek to continually keep the young person and their support person informed and involved throughout the life of the resolutions process.

In the next chapter we will describe how we explore the children's perspectives in ACADE cases and our process for drawing together the multiple stories into the words and pictures story.

Before concluding this chapter, we want to describe a case example from Olmsted County Child and Family Services in Minnesota. In this case, an after hours child protection worker, Donna Smyrk, undertook an investigation regarding an injured 4-month-old baby, who we will call Harry, which involved working with a range of family and professional perspectives about the problem. This case example was prepared following interviews by Andrew with Donna and Harry's parents 'Holly' and 'Richard' and from journal notes Holly wrote about the experience. This is a particularly valuable example at this point since it provides a direct insight into the sort of context that usually gives rise to a denial dispute.

Donna's case

Donna Smyrk was called to a local hospital early one evening in 2004, when doctors discovered Harry had suffered multiple bruises on his face, stomach and leg. The emergency room doctor assessed the bruises to be non-accidental and of different ages, probably related to at least three separate incidents over the previous two to two and a half weeks.

Holly wrote in her journal that: 'The doctor told Richard and I "I'm going to call some people to take some pictures and to come and talk to you". At that moment for the first time I thought someone might have hurt my little baby. Then I realized, they are going to think it is us.'

Holly also knew someone who worked in the emergency ward who came over to the couple and said: 'He (the doctor) has just called the "fricking people"'. At about the same time Holly caught sight of the doctor's notes and saw the words 'child abuse' in the text. She said this sickened her.

Not surprisingly, when Donna arrived at the hospital, Holly and Richard were distressed. Donna described that:

> I told them that what I know from the doctor as well as from training I've had in my job is that when there is bruising in these places, on a baby that's 4 months old it is more than likely that somebody caused the injuries. So what I need to do is start the process of trying to figure out how he got these bruises. So I explained my role and what the process of assessment was in this way.

> The whole time I was always acknowledging; 'this must be really hard for you. I'm sorry that I have to do this, but its my job.'

> We were talking about all the people that had been with Harry over the past two to two and a half weeks and talking about their ideas about how he got hurt. They had ideas they thought maybe the babysitter caused the injuries or that he did it to himself.

> I told them: 'my best bet is that somebody did this to Harry. I've never met you before, or the babysitter or your dad or your friends, so I need to just be open to any one of you doing this to him. So one thing I need to do is to pretend that one of you did it. I just can't go, "you guys are really nice, you look like good parents, you didn't do it".' I said: 'Even if I was your sister I couldn't do that'.

Holly wrote:

> Donna asked us to think hard about any possible explanation for the bruises, she asked us about his crying habits, about people who'd been with him and she asked us about us. I began to feel I could tell her my life story. Donna explained to us that in most situations like this the baby is placed in foster care until there is a full investigation. She said the fact is Harry has bruises on him we cannot explain, but it is not a proven fact that there is child abuse. Then Donna asked me a question that saved the tiny bit of sanity I had left in my body – she asked is there anyone who can stay with you guys or who hasn't had contact with Harry in

the past two to two and a half weeks? Anyone who could be with you 24/7?

The couple suggested Holly's mother, 'Janine'. Holly then rang Janine and she came to the hospital with Holly's sister. After asking Holly and Richard if she had their permission to tell Janine everything that had happened, Donna immediately interviewed Janine when she arrived at the hospital. Donna described:

> First I told the grandmother what I was doing, and then I asked her for 'nuts and bolts' information; her work, where she lives and whether she'd had contact with Harry over the past two and a half weeks, which she had not. Then I got her together with Harry and he just beamed when he saw his grandma and was happy with her. So that was a very good sign. The grandma felt very sad about the possibility that somebody had abused him, and she cried. Then after just general 'visiting' where you can just get an idea of a person, I felt confident that this woman, this grandmother, could be the safe person.

During this process it turned out that the first hospital could not undertake the additional medical tests (full skeletal X-rays, brain scan, opthomology exam and blood test) that would be required until the following day. After inquiries, Donna found that the tests could be carried out that night at another hospital, which the parents were keen to do, so that the process did not drag on, and so Harry would not have to stay overnight in a hospital. This meant everyone decamped to the second hospital. Donna related that:

> The parents each drove in a separate car, and I told them that I needed to ride with whoever was going to take the baby, because you know this is the point we have to start thinking about anybody who's a possibility (of having hurt Harry), can't be alone with the baby. They just thought that was a bit ridiculous. But I said remember, we're pretending it could be one of you. They thought it was kind of dumb, but they said okay.

Holly wrote in her journal:

> I felt like I was walking around with a sign above my head saying 'child abuser', I felt like the world would like to see me dead and take my little precious baby and live happily ever after.
>
> I said to Richard, can you promise me that you have never done anything to hurt Harry? He said never. He is a

wonderful man, he stayed strong for me and didn't get upset that I asked him that horrible question.

By the early hours of the morning the completed tests showed no other injuries or matters of concern, but the doctors at the second hospital were opposed to the idea of Harry remaining in the care of the family, even with Janine taking over the role of primary caregiver. This led to several hours of conversations and an independent assessment of the situation being undertaken by the police. When the police endorsed Olmsted County's safety plan, Donna accompanied Holly, Richard, Janine and Harry to the family home to work through the living arrangements that would now operate in the house. Primarily, this involved moving Harry's cot into the room Janine would be sleeping in and that Janine would be with Harry around the clock. Donna wrote up a contract that was signed by Holly, Richard and Janine that detailed the new arrangements and included an agreement that the county social workers could make unannounced drop-in visits at any time.

In our view Donna's work is a strong and skilful example of investigative practice that kept alive many possible stories about what might have happened to Harry, built around a respectful relationship with the parents, energized by and focused around a safety-organized plan that utilized the family's own network. Andrew asked Donna how she was able to undertake the work in this way, to which she replied:

> Firstly, I had the support of Linda (Billman), my supervisor, who I was able to ring and confer with at every step of the whole eight to nine hour process. As well as that, it was really important to juggle the positions of the doctors and their legal department, the parents and the nurses, the police and everybody because they're all important players in my job. How the parents were going to feel about social services and how this went that night, it mattered. I didn't feel any blame for anybody for anything and I knew I needed to work with all of them again.

Given the parents have provided their permission for this story to be described here, it is appropriate that the final words about this experience should come from Holly, who wrote:

> Donna was like an angel sent to us from God.

> Donna did a very good job of keeping respect for the concern of the doctor.

> She turned into a friend, a crutch for all of us.

Donna stopped over (the following week), but I know she was here because this is the way real child abusers are treated, strangers get to stop by their homes anytime they want to check up on them.

Following Donna's success of working in this way, Olmsted County Child and Family Services now routinely uses this approach in its investigation of ACADE cases involving injuries to infants. In these cases the county will almost always take out an interim care order over the child. With that in place, the parents are offered the choice to either have the child placed in care after being released from hospital or to have him or her placed back at home, but the care must involve round the clock supervision by people from their own naturally occurring network that CPS meets and approves. This second option also always involves a daily visit by a community health nurse. Parents tend to choose the latter and this is usually feasible to set up in the time frame in which the infant is hospitalized. This approach creates an immediate safety network around the family and the process means that the worker can, as Donna did, then get the parents and safety people thinking about how to demonstrate future safety. This sets the scene for ongoing safety-building work that will be required if the parents are to retain custody. This process also makes it more likely that the county can work in partnership with the parents rather than engage in a dispute, which can tend to tie up considerable organizational resources.

Chapter **Five**

FROM MANY STORIES TO THE SHARED STORY OF THE 'WORDS AND PICTURES'

Usually the biggest dilemma for professionals dealing with ACADE cases is to find a means of talking about the seriousness of the concerns with the family and its network when the likely or possible perpetrator is refuting what the professionals believe to be true. In the previous chapter we showed how we use the process of exploring multiple perspectives to create a context in which it is possible to open up differing accounts and explanations of the alleged abuse. Within the resolutions approach, this engagement work lays a foundation from which it then becomes possible to create a shared story with the parents that the statutory authorities can also endorse because it captures the seriousness of the allegations. This explanation or set of 'words' is designed as the means of explaining the concerns to the children and later to extended family and friends. When the words are explained to the children, a set of 'pictures' is also created to match the explanation and facilitate the children's understanding; hence we describe this as the 'words and pictures' process. This is possibly the most important element of the resolutions approach, since it creates a foundation of openness from which a meaningful safety plan can be generated relative to the concerns captured in the words and pictures document.

A little background to the words and pictures process

This approach to getting the concerns out in the open began to be developed in the late 1980s when Susie was chairing child protection conferences. In this role, Susie repeatedly faced the problem that children in child protection cases often knew very little, if anything, about the concerns the professionals held regarding their well-being. Susie found that even when it seemed a child might understand the concerns since they had made the abuse allegation, often their siblings did not know about the concerns, and the youngster themselves was often unclear and worried about who knew and what they knew.

A further problem in all this is that children in families facing allegations of child abuse are usually very aware that something major is happening – because, for example, they can see that their parents are distressed and because they are aware of events such as a sibling being injured and taken to hospital, the police coming to the home, or a sibling or parent having to move out of the family home – but without an explanation from adults they often make up their own. One example of this that Susie will always remember occurred in a situation where a teenage girl had alleged that her stepfather had sexually abused her. This led to the stepfather being arrested, witnessed by his 5-year-old son, but the boy was given no explanation for the event. That night the 5-year-old saw the lead television news story about an IRA bombing and concluded his father had been arrested for that crime. As well as forming their own, often misguided conclusions, when children don't have an appropriate explanation of dramatic events in their family this can tend to propel them toward anxiety reactions and obsessive-compulsive behaviours.

Aware of these problems, Susie began asking parents and carers what the children knew of the concerns. Often the parents had said little to the children, typically they were worried about what to say and where to start if they were to try and explain the events. This is not simply a problem faced by parents. Professionals, perhaps informed by an overly sentimental view of childhood innocence (Ferguson 2005; Parton 2005), are also often at a loss regarding how to communicate the enormity of the events to children caught up in situations of abuse. Whatever the cause of the difficulty professionals have in talking openly to children, research with looked-after children confirms the reality that many of these youngsters do not know why they are in care (Cashmore and Paxman, 1996; Baldry and Kemmis 1998; Cashmore 2002).

The words and pictures process

The process of creating and utilizing the words and pictures involves the following steps:

1. Explaining the process to the parents and their key advisors.
2. Offering a first draft of the explanation to the parents.
3. Refining and finalizing the explanation with the parents, their advisors and social services.
4. Providing the explanation to the children and creating the pictures for the final words and pictures document with the children.

We will explore each step of this process as we proceed through this chapter, drawing on examples relevant to different types of ACADE cases, and will conclude the chapter with an example of a words and pictures document developed to provide an explanation to a looked-after child regarding how they came to be in the care system.

Explaining the words and pictures process to the parents and their key advisors

In training, professionals new to this approach will often state that they cannot believe that parents want their children to have an honest explanation about the alleged abuse. Our experience over more than 15 years tells us that when we are able to introduce the idea of the words and pictures carefully, and successively involve the parents in the process of creating the words and pictures (usually we allow three to four sessions for this), they readily participate in the process. By locating the words and pictures process around the need for the children to have an explanation that is appropriate to their age and development, in almost every case parents are motivated to undertake this work solely on the grounds of being open with their children.

The key here is to involve the parents in a participatory exploration and evolution of the words and pictures and win their confidence that this co-created explanation will not simply enforce the statutory view but will also fairly represent their perspective. Part of this participatory process involves offering the parents the opportunity to have one or two trusted people involved in the discussions, whether a legal representative, a close friend or a member of the extended family. Just as the creation and use of the words and pictures is a journey undertaken over three or four sessions, the development of the parents' understanding of the process is continually revisited during these sessions. In this sense, the explanation of the words and pictures process is an ongoing one that begins when we first introduce the resolutions approach to the family through to presenting the document to the network and its later connection with the safety planning process. Throughout these explanations, we focus on the need to inform the children and also that the statutory authorities need to know that everyone has a fair account of the concerns, as the foundation on which the family can reunite.

The process of explaining the words and pictures process to the family overlaps and flows out of the engagement process described in the previous chapter. This overlap is particularly evident when we explore with the parents what the children know about what has happened, using questions such as:

- What do they think that Sharni makes of what is happening?
- What makes you think she knows or thinks that?
- What has Dawood been told? Who told him and when?
- What questions has Asha asked?
- What difference would it make if George knew a little more about what has happened?
- What difference would it make if Sharni doesn't know any more just yet?
- What stories might Dawood be making up for himself about what has happened? (For example about: having the police come to the home; having Daddy move out; knowing his little sister is in hospital with serious injuries; that his little sister has to live at his grandparents' home; that his older sister has had to move out, and so on.)
- What does Dawood think happened to Asha? How might he know that? What conversations might he inadvertently have overheard?
- Given that Jake is only 18 months and has been living with his grandparents since he recovered from the injuries, and given he will probably have to stay there until he is at least 2, what do you want to tell him later in life about why he had to spend almost two years at his grandparents? When do you think it will be time to give Jake an explanation? What have the grandparents already told their other grandchildren about why Jake is living with them? What explanation would you want the rest of the family to have?
- What does close friend/extended family member/school teacher/ neighbour/best friend of the child know about what has happened? Do you think your children might have heard them talking about the problem? What might they have overheard?
- What does Asha tell her friends at school about why she is no longer living at home? (In a context where she had alleged that her father had sexually abused her.) What do you think it's like for her when she sees her younger brother and sister? What do you think she would like them to be told?

- What do you think social services and/or the court want the children to know?

In our experience, parents who are caught up in ACADE scenarios simultaneously hold a desire to talk to their children alongside shame about what has happened and considerable fear about what to say to their children and how. It is therefore very possible for professionals to use the questions listed above in ways that will intimidate parents. This is particularly so if the professional asks the questions from a stance that communicates a message of 'you've been dishonest with your children' and 'why haven't you told your children the truth already?' For the sorts of questions we have just listed to be effective in recruiting the parents to participate in the words and pictures process, they need to be asked with as much sensitivity and compassion as the professional can muster regarding the parents' vulnerability.

The discussions arising from these questions also tend to work best when the professional allows the conversation to weave between subjects that are challenging and subjects that are affirming for the parents, as explored in the previous chapter. It is not a matter of using these questions to nail down the issue or problem once and for all, but rather they are a means of opening up and journeying with the parents into the dilemmas and difficulties of their situation.

Offering a first draft of the explanation to the parents

Having created a context in which the parents are engaged with the idea of providing an age-appropriate explanation for the children, we offer the parents a draft set of words that we think might work for them, their children and the statutory authority. This draft is presented to them as a document to be worked on and refined so that both they and the statutory authorities are satisfied the words convey the seriousness of the concerns in an age-appropriate manner for the children and also represent fairly the different positions about the concerns.

The words for the words and pictures process cover the following areas:

1. Who's worried about the children?
2. What are they worried about?
3. What happened then? *(This section is not always included.)*
4. Private parts *(This only applies for situations of alleged sexual abuse.)*
5. What we (family and professionals) are doing about the worries.

Alongside introducing the first draft to the parents, we also describe carefully how we intend to go about creating the words and pictures document with the children. This is important to allay fears the parents will inevitably have regarding how we plan to provide the explanation to the children.

1.   *Draft words for a situation of unexplained injuries to an infant*

The following is a typical 'first draft' set of words for an ACADE case involving injuries to a baby, presented here with the sort of dialogue we use to introduce the draft to the parents. For this example, we will imagine that the words are being prepared to explain to 'Billy' aged 5, what has happened to his baby sister, Sharni, (If the injured child is an only child, we create the words and pictures document as a mechanism to explain the events to the child when they are older.)

Andrew: I want to suggest a draft set of words that we can work on over the next few weeks and I also want to explain how I'd be suggesting we use the words to create the words and pictures with Billy. Is that okay?

Mother: Yes, we'd really like to see that, because you'd told us you've done this with other families like us.

Andrew: Okay, good. I've already showed this draft of the words to Helen (social services social worker) and she's said this is what she was hoping for. So, (*pauses*) the explanation breaks down into four sections. The first is 'Who's worried?' (*Writing headings up on whiteboard.*) The second is 'What are they worried about?' The third, 'What happened then?', and the fourth part where we tell Billy 'What we are doing about the worries'. So let's take them one at a time.

- **Who's worried?**

Andrew: To begin the session where we take Billy through the words and pictures explanation, I'll introduce myself and want to get to know Billy a little before getting into the explanation. So I'll probably talk with him about things he likes, something like that, and involve you both in that. Then I'll talk to Billy, saying something like – '*A lot of things have happened in your family in the past two years, for a while you had to live with your grandma and you know Sharni hasn't been able to live with you since she was very little. You've probably wondered why these things have happened.*' In my experience, children always nod at this point! And then I'll say something like – '*I've talked to Mummy and*

Daddy and they've agreed on exactly the words I'm going to use to explain to you what's been happening and we're going to draw (or use) pictures as we go along to help you understand.'

After this I'll ask Billy something like: *'Did you know there were some adults who had been really worried about you and Sharni?'* At that point we'll either draw or colour in a picture of some of the adults who have been worried; the doctor, policeman, the social worker, his mum and his dad. The words I'm suggesting we use to explain who's worried are:

The doctor and the social worker and the police are worried about Sharni and Billy and they have said we must make sure Sharni and Billy are safe now and in the future.

When I do this most children like Billy ask 'what were they worried about?' But if not, I'll simply say 'I'm going to tell you what they were worried about'.

- **What were they worried about?**

Andrew: The words I've drafted for us about the worries are:

Sharni was badly hurt and Mummy and Daddy took her to hospital. The doctors in the hospital said Sharni had been hurt by someone. Sharni had very big hurts on her head and chest and some of her bones were broken. The doctors were very worried; they said Sharni had been hurt at least two times and that she'd been hurt while Mummy and Daddy were looking after her. Mummy and Daddy said they didn't hurt Sharni, but the doctors and social services said they were still very worried and they had to make sure Sharni would be safe in the future.

In this part we'll either draw or colour in pictures of Sharni in hospital with a doctor looking at her and another picture of the two of you, Mummy and Daddy, looking sad and puzzled.

- **What happened then?**

Andrew: After this I'll ask Billy whether he knew what happened then. Probably he'll say he's not sure and so I'll use something like these words to explain:

The social worker said Sharni and Billy couldn't live with Mummy and Daddy after this while they sort out how to make sure everyone will be safe in the future. Aunty Jenny and Grandma said they would help, so that's why you went to live with Aunty Jenny for four months last year. After Sharni got out of hospital she went to stay with Grandma and Grandpa and that why she's still living there. We'll have a picture for this part of Sharni at Grandma and Grandpa's.

- **What are we doing?**

Andrew: Finally, its really important that we finish on a positive note and that Billy knows what we are doing about the worries, so I'd suggest the final words say something like:

Mum and Dad are working very hard with Andrew and Helen (social worker) to show everyone that Sharni will be safe with them in the future and can come home. The final picture would be one of the both of you, Mum and Dad, talking with me and Helen.

In our experience, this will be a lot to take in for the parents so we will often tend only to have a short discussion about the draft words at this stage. We underline that we will not go ahead to tell their children the explanation until they are happy with the words and understand the process fully. We give the parents a copy of the draft words and suggest that they take them home and think about any changes they might want and that we will go through it more carefully in the next session.

2.   *Draft words for a situation of alleged sexual abuse*

In presenting the draft words for a situation of alleged sexual abuse, we follow a similar process of both introducing the draft and explaining the process in greater depth to the parents. Not needing to revisit the second explanatory part of the process again, we simply provide below a typical set of words that we might offer a family facing circumstances of denied sexual abuse. This situation involves 'Jane', aged 8, and 'Jill', aged 5, in a family with separated parents.

- **Who's worried?**

The judge has said in court he is worried about Jane and Jill and wants to be sure they will be safe in the future.

In this instance, Andrew proposed drawing one picture of the mother, father, their lawyers and the social worker ('Maureen') appearing in court which would serve as the picture for both the 'Who is worried?' and 'What are they worried about?' sections. The reason for this was that the initial investigation of the allegations occurred almost three years previously. The mother felt that the children had forgotten the professionals who were involved at that time and preferred that the focus be on the court rather than the initial investigative context. While Andrew would have preferred to add another picture, perhaps of a case conference involving other professionals, this did not detract significantly from the final explanation. This example is demonstrative of the sorts of negotiations that will always unfold in the creation of the explanation.

- ### What are they worried about?

The judge is hearing worries about Jane and Jill. The worries are because Jane and Jill said that Dad touched them on their private parts and also said Dad got them to touch him on his private parts.

Dad said he didn't do these things, but the judge was still worried and can't decide what to think. The judge wants to make sure nothing like that happens to Jane and Jill and that they stay safe.

The judge has asked people to sort out the worries and that's why when you see Dad there have been people making sure everything's okay. The judge has also asked Andrew and Maureen (social services worker) to help too.

- ### Private parts

Your private parts are the parts that your swimming costume covers.

In situations of sexual abuse, we always draw a picture of a boy and girl dressed in swimming costumes and talk to the children about the names they use for their private parts. We do this to ensure everyone knows the children are clear what their private parts are, since in some situations of sexual abuse the abuser deliberately confuses children about this. We accept whatever names the children have for their private parts and then agree together that their private parts are the parts their swimming costumes cover.

- ### What we are doing about it?

Mum and Dad are all working very hard with Andrew and Maureen to show the judge that Jill and Jane will be safe.

There are two additional principles we endeavour to weave into the explanations as we draft and refine the story with the parents and other professionals:

1. Our primary aim of creating the explanation is not to try and tell the children every detail of the situation but rather to represent the seriousness of the concerns and to keep the story simple enough so they are clear about the context and the danger but not over-whelmed by them. We do not go into overly graphic detail about

the alleged abuse, whether physical or sexual, but still describe enough to convey the seriousness of the situation. Children readily understand that if an adult gets them to touch his or her private parts that this is 'yukky' and wrong. Likewise, the description of 'very big hurts to the chest and head' and 'broken bones' is enough to convey to a child the seriousness of a situation in which their sibling has suffered unexplained physical injuries. Using language that is too graphic will tend to worry most parents and tend to generate unnecessary resistance towards the process.

2. We never start the words and pictures with the worries. The first part – who is worried – is designed as a logical lead into the description of the abuse. This way of beginning provides a context for the child to connect the description of the worries to events he or she might have seen or heard about. We also end the explanation with a positive focus. Susie often describes this as 'sandwiching' difficult information between more positive information, thereby communicating to the children that their parents and ourselves are actively making sure the worries are dealt with.

Refining and finalizing the words and pictures with the parents, their advisors and social services

Once a draft of the words and pictures is 'on the table', then a process of refining the explanation can be undertaken. In our experience, most parents are relieved when we present them with this sort of draft. Very often they are worried that the explanation for the children will be more explicit and accusatory. During the refinement process in the following sessions, we are happy to modify the words that are to be used to describe the worries, but we don't allow the message about the seriousness of the worries to be diluted. However, because the description of the worries contains the rider 's/he said s/he didn't do these things', we find parents rarely seek to alter the description of the worries. This is usually the case because the parents are so relieved to have a description that doesn't try and enforce the view that 'they did it'.

Interestingly, it is not uncommon that parents actually request to strengthen the disavowal statement. In one situation of alleged sexual abuse, the father asked for the sentence to read: 'Dad has decided he won't say whether he did this or not'. In a situation involving injuries to a baby, the parents asked for the line to read: 'Daddy and Mummy decided they didn't want to talk to social services or the doctors about what happened'. Once parents realize that they are not going to be shamed and blamed in the words and pictures process, we are consistently struck by how seriously they take the task of communicating as much openness as they can muster in the explanation to their children.

Typical sorts of things that we usually explore with the parents while refining the explanation include:

- The names to use for grandparents, aunts, uncles, and other important people.
- Whether to include a statement about contact being supervised, for example: 'The judge has said that someone else has to be present when Daddy sees Melissa and Karen'.
- Which professionals should be included in the 'Who's worried?' section.
- Parents sometimes will be worried that children, particularly if they are young, might not have names to describe their own private parts or those of the opposite sex. If this is a concern for parents, we agree with them ahead of time what words they would want their children to use for each private part (penis, anus, vagina, and breasts). If indeed it does transpire that the children haven't got names of their own (this is an unusual occurrence, even with young children), then we will use the names the parents have provided.
- How to describe the social services worker – this is often a problem since it is usually very easy for children to understand the role of a judge, police and health professionals, but often the social worker is not so notable, particularly for younger children. This process of refinement sometimes means the social worker might be described by their first name or as 'the lady', or sometimes just 'the social worker'.
- Other details the parents feel are important, such as who took the baby to hospital, or who contacted the police (sometimes, for example, mothers want the story to tell that they contacted the police or their doctor about the alleged sexual abuse).

In all of these ways, the process of refinement personalizes the document for the parents and allows considerable opportunity to deepen their understanding and ownership of the explanation to be provided to the children. Throughout the refinement process we also continually revisit and deepen the parents' understanding of involving the children in creating the words and pictures document. To ensure the parents are as fully prepared as possible for the session, we often write out a full description of each step we intend to take in the session.

If the child protection worker is not observing each resolutions session, we will ask them to attend the refinement session so that they can gauge for themselves the degree of commitment the parents have to the explanation (a key sign of safety). We also do this so we can get feedback from the worker after the session or during a break to ascertain that they are comfortable with any changes. Once the worker has confirmed that the explanation carries the messages social services want conveyed, we let the parents know that we have the green light from the statutory authorities to go ahead. However, even with social services endorsement, we will not bring the children in to hear the explanation until the parents have said they are ready to go ahead with this next stage of the resolutions process.

Briefing a young person about the explanation

In situations of alleged sexual abuse made by a teenager or older child, we will meet separately with that young person to provide them with a full briefing of the explanation and how the words and pictures session is carried out. We involve their support person and, if possible, the likely non-abusing parent in this session. The presence of the likely non-abusing parent provides the opportunity to deepen their insight into the young person's experience and to strengthen their connection with their child around the difficult issue of the allegations.

In meeting with the young person, our primary aim is to make sure that they are comfortable with the explanation and ascertain what arrangements they would like so they feel supported to attend the words and pictures session. Usually their support person will come with them to the session, and on many occasions the young person elects to observe from behind a one-way glass screen or video link. If the young person is uncertain about going ahead with the words and pictures process, we will take as much time as is needed for them to fully understand and feel comfortable with the process. Our experience is that while the young person who made the allegations will inevitably feel anxiety about the words and pictures process, this is always outweighed by their desire to have the story of the allegations out in the open in their family and the family's network. The key point is to involve the young person in the process, and to do this in a way that they feel as supported as possible.

Toward informing others of the explanation

As part of the final preparations for the words and pictures session, we discuss with the parents the importance of building an informed network of people around the family. We explain again that after we've created the explanatory document the next step is for the parents to invite a group of close family and friends to the subsequent session, so together we can present the words and pictures explanation to them. This provides the family with a group of people who know what the children know and who can then participate in an informed way in building and enacting a safety plan that can be approved by social services. In cases of alleged sexual abuse, we explain that these safety people will also be involved to ensure there are no future misunderstandings or allegations that can arise against the alleged abuser.

Following this, we ask the parents:

- Who they think should know?
- Which people the children would most want to know?
- Who would they want to be involved in supervising increased contact after we have created a network of people that social services and the court know are well informed about the professionals' worries.
- Who in their network would be most useful in giving social services the greatest confidence that the children would be safe? Who do they think social services would least expect they would be willing to involve in this way? (We will inevitably suggest that these might be the very best people for them to involve.)

These explorations will usually take up most of one session. If the idea of involving others is too difficult for the parents at this point, we will make sure they understand why this is an essential part of building a safety plan that will satisfy social services and the court. Then we will suggest the parents take some time to think about the issue, perhaps take legal advice, and we can come back to how we build a safety network after the big task of creating the words and pictures is complete. In most cases, we are able to work with the parents to identify and begin approaching friends and kin before the words and pictures session with the children.

The easiest way to facilitate the transition to involving a network around the family is to involve others in the earlier sessions and to have one or two people participating and supporting the parents in co-constructing the explanation that will be given to the children. The exact process and timing of involving extended family and friends tends to differ from case to case, but we have learned time and again that the earlier we involve others around the immediate family, the easier it is to deal with the secrecy and shame that accrues around problems of child abuse.

Our aim at this stage is for the parents to identify four to six people, if possible one or two people from each side of the family and at least one friend or support person of each parent. Once they have created a list of possible names we will ask the parents to approach each person and invite them to come to a meeting after the words and pictures session. Sometimes, parents ask whether we can do both tasks at once and have the safety people come to the words and pictures session. This can work very well because the children have the experience of a whole community of people around them when they receive the explanation of the alleged abuse. This will inevitably lend a greater sense of importance to the occasion for the children.

Explaining the worries to the children and creating the final words and pictures document

The session in which the explanation is presented to the children will inevitably be very tense. Often, one or both parents have attempted to keep the events a secret from the children for a considerable time, and they will usually come to the session highly anxious. For the session to run smoothly, it is best that the resolutions practitioner is well versed and prepared in what they intend to do, so they feel confident they can lead the session in a calm, purposive manner.

Facilitating this words and pictures process with the children involves:

1. Pre-session preparations
2. Greeting and getting to know the children
3. Preparing the children for the words and pictures process
4. Providing the explanation and creating the words and pictures with the children
5. Post-session activities

1. Pre-session preparations

It is important to create a physical space that enables the resolutions practitioner and children to work together effectively and comfortably. We will often use a low table in the centre of a room, where we can sit on the floor alongside the children and work on the words and pictures document together. We make sure we have paper, coloured pencils and marker pens that we can use for the purpose. We provide chairs for the parents, ourselves, each of the children and other adults who are to be in the room, arranged in a circle around the low table.

In advance of her words and pictures sessions, Susie prepares the words and pictures document ahead of time. Susie's method is to pre-draw stick figure pictures corresponding to each area ('Who's worried?', 'What are they worried about?', etc.) on separate A4 sheets that she then gets the children to colour in during the session (see Figure 5.2). Andrew will have the explanation typed out, with notes about the pictures agreed on with the parents (which typically he will provide to the parents in advance so they have the script of the session available to them, and then starts from scratch hand writing the words on to an A3 piece of paper and then creating the pictures together with the children (see Figure 5.3).

It is also important to brief any professional observers who will be attending. We always ask the social services worker to be present, but very often other observers come as well, such as the guardian-ad-litem or child representative, children's therapists and other significant professionals. If we are able, we will have these people sit behind a one-way glass screen, but if this is not possible we will usually seat these people in an outer circle behind the family and their support people. For these observers to get the most out of what they are seeing, it is important to provide them with a comprehensive briefing of the process before they witness the session. If the resolutions practitioner is working as part of a therapeutic team using a one-way glass screen, the team members behind the screen can often undertake a lot of this interpretation work with the observers as the session unfolds.

2. *Greeting and getting to know the children*

The children are the primary focus of the words and pictures session, so if the resolutions practitioner can quickly demonstrate to the family that they can engage with the children, this will go a long way to putting the parents at ease. For this reason, we are both very hospitable and energized in greeting the children, thanking them for coming to see us and introducing ourselves simply by saying something like: 'I'm working with your Mummy and Daddy so that _____ (daddy, or child) can come home again'. At the same time, we are often playful about who should sit where and often involve the children in directing this. Then we ask a little about each child's life, starting typically with the youngest or liveliest child, usually focusing on things the children like doing most. While getting to know the children is vital for the session to be successful, we are also mindful of not prolonging the process, since that will tend to create a situation where the parents' anxiety can start to rise. It is important to keep a sense of forward momentum throughout the session.

If, as in the example we are about to consider, a young person who has made allegations of sexual abuse is attending and has chosen to sit behind the one-way screen or watch by video in another room, the practitioner also needs to manage these arrangements. In the example below, 'Mary', aged 14, who had 18 months earlier alleged that her stepfather had sexually abused her, chose to be in the room with her support person. This scenario also involves mother, 'Marion', and 'Damian' who is Mary's stepfather and Milly and Sam's father, the younger children 'Milly', aged 8 and 'Sam', who is 5 years old.

3. Preparing the children for the words and pictures process

Once we feel we have built a connection to each child, we will shift the conversation towards the words and pictures process by saying something like:

Susie: A lot of things have happened in your lives in the past two years, for a while you all had to live with your grand-parents. Then you moved back home, but only after Daddy moved out and went to stay with Aunty Karen.

(Obviously these sorts of details need to be adapted to be relevant to each different case.)

Susie: You've probably all wondered why these things have happened and you've had to live in different places. (*Pauses here and waits for nods from the children.*) Can you stand up Sam and Milly? (*They stand.*) Wow you two are big! How old are you now?

Sam: I'm five and three quarters!

Milly: I'm nine in November.

Susie: (*Getting out of her seat and crouching down beside them.*) I see, well the two of you are certainly big enough now to know what's been happening. I've talked to Mummy and Daddy and Mary and they've agreed on exactly the words I'm going to use to explain to you what's been happening. So, we have to go really slowly and make sure you both understand everything, and we're going to use some pictures as we go to help make sure you understand everything. Can I get you to sit down at this table and help me draw something?

Sam: Okay, what? (*Sam sits at the table quickly and Milly moves in beside him, while looking at Susie quizzically.*)

Susie: I want you to help me draw some traffic lights, three sets actually, so let's do one each. (*Susie takes three A5-size pieces of card, either pre-prepared or quickly makes a line drawing of a traffic light as in Figure 5.1.*)

Susie: Sam, can you colour in the red light on yours?

Sam: Which one?

Susie: Good question! Which light is the red one on a traffic light?

Sam: The top one.

Susie: Exactly right! So use that red pencil there and colour in the top light red. Milly, can you colour in the bottom light? What colour is the bottom light?

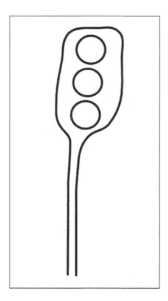

Figure 5.1   Traffic lights

Milly: Green.
Susie: Of course, I knew you'd know that! (*Milly quickly starts colouring, seemingly to show Sam she knows what to do.*) That's great colouring both of you! I'll do the amber one.
Susie: (*After the colouring is done.*) Okay, let's put all three cards on the table. So Milly, if I was explaining something and you didn't understand what I was saying and you wanted me to stop, which traffic light would you hold up to me? (*Milly picks up the red light and shows it to Susie.*) That's right, exactly! And Sam, if I asked you whether you understood and whether I could keep going and you wanted me to keep going, which traffic light would you hold up? (*Sam thinks for a moment and then picks up and shows everyone the green light.*) That's it! Okay then, let's test out Mummy and Daddy. You see the other thing is that Mummy and Daddy can use the traffic lights too, they can ask me to stop or slow down at any time. So Damian, which traffic light would you hold up if you weren't sure whether Milly or Sam were understanding what I was saying and you wanted me to slow down and check with them?
Damian: Well I guess I could pick up the amber one or the red one.
Susie: That's right, whichever one of those you think is best. The point is, at any time, if you Damian, or Marion, think Milly or Sam aren't understanding me, or if you're

thinking I'm not doing it the way we agreed, then you can stop me. Is that okay with you? (*Mother and father nod.*)

In this way the traffic lights exercise does double duty as a playful segue into the words and pictures explanation but also lets the parents and the children know that they can control the process.

4. *Providing the explanation and creating the words and pictures with the children*

At this point we start in on providing the explanation to the children in the following sort of manner:

Susie: Sam and Milly, did you know that there were some big people who were worried about the two of you and Mary?

Milly: (*Sam is looking quizzical.*) Um no, who do you mean?

Susie: Mary, you know don't you who the big people were, because you talked to some of them.

Mary: First there was my teacher and then the police.

Susie: (*Putting the first A4 sheet, titled 'Child protection case conference' on the table in front of Sam and Milly.*) Let me show you both. You see all these people had a meeting, they call it a case conference, and they were talking about all of you. Milly, let's see if we can help Sam read the names of the people at the meeting. Sam, can you read them? (*Pointing at 'Dad'.*)

Sam: Um, um.

Milly: Dad!

Susie: Okay great Milly, good helping! Let's see if Sam can get the next one on his own. (*Pointing at 'Mum'.*) What does that look like?

Sam: Mum?

Susie: That's right! Milly let's see if Sam can get the next one before you read out the other names. (*Pointing at the policeman.*) What does that man look like?

Sam: A policeman? (*A little wide-eyed.*)

Susie: Well done Sam! Okay Milly can you read the rest?

Milly: (*With Susie pointing at each drawn figure.*) 'Social worker, Helen Jones', 'Doctor Ray, Family doctor', 'Mrs Johnson, Teacher', 'Mr Webb, chairperson' and 'Margaret Smith, School nurse'. We've got a school nurse at our school too.

Susie: Thank you Milly, that's great! And you see these words just here, Sam, they tell what the people are saying to each other. They're saying: 'We are very worried about Mary, Milly and Sam and we must make sure they stay safe.'

Milly: What are they worried about us for?

Child Protection Case Conference

We are very worried about Mary, Milly and Sam and we must make sure they stay safe.

Court

The judge is hearing worries about Mary, Milly and Sam. The worries are because Mary said Dad touched her on her private bits and said he got her to touch his private bits. Mary told the judge this happened a number of times but couldn't remember the exact times and dates.

Dad told the judge he didn't do these things but the judge couldn't quite decide what to think. The judge wants to make sure nothing like that happens to Milly and Sam and that they stay safe. The judge said until the worries are sorted out Dad must live seperate from the family.

Private Bits

Your private bits are the parts your swimming costume covers.

What Are We Doing?

Mum and Dad are working really hard to show everyone that Mary, Milly and Sam will be safe so Dad can come home.

Figure 5.2

One of the children almost always asks this, which automatically leads us into the 'What are they worried about?', part of the explanation. Obviously, if the children do not ask, we explain that we're now going to tell them what 'these people' are worried about. Again, we are looking to maintain the forward momentum and to get to the worries as quickly as is reasonably possible, which will release the tension for the parents and Mary.

Susie:	Really good question Milly! (*Putting the 'Court' A4 sheet on the table in front of Sam and Milly*.) After the meeting with all those people, the policeman and the social worker told a judge in court all about the worries they had about you. The judge is hearing worries about Mary, Milly and Sam. (*Reading slowly and carefully, but with no emotion*.) The worries are because Mary told her teacher Mrs Johnson that Dad touched her on her private bits and said he got her to touch his private bits. Mary said this happened a number of times but couldn't remember the exact times and dates. Dad told the judge he didn't do these things, but the judge couldn't quite decide what to think. The judge said, 'This is very serious. I need to be sure that all the children in this family will be safe.'
	Does that make sense to you both? (*Both Sam and Milly are wide-eyed, but Milly nods*.) Okay, good, can I keep going? Which card do you want to hold up? (*Sam picks up the green card and shows it to Susie*.) Is that okay with you, Mum and Dad and Mary, if I keep going? (*They all nod*.)
Susie:	Okay, Sam and Milly, I want to make sure you know where your private bits are. (*Milly giggles and Sam looks at her and starts to smile too as Susie puts the 'private bits' A4 sheet on the table*.) Now look at this picture, I know it's not a very good drawing but it's meant to be a drawing of a boy and girl about your age who are wearing their swimming costumes.
Milly:	Yeah but I'm bigger than Sam and my hair's blond, his is brown.
Susie:	Good point, well why don't you colour in the hair on the girl with a yellow pencil, and Sam, what colour do you want to do the boy's hair?
Sam:	I'll do it brown. (*Both do the colouring in*.)
Susie:	Okay, what colour would you like to do the swimming costumes?
Milly:	I'm going to do mine with flowers.
Susie:	What about you, Sam?
Sam:	Um, just red, I like red.

Susie: Red, that's a great colour! (*Helps them choose their colours and start colouring in.*) Okay, can you answer questions while you keep colouring in? (*Both nod.*) Okay, Sam, what do you call your private bits?

Sam: (*Looks at Susie and then at his mother, who nods to him.*) Um, my weenie. (*Milly giggles.*)

Susie: Okay, your weenie, good name for it. And what do you call your private bit behind your weenie, at the back? (*Patting her bottom.*)

Sam: Um, (*looks a bit uncertain*) just my bottom.

Susie: That's great, good answers. Let's write them on the picture (*Susie writes the names*). Okay Milly, your turn now. What do you call your private bits?

Milly: (*Giggles again.*) Um, my tuppence.

Susie: Okay tuppence, where did you get that name?

Milly: It's what my Mummy says (*Milly looks at her mother, who smiles*).

Susie: Okay, good, tuppence. What name do you use for your back bit?

Milly: Ahh, arse (*she looks around as Sam giggles and her mother frowns*), ah no, I mean bottom.

Susie: That's okay, I bet all your friends have lots of names for that bit, but let's just say bottom, that's safest. Okay, so one last question about private bits Milly, what are the private bits that big girls have? What do you call them?

Milly: (*Looking at her mum again, who nods that it's okay.*) Um boobies (*Sam giggles again and so does Mary*), um ahh, I mean breasts.

Susie: That's good, that's two good names for them, let's write them both down. Thankyou! Okay, you've just coloured in the swimming costumes really well, so you see that those words say, 'Your private bits are the parts your swimming costume covers'. Do you think that's right, Sam, that your swimming costume covers your private bits?

Sam: Yeah it is.

Susie: Boy, you're really smart, you know that. (*Turning to Sam's parents.*) I think he's going to do really well when he starts school. Okay, so last picture (*putting the last A4 sheet on the table*). This one tells you what we are doing about the worries the judge and those people have. You see this is a picture of me with your Mum and Dad and with Andrew, behind the one-way screen, who you met before. So this picture tells you that your 'Mum and Dad are working hard to show everyone that Mary, Milly and Sam will be safe, so Dad can come home'.

Mary has this been OK for you? (*Mary nods*.) Is there anything else you wanted me to say at the moment? (*Mary shakes her head*.) Would you like to help Sam and Milly do more of the colouring Mary? (*Mary nods*.) So Sam and Milly, we're going to finish very soon, but while I talk to your Mum and Dad a little bit could you choose one of those three other pictures each and colour them in? (*Sam chooses the 'We are all working together' sheet and Milly starts colouring the 'Case conference' picture. Mary gets down next to Sam to help him colour in, Milly passes her a blue pen*.)

This session is often fairly short since the parents, in particular, will often feel quite exhausted. Typically, we will begin to draw things to a close by asking the parents whether the session was what they expected and whether they have anything to ask or add. Usually they have little to say.

Following this, we will usually clarify whether everything is in place for the safety people to come to the next session. If the parents haven't yet invited all the people on their list, we'll check how much time the parents need to get this done. Building on this discussion, we then re-engage the children in the conversation, talking with them about who will know what. We do this using a series of concentric circles that we draw on a white board or flip chart, equivalent to Figure 5.3.

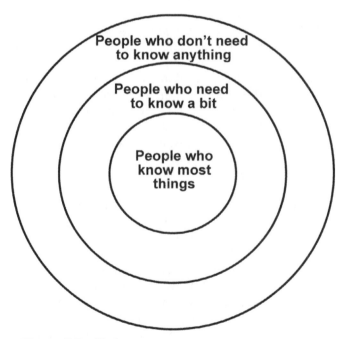

Figure 5.3 Circles

We explain that there will be some people, such as grandparents, other close family and friends, who will be helping their parents show the court or social services that the children will be safe. To illustrate, we write in the names of the people the parents are inviting to the next session and explain that all these people will be seeing the words and pictures that we have just created together and that they have now 'beautifully coloured in!' We also talk briefly about people who don't need to know anything, such as the postman or shopkeeper, and explain that some people will need to know some things and that's part of what we have to figure out with their parents (and older siblings in sexual abuse cases).

We explain to the children that we will also copy the four big pictures with their words and make them into one document on a single A4 sheet of paper (as in Figures 5.2 and 5.4) and that we will laminate this for the family. We suggest that this will be a really important document to have available for everyone so that if the children or anyone else who needs to know is wondering why all these strange things happened, the family can get out the document and look at it together. We check at this point that the parents agree for us to provide a copy to all the relevant professionals involved in their case.

The final thing we will then ask the family to decide upon is an easily accessible but private place where the words and pictures document should 'live' so that everyone can find it. Once the location is agreed upon, we ask if we can ask the social service worker to bring the laminated document out to the home before the next session and they can all show the worker where it will be kept. Once these final items of business are complete, we thank everyone, particularly the children, and end the session.

5. Post-session activities

With the words and pictures process complete, this will usually generate a sense of achievement and progress in what has previously been experienced as a stuck situation. Typically, it is not just the family that finds a new sense of hope about moving forward; very often the key professionals also experience renewed optimism about the case. It is important to capitalize on this shift of sentiment and, in particular, to meet quickly with the social services worker after the words and pictures session to plan for handing increasing responsibility for the children's safety over to the family and its network. It is imperative that the social services worker and the resolutions practitioner share the same expectations and work together closely from this point since the incremental reunification process starts in earnest once the words and pictures process is complete. Since the social services worker will be in regular contact with the family and safety network from this point on, it is also important to help the worker to shift what may have been a quite fraught relationship with the family towards a more purposive safety-building task. In the first instance, this can be focused around the worker taking the laminated words and pictures plan to the home, providing compliments to the parents and children for having completed it, and being involved in the constructive task of giving the document physical residence within the family home.

As mentioned above, copies of the completed words and pictures document also need to be provided for the other professionals involved in the case and for foster carers if any of the children are in the looked-after system. A copy should also be made for the young person in situations of alleged sexual abuse. It is worth observing here that, in our experience, when words and pictures documents are brought into a court context, judges are typically very pleased to see that this sort of concrete work has been undertaken with the family and will usually readily endorse contact changes based on this work.

The primary task of the resolutions practitioner following the words and pictures session is to utilize the new energy to see that the network meeting happens as quickly as possible. To this end, it is often important to contact the family a day or two after the session to ensure arrangements are in hand for drawing the network together. This is an additional challenge for the parents, but the fact that once this task is completed contact arrangements can be significantly increased and supervised by the family's own network helps to motivate this endeavour.

A words and pictures example in an ACADE injured infant case

We employ essentially the same process for creating the explanation and presenting it to the children through the words and pictures in all our work with ACADE-type cases, adapting the process to the particularities of each particular case. The following is a constructed but typical example of the sort of words and pictures document that we create for ACADE situations involving injuries to an infant. In this example, the infant's name is 'Sharon' and her elder sibling, who helped do the drawings, was 'James', aged 8. Sharon had suffered skull and rib fractures, retinal haemorrhaging and a subdural haematoma. These injuries left the child with a mild developmental delay. The injuries had occurred two years prior to Andrew undertaking the words and pictures process with the family, during which time, following release from hospital, Sharon had been living with her grandparents. James had little idea as to why his sister no longer lived with his family. The words and pictures document presented in Figure 5.4 is typical of the sort Andrew creates by writing the words and creating the drawings with the children during the session.

<u>Who's Worried?</u>

<u>What Are They Worried About?</u>

Sharon was sick and very badly hurt and had to go to hospital. Sharon had very big hurts all over her body. The doctors were very worried, they said Sharon had been hurt while Mummy and Daddy were looking after her. Mummy and Daddy said they didn't hurt Sharon but the doctors and the social worker were still worried and said they had to make sure Sharon would be safe before she could come home.

<u>What Happened Then?</u>

After this the social worker said Sharon couldn't live with Mummy and Daddy. Nan and Pop wanted to help so Sharon went to live with them after she got out of hospital. Sharon has lived with Nan and Pop for more than two years since then.

<u>What Are We Doing?</u>

Mummy and Daddy are working very hard with Andrew and Karen (the social worker) to show everyone that Sharon will be safe when she comes home.

Figure 5.4

A words and pictures example for a child in the care system

As we identified earlier in this chapter, many looked-after children are uncertain why they are in the care system, and parents, carers and professionals are often uncertain how and what to tell the children. In the past few years we have begun to use the words and pictures process to address this problem. In our view, a words and pictures-type process should be undertaken with every looked-after child as expeditiously as possible after they come into care. The following is a composite example of a words and pictures explanation Susie prepared, together with the parents, professionals and carers for 'Jodie', a 5-year-old. We typically create pictures for most or all of the explanation points, but to save space here we have included only five drawings. In cases of children in the care system, we are careful to identify the first names of the biological parents alongside the titles 'Mummy' and 'Daddy', since it is not uncommon for looked-after children to have ascribed a succession of carers with those appellations.

1. Mummy (Lisa) and Daddy (Shane) met when they were teenagers. They both had lots of problems. Daddy (Shane) had been in trouble to do with cars and both had struggles with drugs. Mummy (Lisa) and Daddy (Shane) both wanted a baby as they thought this would help them keep together.
2. Mummy (Lisa) and Daddy (Shane) worked very hard to make a nice home for Jodie when she was born. Lisa spent all their money on things for the home, she wanted it to be nice for Jodie. There are some pictures (which Granny Irene has) of baby Jodie in their nice flat.
3. Mummy (Lisa) and Daddy (Shane) then found they were having big problems again. When Jodie was 5 months old they lost their flat. They had to move lots and lots. They had no money to buy food for Jodie because they were spending all their money on drugs. They were all tired and sad.

Figure 5.5

4. By now, everyone was very worried. Mummy (Lisa) and Daddy (Shane) couldn't look after Jodie properly because of all their problems. Aunty Maddy knew Mummy (Lisa) and Daddy (Shane) needed help and she rang the social services, but they didn't seem to be able to help much. In the end, when Jodie was 8 months old, Nanny Bev and Pops Pete said Jodie could stay with them until Mummy (Lisa) felt a bit better.

5. After a while, things seemed a bit better and Jodie went back to stay with Mummy (Lisa) and Daddy (Shane). They sometimes went to the park and Jodie learned to ride her trike.

6. But things didn't work out because, however hard they tried, they couldn't get away from the other people who also had big problems with drugs. Everybody still wanted things to get better so Jodie could be with Mummy (Lisa) and Daddy (Shane). So everyone tried to help again and Jodie went to live with Nanny Bev and Pops Pete lots more times, from when she was 8 months to when she was 2 years old.

7. There were good times, and Jodie had her second birthday party with Mummy (Lisa). Jodie stayed the night with Mummy and Auntie Maddy and two friends. There is a photo of them all having fun.

Figure 5.6

8. About a month after the birthday, things got really difficult and a neighbour called the police because Jodie was outside the front door. Jodie was sitting all alone on the pavement and could not get back in the house. Mummy (Lisa) and Daddy (Shane) didn't hear her crying. This was very dangerous and everyone was very worried about Jodie.

Figure 5.7

9. This time there was a court case. The judge listened very carefully to all the worries about Jodie's life, and heard from all the different people who knew Jodie (Mummy, Daddy, Nanny, Auntie Maddy and Jodie's health visitor and her social worker). In the end, the judge decided it would be best if Jodie went to stay with Nanny Bev and Pops Pete, and not keep coming and going to different houses, he said she must stay in one home with her Nanny and Pops.

Figure 5.8

10. Jodie has lived with Nanny Bev and Pops Pete ever since, with visits to Granny Irene (Shane's Mum) every other weekend. Jodie sometimes sees Mummy (Lisa), Daddy (Shane) and her baby brother John, and Nanny always comes too. Sometimes Nanny has to help look after John.
11. Mummy (Lisa) still has problems with drugs and so does Daddy (Shane). Sometimes Shane has been in trouble with the police. Although he has been in prison, Shane is working hard to make his life better. Mummy (Lisa) and Daddy (Shane) have both said they want to always see Jodie, and the judge has said as long as it is safe Jodie will be able to see them.
12. Helen (social worker) is making sure Jodie is with people who will look after her safely. Nanny Bev and Pops Pete have said that Jodie can live with them until she is grown up. Helen and Nanny Bev and Pops Pete often talk together to make sure Jodie is safe and is getting everything she needs to grow up happily. Jodie is a good swimmer and Nanny and Pops take her to swimming club, she is going to swim in the county gala soon.

Or point 12 might be:

Nanny Bev and Pops Pete have been very poorly recently. So Helen (social worker) is making sure Jodie is with people who will look after her safely and is getting everything she needs to grow up happily. Jodie will live with the Bland family until Helen can find a new family that Jodie can live with until she is grown up. Jodie will still see Nanny and Pops at the weekends, and her new family will help her see Mummy and Daddy as long as a safe adult can be there too. Everyone knows Jodie is a good swimmer, so they will make sure she can go to swimming club and swim in the county gala.

We create this sort of story for the child through the following process:

1. Begin by briefing social services on the process. Obtain their permission and endorsement to undertake the process and commitment to use the words and pictures within the looked-after system.
2. Check with the parent or parents about the problem (for example mental health problem; severe illness; child protection concerns; drug or alcohol misuse) regarding what would

Figure 5.9

be most helpful for their children to understand about the situation.

3.   Explore these same issues with the other parent, kinship system, and significant adults in the child's life.
4.   Explore with the child/children what they already know and what they are concerned about (depending on the circumstances include the parents in this discussion if possible).
5.   Draft the explanation, utilizing the family's own language and ways of expressing concerns wherever possible and bearing in mind the family's race, culture and religion. Link all of the above to any worries/concerns about the children at home, at school, with peers, that is, the context in which the child might be expressing some of the worries or confusions.
    The explanation should be balanced and not solely focused on the negative. The explanation should be framed with a neutral or affirmative beginning and a positive message at the end. The explanation should be interspersed with meaningful positive events in the child's life that fit and add to the overall story.
6.   Present the first draft to the parents. Develop and refine the words so that they are comfortable with it and the explanation reflects what they feel the child should know.
7.   Once the parents take ownership of the explanation, the next task is to ensure that the explanation captures everything social services would want the child to know.
8.   Provide the explanation to the child/children with their parents, extended family, carers and social service workers present.

9. Ensure that all other significant extended family members and adults in the child's life have seen the explanation and will draw upon it if they need to talk to the child about the problems the parents face and the reasons the child is in care.

In the United Kingdom it is common that looked-after children have undertaken a life storybook process. 'Life story work', as it is often termed, has a similar purpose to the words and pictures process just described, but in our experience most life storybooks are different in a number of key ways:

1. They tend to primarily focus on the negative events that led to the child being in care.
2. The parents and extended family are usually not involved and have little control or say in developing the story for their children.
3. The life storybook work tends to be professionally driven and therefore the story is often told from the perspective of explaining the professionals' interventions rather than focusing on the child's need for understanding in the context of the family's experience.

The importance and power of pitching the explanation to the child's level and broader life context was demonstrated to Andrew recently, in constructing a story around a situation in which a mother had suffered from a prolonged serious mental illness. The story's creation involved the mother, the child, aged 9, two sets of grandparents, an uncle, the father, the social services social worker and the psychiatrist. After the words and pictures session, the paternal grandmother stated it was the first time she had actually 'understood' her daughter-in-law's difficulties – this insight for her coming in part because the explanation was created with and for her granddaughter. The mother chose not to attend the session when the explanation was given to the child, since she felt it would be too distressing for her. Later, when the completed words and pictures document was shared with the mother and her mental health social worker, the evident child-focused nature of the document led the mother to talk for the first time of her own childhood experience of abuse by a family friend.

Conclusion

The words and pictures process involves the parents, professionals and children in creating a shared, age/stage-appropriate narrative of the events surrounding the alleged abuse. The words and pictures document provides the foundation on which to build the safety plans that will follow, but it can also serve as an important ongoing historical document for the family regarding these past events. The document is something that the children can always look at later in their lives and see that the professionals were making every endeavour to involve them and explain to them what was happening, at their own level.

We turn in the next and subsequent chapters to using the words and pictures document as the basis for moving towards reunification and building future safety arrangements for the children. The child-friendly process we use in creating the words and pictures document will also be replicated when we come later to create the final safety plan.

Chapter **Six**

CREATING AN INFORMED SAFETY NETWORK AROUND THE FAMILY

The creation of the words and pictures document provides a clear demonstration to the statutory authorities that the immediate family shares a common, professionally endorsed understanding of the concerns. The next step in the resolutions process involves utilizing the words and pictures document to inform a wider network of people who are close to the family. Once an informed network has been created, these people can then be actively involved in ensuring the children are safe and the possible perpetrator is protected from future misunderstandings or allegations. This group then forms the basis of a safety network for the family that will grow in numbers as the resolutions process progresses towards creating the final safety plan. In this chapter, we will describe how the process of involving an initial group of people from the family's own network usually unfolds.

Professional commitment to building a family safety network

When we train professionals in the resolutions approach, they often express scepticism that parents disputing allegations of child abuse will involve other people in their problems. In our experience, however, at least part of the difficulty in building a safety network is that child protection professionals are unused to involving an extended family and friendship network around such families. While this is an atypical orientation for child protection professionals more used to emphasizing individual change, a network emphasis is by no means unique to the resolutions approach.

Probably the most sustained professional application of locating the welfare of vulnerable children within their naturally occurring community comes from the use of Family Group Conferencing in child protection systems around the world (Lupton and Nixon 1999; Burford and Hudson 2001). International research regarding Family Group Conferencing articulates a recurring lesson that the most important precursor to effectively involving a network around a family facing child abuse allegations is the amount of time the convener gives to engaging and preparing the individuals who will be in the network (Gunderson 1998; Lohrbach 2003). This same principle applies when involving a network of people around a family undertaking the resolutions process. While parents often do express anxiety about involving others, the key to overcoming this is the persistence of the resolutions practitioner and the time they give to the task. It is important to prepare and assist the parents in approaching others, and it is equally important to maintain leverage by insisting that the journey towards reunification cannot proceed without building a safety network.

Following the words and pictures session and to honour the considerable efforts of the family in the resolutions process to date, the contact arrangements for the likely abusive parent with the children increase, but remain externally supervised. Once the network meeting has occurred, members of the safety network can supervise the contact visits and the staged reunification process can proceed in earnest. If the parents were not able to complete the task of inviting a group of four or six people to become part of the safety network, then the resolutions practitioner should help the parents undertake this task as quickly as possible once the words and pictures process is concluded. Sometimes parents do hesitate in bringing together a network, but if the resolutions practitioner has underlined the importance of building the network from the preparatory stages and involved advisors and support people in earlier sessions the task is always much easier.

The network session

The initial family network meeting involves the following steps:

- Explaining the resolutions process
- Presenting the words and pictures document
- Discussing the network's role in the safety-building process
- Creating the first safety guidelines for contact

Explaining the resolutions process

The first step in meeting with the family network is to explain the resolutions process to everyone present. Some of the group may have heard the explanation before, and the parents certainly will have heard it numerous times, but this remains a useful process for everyone involved. The people who have not heard the resolutions process explained obviously need to understand what they are being asked to participate in, but in our experience those who have heard the explanation before, including the parents, deepen their understanding of the process each time it is described. Following this explanation we make time for discussion and questions. Inevitably, the people who are new to the approach challenge the process and often assert the innocence of the possible abuser. As in the earlier engagement stage, we interpret this not as resistance but as an additional opportunity to better inform the family and its network about the professional concerns and to deepen their capacity to take those concerns seriously and build a meaningful safety plan to address them.

Presenting the words and pictures document

To set the scene for presenting the words and pictures document, we explain to the network members that it is vital they understand the concerns social services hold for the children's safety and also that they know what the children know. In advance of this session we ask the possible abusive parent if they would be willing to read the words and pictures explanation to the network. We explain to them that if they are willing to take on this role, this is an evident way of demonstrating to social services their openness about the concerns. In the majority of our cases, the possible abuser agrees to take on the task. Where they are not willing to do this we endeavour to have the likely safer parent or a close relative read out the description. Asking a parent or family member to read the explanation is another way of underlining and building the family's ownership of the words and pictures document. At this meeting we provide photocopied reproductions of the words and pictures document to all the people in attendance, which helps them to follow and take in the explanation.

Discussing the network's role in the safety-building process

Having presented the words and pictures explanation and fielded any questions related to it, the next task is to explore how the network can help the family reunite by supporting the family in changing its living arrangements. At this stage, we often show the network an anonymous, composite final safety plan created for a family facing similar circumstances. We use this document to explain the staged process that will underpin the creation of the final safety plan. The steps in this process are:

- The first version of interim safety guidelines are created relative to the current contact arrangements between the possible abuser and the children.
- Contact between the possible abuser and the children is supervised by members of the safety network and the interim safety guidelines are progressively made more detailed as that contact increases towards full reunification.
- The social services worker maintains regular contact with the network members, the children and parents to monitor the implementation of the evolving safety guidelines.
- As contact between the possible abuser and the children increases and the safety guidelines become more detailed, the parents choose additional people to be part of the safety network.
- The staged reunification process and successive evolution of the safety guidelines ultimately lead to the creation of the final safety plan that forms the basis of the family's future living arrangements and can satisfy the statutory authorities that the children will be safe.

At this point, we typically revisit the concentric circles diagram we began to explore with the family in the words and pictures session, pointing out that the more people who can be involved in the inner circle, the more confidence social services will have in the reunification process. We will often then explore with the parents and network who else they think could and should be part of the safety network.

In this session, the family and network will usually, and not surprisingly, want guidance about how long the reunification process will take. To be able to field this question, we clarify what time frame the social services worker is envisaging in advance of the session. Given the realities of social services involvement, the time frame at this stage is usually in the range of three to six months.

Creating the first safety guidelines for contact

The final stage of this session involves creating the first set of safety guidelines that will apply to the network-supervised contact arrangements between the possible or alleged abuser and the children. The whole purpose of this process is to help the parents and the network think through the issues that need to be addressed in building a comprehensive safety plan that they can take responsibility for. As we will repeatedly emphasize in the two safety planning chapters that follow, the most important aspect of creating a meaningful safety plan involves exploring the minutiae of contact and living arrangements together with the parents and network. By delving into the details of the contact activities, this provides fertile ground to encourage the network and parents to think through the nitty-gritty of what is required to demonstrate that the children are safe and the possible abuser is protected.

The safety guidelines are created by exploring the details of contact visits – what will happen, who will be involved, where will this occur and what are the specific safety issues that these activities might pose. In sexual abuse cases, the safety guidelines and plan will be organized around the alleged abuser not being alone with any children – the issue then is to involve the parents and network in thinking through how this can be ensured and to consider any challenges to this primary rule. Whatever activities the parents are considering during the contact visits, we ask as many questions as we can think of about possible challenges to ensuring the likely abuser is not alone with any other children. Typically, we will ask about situations in which children need assistance with toileting or if they become sick, or if one child becomes lost, who will do what to ensure the rule is followed. Contact visits that involve outings such as attending fairs, parties, video game halls, concerts, places of worship, swimming pools or the cinema always provide fertile ground to deepen the family and network's thinking.

In ACADE cases involving injuries to an infant, we explore the contact arrangements around the possible abusive parent not having sole responsibility for the care of young children. Where there is little sense of who the more worrying parent might be, the safety plan will require the parents always working together as a team with the supervisor also present. With these cases we also focus the safety guideline discussions on situations that might be stressful for the parents, such as the conclusion of an exhausting day, times when parents are sick, depressed or using alcohol or drugs, and events such as anniversaries, religious festivals and community celebrations.

Faced with the detail of these sorts of conversations, some family or network members may feel the resolutions practitioner is being overly intrusive into the private life of the family. When this sort of concern is raised, we make a point of thanking the person who raised the issue and then acknowledging that this indeed is an uncomfortable and intrusive process. We usually explain the reason we have to intrude in this way is because child abuse happens during everyday/everynight family life and because of this we have to explore with them the minutiae of the family's interactions with the children so that together we can create a meaningful safety plan. We also continually frame our intrusiveness as being a big part of helping the family to get social services out of their lives. It is often powerful at this point to ask the parents in front of the network whether they would prefer the discomfort of our obsessive questioning and nosiness or the discomfort of social services coming around to investigate them again in the future.

We are constantly seeking to reinforce to the family and network that building a meaningful safety plan that satisfies social services and protects the reunified family is challenging work. In this light, every objection or query people in this session raise about the process, we interpret not as resistance but as these people genuinely grappling with how they can engage with the task of creating meaningful safety. This is an approach to challenges and 'resistance' that draws on Milton Erikson's notion of 'utilization' – always endeavouring to find ways of making use of the client's views and experiences (Rossi 1980; de Shazer 1984; Dolan 1985). The idea of utilization helps us sustain a grounded optimism that there is within the resources of the family, its network and the professionals the capacity to deal with the challenges involved in creating a meaningful safety plan to address the problem of the denied abuse.

The sorts of detailed conversations involved in creating safety guidelines can at times seem very mundane, but in our experience each successive conversation focused around the minutiae of ensuring safety in a particular scenario serves to deepen the network and family's engagement with the safety-building process. Informing the network of the concerns and engaging them in beginning the safety-building work in this way sets the scene for the evolutionary and participative process of progressively co-creating the final safety plan. To conclude this session we always return to the specific who, where, when and what details of creating safety guidelines for the most immediate contact arrangements.

As the family's network begins supervising the contact arrangements, it is vital that social services follow up the network people involved, the children and the parents separately after each of the initial contacts to demonstrate that social services are serious about ensuring the safety guidelines are followed. For this reason, it is also important that the social services worker attends this session. To allow the family and network time to focus on the task of making the contacts demonstrably safe and time to interact with the social services worker we often propose that several rounds of contact are undertaken before we proceed further with the resolutions process. During this period we typically keep in close contact with the social services worker to enable them to constructively step into the role of monitoring the contact arrangements.

An interim safety guidelines example

The injured infant case example presented at the end of Chapter 4 is a good example of a practitioner developing a straightforward and detailed set of interim safety guidelines. Donna Smyrk's work displayed the sort of attention to detail we consider to be at the heart of creating a meaningful set of interim family safety guidelines which included:

- Visiting the home to discuss with the parents and grandmother how the guidelines could be enacted in this specific physical environment.
- Talking in depth with the parents and maternal grandmother about the new living arrangements where the grandmother would adopt the role of primary caregiver.
- Emphasizing the need for the parents not to be alone with the baby and underscoring this in focusing on the specific arrangements for the car journey when transferring between hospitals.
- Establishing a process of unannounced social services drop-in visits and through this communicating the seriousness her agency ascribed to the concerns and the safety arrangements.
- Continually emphasizing the need to follow the safety guidelines to protect both the family's and social services' interests.
- Writing up these arrangements into a straightforward contract.

Timing of involving the network

In this and the previous chapter, we have presented a process for involving the network that is more-or-less separate from the children's words and pictures session. Primarily, we have done this to separate out the purpose, tasks and steps of involving a network within the overall resolutions approach. Often, this is exactly how things transpire in practice. Frequently, however, as we have already alluded to in the previous chapter, we, and the parents, find it possible and preferable to bring together all of the members of the initial safety network in the words and pictures session. Involving the network in this way has many benefits, including the fact that the words and pictures session then serves the double purpose of informing the children and the network members about the concerns simultaneously. If the parents and practitioner decide to involve the network in this way, it is important that the practitioner meets the network members, briefs them and responds to their questions before undertaking the words and pictures session, so that that part of the session can be solely focused around the children. If the words and pictures and networking tasks are brought together in this way, we usually schedule two hours for the session, taking a break half way through to demarcate the work with the children and that which focuses on the network. Our point here though is to underline that the exact timing and method of involving the network tends to vary from case to case. The timing will depend on how quickly the practitioner can involve others alongside the parents in the early sessions, what the parents want, and when they are ready to involve others.

The network as the vulnerable child's 'village'

A well-known African folk wisdom asserts that 'it takes a village to raise a child'. Each element of the resolutions approach weaves and feeds into the others; thus the words and pictures work creates a context for informing the network, which in turn creates a context where the safety planning can be more robust and 'a village' can be created around vulnerable children in situations of disputed abuse.

The involvement of an informed network fulfils many tasks in the resolutions work, including breaking down the sort of secrecy and shame that tends to accrue around a problem such child abuse, and also demonstrates to the children that many important adults in their lives are taking their safety seriously. Conte et al. (1989) interviewed convicted child sexual abuse offenders and one of the messages that came across clearly was that a major, and possibly the principal, thing that would stop offenders' attempts to sexually abuse a child would be if they knew the child would tell and that the child would be believed. Bouchel (1994) emphasizes that building networks of safety around vulnerable children is invaluable but usually overlooked work. Bouchel highlights that the notion of the child raised by the village is an important part of most traditional cultures and therefore should be seen as an important component of constructive cross-cultural child protection practice. The next chapter, and the ninth, will describe how the resolutions process deepens the involvement of an increasing network in evolving the safety guidelines towards the final safety plans.

In our experience the emphasis on collective responsibility for the child's safety rather than pursuing individual acknowledgement, has been a key attribute that has enabled us to successfully use the resolutions approach with families from many different cultures including indigenous families.

Chapter **Seven**

FAMILY SAFETY GUIDELINES: BEGINNING THE JOURNEY TOWARDS THE FINAL FAMILY SAFETY PLAN

Every aspect of the resolutions approach is designed to create a context in which the professionals can work with the family and its network to construct a specific and detailed safety plan that addresses the seriousness of the maltreatment concerns. Completing the words and pictures, and using this document to inform a network of people around the immediate family, signals the point at which the first significant moves are made in the resolutions programme to increase supervised contact between the alleged abuser and the children. Having arrived at this point, the resolutions practitioner begins the process of working with the family and their network to create a workable family safety plan that will ensure that everyone is confident that the children are safe and the alleged perpetrator is protected from future allegations. The journey towards the final safety plan begins by preparing a set of family safety guidelines, which are created first to meet the requirements of demonstrating and ensuring safety during contact visits. Then, as the reunification process advances and contact increases, these guidelines are successively extended into the final safety plan. Generating the safety plan in this evolutionary and participative manner increases the likelihood that it will become the basis for ongoing living arrangements in the reunified family.

Between this chapter and the ninth, we hope to provide a comprehensive description of the process we use in creating safety plans and give a number of examples of such plans. In this chapter we will focus more on how we think about safety planning and the development of the initial family safety guidelines to be used at the initial stages when contact between the likely or possible perpetrator and the children is beginning to increase.

The challenge of organizing practice around clearly defined future safety

As we have suggested throughout this book, child protection practice, whether in statutory or treatment contexts, tends to be over-organized by everything that is perceived to be wrong with the family. In Colin Luger's research, with professionals who referred families to the resolutions programme, one guardian-ad-litum commented:

> Who is going to be brave enough to make the decision that a child can go home and on what basis are they making it? It's far easier to find evidence to support the child not returning than to find evidence that a child should return home, and that's if there is the will to work towards rehabilitation.
>
> (Luger 2003: 21)

Child protection authorities, of course, do create case plans all the time, but in our experience these very often fudge the issue of what is trying to be achieved. Child protection case planning often tends to document services that families must attend, rather than being a process that purposively describes and creates future safety. This problem is reflected in research with service recipients. For instance, Farmer and Owen (1995), McCullum (1995), Thoburn et al. (1995), MacKinnon (1998), and Dale (2004) all found that service recipients often feel child protection professionals do not clearly define what they want and frequently engage in shifting the goal posts. One service recipient expressed it this way:

> It always felt like they had a hidden agenda because they'd get me to do one thing, then they wouldn't be certain that that was enough so they'd come up with another thing. And they are really creative in a way because they would try to find something impossible for me to achieve. To me that was not in the children's best interests, because they are working towards nothing, towards the hope that I fail.
>
> (Teoh et al. 2003: 151)

In our view, part of this case planning problem arises because professionals confuse means (the services and other mechanisms to get to safety) with ends (the safety that is required to close the case). The practice of creating plans that document lists of services rather than specifically defining safety also comes about because delineating the endgame of a child abuse case in an explicit way is very challenging. In the defensive culture that tends to surround child protection casework, it is far easier to list services for service recipients to attend, rather than go out on a limb and make a clear claim regarding what constitutes enough safety to close a high-risk case.

There is at least one additional inhibiter to the enactment of detailed safety planning in child protection practice. The guardian-ad-litum quoted above distils this well when she states 'It's far easier to find evidence to support the child not returning than to find evidence that a child should return home.' This situation pertains at least in part because most of the research endeavour in the child protection field tends to focus on the causation of maltreatment rather than on what solves the problem. For any given category of child abuse (for example, children neglected by addicted parents or children deemed to have been abused in the face of violence between their parents), there is vastly more research and writing available regarding the incidence, aetiology and maintenance of such abuse than research that seeks to define what constitutes meaningful safety relative to that area of concern. When professionals endeavour to organize their practice around future safety, it is important to recognize that in analysing the problem they can draw upon a considerable and well-documented evidence base to inform their practice. However, when seeking to identify what constitutes sufficient safety to reunite a family relative to any specific form of maltreatment, the professionals are in more vulnerable territory and are relying, in the main, on professional judgement rather than a strong evidence base.

For all these reasons, there is considerable additional work that needs to be done in the child protection field to more effectively research, define and describe what professionals mean when they endeavour to conceptualize safety. Since safety planning is such a critical area of child protection work, and simultaneously such a vulnerable, challenging and under-researched aspect of practice, it is important to define here how we think about safety before we explore specific safety plans and the processes we utilize to create them.

Safety defined and exemplified

In defining safety, we draw on work undertaken in developing the Victorian Risk Framework (DHS 1999), which is the statutory risk assessment system used in the Australian state of Victoria. The

Victorian Risk Framework undertakes the risk estimation task through a balanced analysis of danger, strengths and envisioned safety, and defines safety as 'strengths, demonstrated as protection over time' (see Boffa and Podestra 2004 for further discussion). To interpret this definition in a grounded way we want to draw upon a practice example undertaken by Cindy Finch, a child protection worker on the long-term child protection team from Olmsted County in Minnesota. Olmsted County Child and Family Services also draw upon the Victorian definition of safety in their child protection practice (Lohrbach and Sawyer 2004).

This case involved separated parents who we will call Sharon and Gary, both in their early 20s. They have a young son, Jack, who is 14 months old. Sharon, who suffers from a mild learning disability, had lost her parental rights to a child from an earlier relationship when she was 17 years old. In the US system, termination of a parent's rights regarding a previous child means that any future child protection matters involving that parent will almost always be dealt with through a concurrent planning process. Thus when Cindy received this case the parents only had four months left to demonstrate to the court that they could care for the youngster (Plan A of the concurrent planning process) before termination proceedings would ensue (Plan B).

The concerns regarding the current situation involved exposing the infant to repeated situations of fighting and violence between the couple (Gary had served a jail term regarding this) and failure to meet Jack's medical needs – he suffered from severe long-term health problems. Sharon and Gary would typically deny the significance of these maltreatment concerns and each would regularly blame any problems on the other parent or accuse the professionals of being out to get them and being hypercritical. In an endeavour to support the parents to be able to retain Jack in their care, the previous child protection worker and the court had directed the parents to participate in a range of professional services. These included couples' and separate individual counselling, separate parenting education for both parents, and regular involvement with a community child health nurse. The court had also appointed a guardian-ad-litum to represent the child's interests. When Cindy received the case, the parents were involved with all these services, however there was little coherence between the professionals regarding case direction and what needed to be achieved to allow the parents to retain the long-term care of their son.

Mindful of the short timeline that was operating in this

situation, and that the professionals had not formed shared goals, Cindy instituted bi-weekly meetings with the professionals and gatherings on the alternate weeks that brought together the parents with the professionals. These meetings were designed to clarify the key areas of concern and maintain an ongoing focus on what safety would be required to satisfy the guardian and the court.

For our purposes here, we will focus on two of the five key risk statements that the county and the guardian had identified which needed to be addressed before the parents could retain custody. Following each risk statement, we will describe the safety plans that Cindy, working with the family and professionals, developed to address these risk statements. At certain points we will interrupt the narrative of the case description, drawing on the definition of 'safety as strengths demonstrated as protection over time' to offer an interpretation of what the definition can mean in practice.

The first risk statement read:

> The county and the guardian are worried that Jack could be physically or emotionally hurt when Gary and Sharon get into arguments and fights and they become so wrapped up in the argument they forget to pay attention to Jack.

Safety plans created to this risk statement:

In discussions with Cindy and the guardian at several planning meetings, Gary stated that he wanted to walk away from Sharon when he felt the fighting between them beginning to get out of control. However, Gary also described that when he had attempted this in the past, Sharon would usually follow him to continue the fight wherever he went. Sharon also engaged in discussions about this problem at the planning conferences and worked with the family counsellor to identify when, why and how she gets into fights with Gary and how she might pull herself out of this escalating phase.

From this preparatory work, a written, signed plan was drawn up which proposed that Gary would walk away when fights started to escalate and that Sharon not follow him.

In regards defining safety as strengths demonstrated as protection over time, the work so far described can be understood as having created and crystallized significant strengths that have the potential to reduce the identified risk. At this point, however, the strengths have not evolved into demonstrations of protection. This distinction between a strength and demonstrated protection is critical, because child death inquiries often find that professionals in serious cases of child abuse fall into the error of over-rating positive attributes and good intentions, particularly when the professional has formed a constructive relationship with the parents (Reder et al. 1993; Department of Health 2002). This is part of what is meant by the idea of professional dangerousness (Dale et al. 1986) or naïve practice (Dingwall 1983). To bring rigour to relationship-grounded, strengths-based, safety-organized practice requires careful and clear-eyed attention be focused on the enactment of the good intentions in clear demonstrations of protection, over time. In Gary and Sharon's situation protection was demonstrated in the following ways:

> As part of the written agreement, Gary contracted to keep a journal of times when he and Sharon began to argue and he was able to walk away. The journal entries were then followed up with Gary and Sharon by the family counsellor. As a result, when Cindy prepared her report for the court in which she recommended parental custody continue, she was able to report on at least ten documented and reviewed occasions, when Gary had successfully walked away and Sharon had not followed. Sharon and Gary independently verified each occasion with Cindy, and the leader of the fathers' education programme had confirmed witnessing several of these instances and a family member had witnessed several others. The professionals, extended family members and the couple themselves also observed that it had become easier for Sharon to allow Gary to walk away.
>
> Regarding the same risk statement, Cindy had also asked the couple what should be done about the problem of Sharon grabbing sharp knives or scissors to threaten Gary during their fights. On a number of occasions this had occurred when Jack was present. At Sharon's suggestion, a secure locked box was purchased in which all her sharp kitchen knives, scissors and the like were to be stored. During home visits, Cindy and other professionals would check that the box was still being used to secure the sharp implements. Gary, Sharon and Sharon's mother, Biddy, all stated that it is safer for Jack that Sharon did not have ready access to those items.
>
> The final step of this plan involved Gary and Sharon agreeing that if they were unable to step back from a fight, either of them could call Biddy. Biddy agreed that she would then come

immediately and take Jack away, at least until Gary and Sharon had calmed down. Cindy met with Biddy, Sharon and Gary before this idea became a formal part of the plan, and Biddy stated she was very happy to help out in this way and stated that she had taken Jack away when his parents were arguing in the past. In the four months between when this plan was put into place and the case went back to court, Gary and Sharon never needed to ring, but both felt more comfortable knowing that Biddy would help them out if needed.

The second risk statement read:

> The county and the guardian are worried that Jack's illnesses may get worse when Sharon does not follow medical recommendations.

This risk statement arose because at times Sharon was not providing the medicines and care that Jack needed for his health conditions. The problem was further complicated by the fact that Sharon often became very defensive and argumentative in the face of medical staff, particularly doctors. On several occasions, Sharon had removed Jack from hospital against doctors' recommendations after she had fought with them. As a result, several doctors had documented their belief that Sharon could not meet Jack's health needs.

Safety created to this risk statement:

Cindy brought together the guardian and the parent health nurse to concretize the nature of this concern and then involved Sharon in the deliberations. From these discussions Sharon agreed to keep a log of all the medical interventions she used with Jack. The parent health nurse reviewed the log with Sharon on a weekly basis to ensure her interventions were in agreement with doctors' recommendations. Alongside this, the parent health nurse prepared a series of straightforward cards that provided very simple directions as to what Sharon was to do in certain medical situations (such as asthma attacks, coughing spells, vomiting, diarrhoea, and so on).

After the log and cards were prepared, Sharon used the log to document every medical intervention she used with Jack in the four months leading up to the court hearing. During this period, Jack's key doctor and the parent health nurse were completely satisfied with the care Sharon was providing for Jack and this was also demonstrated in Jack's general well-being. Having the log available also changed the dynamics for Sharon when she had contact with medical professionals. Sharon told Cindy that having the log helped her feel calm and confident when Jack had regular check-ups with their doctor as well as when she had to take Jack to the emergency room.

This case is a clear demonstration of the interactional dynamics that often intensify the problem of the alleged 'denial'. At the outset, Gary and Sharon were identified as denying both the severity of and responsibility for the problems. As Cindy was able to get all the professionals focusing together on what would constitute sufficient safety to return custody to the parents and then used the meetings to regularly communicate and develop this focus with Gary and Sharon, the parents' 'denial' dissolved. We would suggest that the problem of 'denial' in this case had at least as much to do with the professionals not being 'on the same page' as it was to do with Gary and Sharon's responses and psychological makeup. This case also demonstrates well how focusing on future safety can enable professionals and family members to purposefully work together and step away from blaming and defensiveness.

To further assist the reader to understand the logic that informed the creation of this safety plan, we want to offer our ideas regarding what constitutes an effective comprehensive safety plan.

Attributes of an effective safety plan

The following list describes the attributes we believe make for a comprehensive and effective safety plan. While we would see some differences in emphasis between cases deemed to involve 'denial' and those that do not, we think the attributes described in this list apply to most situations of child maltreatment.

1 The safety plan must be constructed relative to clearly identified and commonly understood dangers.

For a meaningful safety plan to be created, the child abuse dangers it is to address must be identified in clear, straightforward language that is understandable by everyone involved. Once identified in this way, the safety plan is then constructed to directly address these concerns.

2 The safety plan must describe specific behaviours that address the dangers.

The safety plan must describe a specific set of detailed behaviours and actions that everyone (parents, children, family network and professionals) agrees will demonstrate that the children will be safe from the dangers and will also protect the alleged abuser from further allegations or misunderstandings.

In circumstances of sexual abuse, the plan will typically address the following key areas:

- Alleged perpetrator to not be alone with any children at any time.
- Identify the primary carer.
- Privacy.
- Clothing at night and after baths.
- Intimate care and appropriate physical contact for the alleged abuser.
- Who is where in the house, garden, garage, etc., when the children are home.
- Transport arrangements.
- Arrangements at school, clubs and other activities.

In circumstances of physical abuse, the plan will typically address the following key areas:

- Intimate care.
- Care during stressful times, such as feeding times, night waking, times of financial hardship, anniversaries of previous injuries or deaths, unexpected illness, particularly to the primary caregiver.
- Medical care and medicines.
- Rough play.
- Communication about disagreements.

The safety plan will typically address the following key areas in both physical and sexual abuse situations:

- Identifies key safety people who the children can contact if they have any concerns.
- Identifies people to assist the parents and who will monitor children's safety.
- Identifies people who will help out particularly if/when the primary carer is ill, under stress or unavailable.
- Arrangements in situations such as anniversaries, parties, celebrations or when parents wish to use alcohol and/or drugs.
- Arrangements regarding other children when relatives or friends are visiting or babysitting.
- The age at which infants/young children will have the words and pictures and the safety plan explained to them (for the first time or as a regular refresher) and who will take responsibility for the task.
- Child development and how the plan needs to change as the children grow.
- Incorporates a family safety object.
- Addresses the issue of how long the safety plan is applicable for.

3 *The safety plan must be developed, refined and implemented successively and over time.*

The safety plan will necessarily involve the family arranging their daily lives in different ways to their previous living arrangements. These changes cannot be put in place in one fell swoop. Rather, an effective safety plan requires time to be developed, refined and demonstrated. At a minimum we would suggest it usually takes at least four months to refine and bed down an effective safety plan that stands a realistic chance of being implemented by the family after the professionals withdraw from their lives. The safety plan is developed over time in negotiations between the family and professionals as the family moves successively towards reunification. The plan is progressively refined and evolved as the family faces the challenges involved in demonstrating that the children are safe and the alleged or possible perpetrator is protected from any further allegations. The social services worker must be involved in regular monitoring and follow-up with the children and all the adults involved in implementing the safety plan to provide statutory verification of implementation and feedback regarding improvements of the plan.

In this way the family and professionals are implementing the definition of safety as strengths demonstrated as protection over time.

4 *The safety plan must be endorsed by the statutory authorities involved in the case.*

The safety plan must be developed in conjunction with, and endorsed by, the professionals who exercise statutory authority over the matter, usually social services workers and professionals involved through the court such as the guardian-ad-litum and solicitors. Social services also undertake the role of checking and approving each of the people nominated as safe adults for the family's network.

5 *The safety plan must involve everyone in the family and as wide a network as possible.*

Adults

The preparation and refinement of the plan will usually involve the parents and one or two support people. In sexual abuse cases we do most of the development work with the likely non-abusing parent and older children, and after the plan has taken shape we then invite the alleged abuser to be part of further refinement.

Once developed, the plan should involve as many people as possible; usually we are looking for a network of at least 10 extended family members and friends, to be involved in its ongoing implementation and maintenance.

Children

The safety plan should be developed with as much involvement of the children as possible. The older the children are, the fuller their involvement can be. We always negotiate the children's involvement with the parents, privileging the judgement of the likely non-abusing parent.

As a minimum we want the children to be aware the safety plan is being created, and of the people who are involved in the process. The safety plan needs to be created in language understandable to the youngest children so that it can then be presented to them and they can be involved in its subsequent implementation and refinement.

Safety planning as a process, beginning with initial safety guidelines

One of the strongest messages we want to get across in this chapter is that a safety plan is not something akin to a box of soap powder, that can be taken off the shelf as some sort of pre-prepared product, applied to the family and problem solved. Creating a safety plan that is rigorous and stands a good chance of being implemented after the professionals close the case is a developmental process that requires time and the involvement of many people: professionals, family and their network. Within the resolutions approach the journey of creating a meaningful safety plan begins in earnest once we have completed the words and pictures process and we have seen that a simple explanation of the problems is now shared among the family and a network of people who surround them. This provides us with a group of people around the children who we know are informed about the alleged dangers.

Our safety guidelines and safety plans, particularly those developed for cases of alleged sexual abuse, always involve a 'most important rule' which states that the likely perpetrator will not be alone with any children. In developing safety guidelines and the safety plans we will usually have several sessions which involve the likely non-abusing parent and one or two support people to draft the rules of the guidelines. After the draft is prepared, we involve the likely perpetrator in refining the plan. In these drafting sessions it usually does not take long before someone will say something like:

Dan: This is a bit crazy you know, are you seriously suggesting we have to take responsibility to ensure Bill (mother's

partner who was convicted of sexually abusing a neighbour's child, but continued to maintain his innocence) is
never alone with any children? It's too much, I don't
think it can be done.

For us the fact that 'Dan', who is the maternal grandfather, has
voiced this concern overtly is a fantastic resource in our journey
towards developing a robust safety plan. At this point he is offering a
challenge that invites pessimism, but if we respond in this way we will
only be adding to the logic that this problem is too difficult to address.
These are very real challenges and the practitioner will feel the weight
of them when family or professionals issue them. To not be consumed
by the challenge and utilize it as an opportunity, we might proceed like
this:

Susie: That's a great question! Exactly the right question for us to
            struggle with really, so let's think about it some more.
            What do you think Fran (*mother*), do you think it's
            possible to make sure Bill is never alone with any children?
Fran :   (*thinking and speaking carefully*) I don't know, it'd be hard.
Susie: Absolutely! That's why we need to think through all the
            issues. Let's say we work on this over the next couple of
            months and we can set up a safety plan, in which you'll
            have to play a central role but which also involves lots of
            others, that does makes sure Bill is never alone with any
            children, would that make you more relaxed about these
            problems?
Fran: (*speaking slowly*) I would be more relaxed, I think, I have
            been so worried about everything since all this started, I
            never stop worrying. It might be something positive to do
            rather than just worry.
Susie: You've heard me say many times to you and to Bill that this
            is not just about showing that the children are safe but also
            setting your life up so that no one can ever accuse Bill of
            abusing children again. Do you think Bill buys that idea?
Fran: (*slowly*) Yes, I do actually, he even said it to you last week,
            remember? Remember he got upset at you because you
            didn't want him in this meeting, particularly with my
            Mum and Dad coming, but he also said he needed this sort
            of plan because those people (social services and police)
            are always going to be suspicious of him?
Susie: Yes, I do remember. Okay, so do you think it's worth
            going to all this hard work to create a plan that can show
            social services and the police that the children are safe
            and Bill is protected from any future allegations or
            misunderstandings?

Fran: We have to, otherwise he's never going to come home.

Susie: Okay, so coming back to you, Dan, you raised the issue for us. What do you think of what Fran is saying?

Dan: I think it's right we have to do this, I said to you before (following the meeting in which the words and pictures were presented to the network) that I know what you're doing and I agree with it completely. I just think it's a big thing to ask and I'm worried that it's asking an enormous amount of Fran.

Susie: I think that's absolutely true, it's why we have to take it slowly and make sure what we come up with is something that can really work. I don't want to go any faster than what you all think you can cope with. Dan, I think it's really important you asked this question; I'd ask you to keep raising your concerns if you think the plans we come up with aren't realistic as we get into the detail of them. It's why I want to go slowly and that's why at the moment I want us just to see whether we can make the rule that he's never alone with any children stick during the contact visits and keep reviewing it and see how we go. Does that make sense?

Dan: Yes it does. (*Fran also nods.*)

In this way Susie has taken Dan's challenge and utilized it to enable Dan and Fran to think through more carefully what the safety planning process is all about for them. Following this dialogue, Susie then moved the conversation on to exploring in considerable detail the sort of contact visits that would be most manageable as they started out on the process of taking responsibility for Bill's contact with his and other children. The particular aspect of the safety guidelines that took the longest to sort out in this session revolved around the issue of what would happen if the youngest daughter, of 18 months, wanted to go to the toilet. Dan had foreseen this issue when Susie had asked what were possible situations that would make it hard to ensure Bill was never alone with the children. After talking this through for about ten minutes, during which Susie continued to ask questions that caused Fran, her mother and Dan to decide what they wanted to do, they were able to come up with their rules. If there was only one other adult with them, they would ask the oldest daughter (9 years old) to go with the toddler to the toilet, but if this wasn't possible they would get Bill to walk at least a 100 metres away and sit where he could be seen while the supervising adult dealt with the toddler's needs. It was also agreed that if the contact was happening at the home, the older children would be sent upstairs to be in their rooms until the toddler was sorted out, or Bill would go to the shops for some milk to make it look more natural to the children.

This is the sort of detailed work we undertake with the parents and safety people as we successively refine and increase the specificity of the safety guidelines towards the final safety plan. The safety plans created within the resolutions programme readily transfer to families from different cultures, as the plans are always based on the family's own ideas, network and customs. Our questioning is designed to highlight potentially difficult areas and help the family to find solutions that work well for them. We will explore these processes in more detail in Chapter 9, but before we conclude this chapter we want to look at one particular set of safety guidelines developed in a different situation of alleged sexual abuse.

A family safety guidelines example

This example involves a separated couple, who we will call John and Mandy, who were involved in a protracted custody and access dispute before the court. The case was made more heated and difficult by the fact that their two preschool daughters, Alexandra and Amelia, had made statements to social services and to a forensic psychologist that led the psychologist to be convinced John had sexually abused the girls and led social services to substantiate a child sexual abuse finding against him. The police investigated but decided there was insufficient evidence to prosecute the matter. John denied the allegations and asserted that Mandy had coached the girls to make the allegations so that she could gain sole custody and get revenge against him for the separation. The case had dragged on with social services and in the family court for over two years when we became involved at the request of the guardian-ad-litum. Our involvement followed the court making an order that John be granted a minimum of four hours' contact per week. Social services were particularly keen on our involvement since John was remarried to Rebecca, their new baby had just been born, and social services were not sure how they should deal with this situation.

Rebecca and John undertook the entire resolutions programme, initially motivated by John wanting to demonstrate his willingness to undertake treatment (he had refused treatment that required him to admit he was a perpetrator of child sexual abuse) and because he wanted to pursue shared custody of his daughters. Mandy, in the company of her sister as her support person, was involved in about half the number of sessions that Rebecca and John attended. Mandy's involvement in the process, particularly at the beginning, was focused around negotiating the content of the words and pictures, which we prepared with Rebecca and John and then checked with Mandy. More generally, Mandy's involvement was about keeping her abreast of progress and to negotiate with her the contact arrangements and the content of the safety plan. Alexandra and Amelia were involved in drawing the pictures for the words and pictures document and then in doing the same thing with the safety plan document. Mandy was particularly appreciative of the development of the words and pictures document because she had been unable to find a way to talk to the girls about the issues for almost three years, after she had been told by the forensic psychologist and also her lawyer not to talk to her daughters about the matter.

As we proceeded through the resolutions process with Rebecca and John, they voluntarily decided that they would withdraw from pursuing joint custody of Alexandra and Amelia. This decision crystallized for them during the process of looking to further develop the initial family safety guidelines that were designed to protect the children and John during the four-hour contact visits into a final safety plan. At this point, Rebecca and John made the decision that to attempt to increase their contact with Alexandra and Amelia, particularly on to overnight stays, would create more problems for them than they wanted to handle. Thus, in this case, the initial safety guidelines became the final safety plan. Our sense of how this shift in John's goals came about was that because the resolutions process provided a space where he felt listened to regarding his position, he stepped back from simply fighting his corner, and Rebecca was able to have more influence on his thinking.

The safety guidelines as they were prepared with Amelia and Alexandra are presented in Figure 7.1 in the format Andrew uses to create safety plans – drawing the pictures together with the children and hand writing the words on the document.

In this plan the first rule, which states 'Daddy is never to be alone with Alexandra and Amelia', is the 'most important rule' and informs all the remaining rules. The second rule identifies the five safety people from Rebecca and John's network and that at least one of them will always be present during the contact visits.

It is worth noting that the picture that Alexandra and Amelia drew with us to this rule involves going to the cinema. This was a favourite activity that the children and John liked to do during contact. Being aware of this, we had undertaken quite a lengthy discussion with John and Rebecca about what it might look like to Mandy, her parents or one of her friends if they saw John and Rebecca taking the girls into the cinema. When we initiated this discussion, John became quite angry, accusing us of thinking he might molest his daughters in the cinema. Over the period of a 30-minute discussion we were able to respond to John's anger so that we could discuss further what he and Rebecca thought they needed to do so John was protected in this situation from people's worst fears about him.

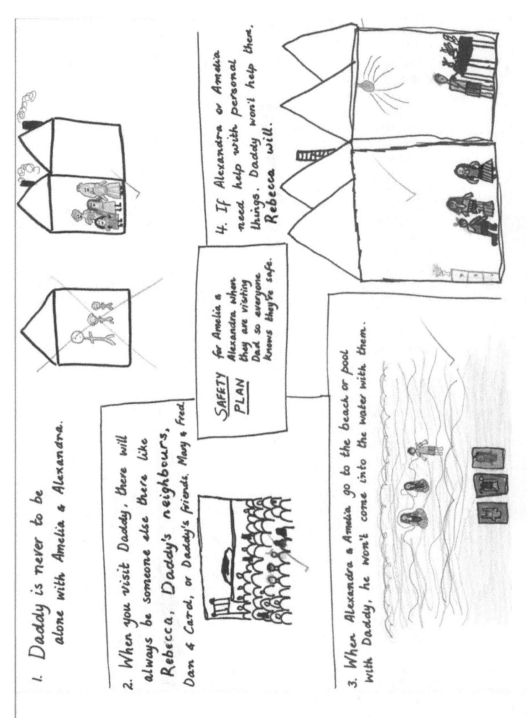

1. Daddy is never to be alone with Amelia & Alexandra.

2. When you visit Daddy, there will always be someone else there like Rebecca, Daddy's neighbours, Dan & Carol, or Daddy's friends, Mary & Fred.

SAFETY PLAN for Amelia & Alexandra, when they are visiting Dad so everyone knows they're safe.

3. When Alexandra & Amelia go to the beach or pool with Daddy, he won't come into the water with them.

4. If Alexandra or Amelia need help with personal things, Daddy won't help them. Rebecca will.

Figure 7.1

The couple considered the possibility of not going to the cinema, and also of John not going, but these ideas were set aside as both decided the visits to the cinema were something the girls liked and that the couple wanted to continue, in part because it relieved some of the tension often associated with the contact visits. As a result, it was agreed that John would never sit next to the girls in the cinema and the girls' drawing in the safety plan represents this commitment. We discussed this arrangement with Mandy in advance of preparing the document and she accepted the proposal. We also discussed it with Alexandra and Amelia during the picture drawing safety plan session. John and Rebecca were involved in this session, as were Dan and Carol, Mary and Fred. We had decided to involve these four as observers in the safety plan drawing session at the request of John as a way of avoiding an additional session where he would present the plan to the network. We discussed this and all the other rules once again with the girls when we presented the completed safety plan with them to Mandy and her parents.

When we look at this safety plan as we are preparing this book, we wonder why we didn't simply write up another rule with words that explicitly covered the cinema situation. One of the very pragmatic reasons this did not occur is we ran out of time in the number of contracted sessions to develop the safety plan further in this way. But this points to the fact that we are actually never happy with any safety plan we develop; there is always more that could be done to strengthen and further refine it.

Rule 3 identifies that John will not go in the water with the girls at the beach or pool. This is a very common rule that we create in safety plans dealing with sexual abuse issues where families regularly go swimming. Again, this was developed in a similar discursive process with John and Rebecca to that of rule 2. John also became angry (though not as strongly or for as long as he was regarding the cinema issue) when we explored what it might look like to an observer if they saw John in the water with Alexandra and Amelia. We asked that question after having discussed with the couple the fact that some men who sexually abuse children are particularly tempted to be sexually abusive in public situations such as the beach, and that this location is therefore one that social services are often very concerned about.

Rule 4 identifies that John will not help the girls with personal things, such as dressing, washing or the like, but that this will be Rebecca's responsibility.

The couple also undertook to keep a journal in which they recorded the details of each contact visit, for example what they did, which other adults were present, and also included details such as who went in the water with the girls if they went swimming or who sat where when they went to the cinema. The journal was sent back to Mandy for her to review after each contact. This is a process we will commonly institute alongside the safety plan, particularly in situations in which parents are separated.

After each of the first four weekly contact visits, the social services worker made direct contact with Alexandra and Amelia on their own after school, then Mandy and whoever else was involved in the contact visit. Finally, the worker would meet with John and Rebecca about the visit. The social services worker also reviewed the contact journal. After the first four contacts, the social service worker's follow-up dropped back to bi-weekly direct contact and then after eight further contacts the worker undertook direct follow-up once every four weeks and phone follow-up following each second contact. The monitoring arrangements allowed the social services worker to verify that the children felt safe, that the rules of the safety plan were being followed, and to draw out any issues that needed to be addressed to ensure the safety plan was effective and satisfactory for all involved. This follow-up regime was sustained over a six-month period, following which social services closed the case.

What we most want to highlight through this example is the careful and detailed process we engage in with the family to develop each rule. The rule itself is not the be-all and end-all, rather it is simply the end product. What is most important is the rigorous exploration of the issues with the family and their network and the process we undertake to involve everyone in developing and understanding the rules. This we believe makes for a robust safety plan. Each rule inevitably involves difficult conversations that require equal measures of care and courage on the part of the resolutions practitioner to initiate and sustain the family's focus on the issue at hand. Often enough, these discussions become heated, but by sustaining the focus on creating a meaningful safety plan this process strengthens the thinking and capacity for the adults surrounding the children to deal with the hard issues involved in protecting people like John from further allegations and demonstrating that the children are safe.

Pragmatic social services concerns about safety planning

When social service workers come to understand our approach to safety planning, they will typically raise two issues: one is about confidentiality; the other is about finding the time to be part of the monitoring and development of these sorts of safety plans.

With regards to confidentiality, social service workers are usually concerned about whether they are breaking client confidentiality by seeking to involve people around the family in such a sensitive matter. The point to be made here is that the parents are always in charge of deciding whether and who to involve. Certainly, we utilize social services and court leverage to motivate the parents to involve as wide a network as possible, but it is always the parents' decision as to who to involve.

Safety planning in the way we see it always involves monitoring of contact between the likely abuser and the children, because quite simply, this is where all the important action occurs regarding enacting meaningful safety. This emphasis inevitably raises the time factor for social services. The amount of time social services practitioners can make available is always a conundrum that has to be faced in every case. Of itself, it is an issue about how much the system can collectively turn to face the challenges of creating meaningful safety within each case. If we had our way, in most serious ACADE cases we would want something like a two-year process for developing, refining and monitoring the implementation of a safety plan. However, the pragmatics and real-politics of what is possible within a highly pressurized social services system always impacts on the monitoring of safety plans, and in each case we have to negotiate the worker's involvement in the process. In John and Rebecca's situation we were comfortable with the length of monitoring for the contact arrangements with Amelia and Alexandra. However, while social services were initially worried about the couple's own child, they did not take this infant's safety on as an issue they would involve themselves in, despite our encouraging them to do so.

As we suggested in Chapter 4, for social services' involvement to be maximized their participation must be negotiated and agreed upon before the commencement of the resolutions work. At this point, the resolutions practitioner has the leverage of their service involvement to negotiate with, in return for social service commitment in the ongoing process. Having said all this, we are constantly surprised how readily social services workers make extra time to do everything they can to help strengthen and refine the safety plan when they realize that the process is a meaningful rather than token undertaking. As well as seeing that the safety plan is helping keep the children safe, the workers are often very motivated to 'go the extra mile' because in doing this they learn a great deal for themselves about how to create meaningful safety plans.

Conclusion

If the reader is feeling in any way sceptical about the process and the plans we describe, we would encourage them to maintain their scepticism! Approaching safety planning with a lively, rather than pessimistic, sense of scepticism is an invaluable resource for building the rigour and detail of the plan with the family. We also want to underscore a point we have implied several times during this chapter, namely that even after we have created what we regard to be the best safety plans we have been a party to, we are never happy. These safety plans remain for us the best 'dirty' solutions we can come up with to the complex problem of the ACADE dilemma, and we know we can never be certain that they will be comprehensively implemented after all the professionals withdraw their involvement. For us to seek to claim more than this would in our view be to engage in our own denial of the complexity and challenge of building meaningful safety in serious ACADE cases. However, it is far better to involve as many people as possible in the family's naturally occurring network and facilitate thenm to take as much responsibility as possible to ensure the children are safe, and the likely perpetrator is protected from future allegations, than retreat into the sort of pessimism that saw the professionals withdraw their involvement in Rosemary's situation which we presented in Chapter 1.

There remains more that we want to describe about how we approach and undertake safety planning, particularly the process of moving towards and bedding down the final safety plan. We will return to that topic in Chapter 9, but before that we need to turn to the similar-but-different process we utilize to strengthen the insights and position of the likely non-abusing parent. It is important to underline that the four or five similar-but-different sessions are usually spread out over two to four months before we enter the process of developing the final safety plan. At the start of each similar-but-different session, we continue to review, refine and evolve the safety guidelines commensurate to the contact arrangements. As indicated in the overview chart in Chapter 2, contact steadily increases over this period, with the first overnight stay usually commencing towards the end of the similar-but-different process.

Chapter Eight

WORKING HYPOTHETICALLY: THE SIMILAR-BUT-DIFFERENT FAMILY

Introduction

In ACADE-type cases, statutory authorities will typically create case plans that include a key statement that reads something like: 'the parents must demonstrate an understanding of what led to these allegations and an understanding of the dynamics that surround situations where children are sexually (or physically) abused, before reunification can be considered'. This issue often becomes a substantial sticking point in progressing the case, because while the abuse allegations are disputed, it is usually uncertain how this goal can be achieved. In this chapter we will describe the resolutions process of meeting this goal.

In the resolutions approach, exploring dynamics seen by professionals to surround situations of child abuse is undertaken by directly involving the parents in a hypothetical, or similar-but-different, role-play process. In the hypothetical scenario, the parents role-play a different couple, in a similar family, facing similar issues of substantiated abuse, with the primary difference that in this hypothetical family the alleged perpetrator has admitted responsibility. In the role of the similar-but-different parents, the couple is then usually able to discuss hypothetically the issues they have been unwilling or unable to overtly discuss in their own situation because of the 'denial' dispute. This similar-but-different process provides them with the opportunity to demonstrate to the child protection authorities that they can meaningfully explore issues associated with the alleged abuse.

This hypothetical method of discussing difficult issues is not unique to the resolutions approach. Furniss (1991), Winn (1996) and MacKinnon (1998) describe the use of 'as if' and 'what if' conversations in child abuse cases. Scott (1993) uses a different sort of hypothetical scenario in creating an imaginary stereotypical sexual offender as a phantom group member in sexual offenders' group work. Probably the aspect of utilizing hypothetical conversations that is most unique to the resolutions approach lies in the length of time for which the discussions are sustained. Also, the clients themselves are asked to take on the hypothetical roles. This process, undertaken over three to five sessions, provides the opportunity to undertake a detailed and sustained exploration of the issues.

In summary, the similar-but-different process:

1. Creates a unique context in which it is possible for the caregivers to speak about issues surrounding child abuse that have previously been untenable conversations while the couple have been caught in disputing the allegations made against the alleged abuser.
2. Allows the likely non-abusing parent to consider other possibilities, and thus space is created to focus on strengthening the role and position of the likely non-abusing caregiver.
3. Creates a context to explore in detail issues seen to typically surround situations of child abuse, such as grooming processes, cycles of violence, issues of trust and responsibility, and the impact of abuse on children.
4. Allows the exploration of difficult relational dynamics such as how to go on when one of the parents has acknowledged abusing a child, trusting the perpetrator and intimacy with a partner who has abused children.
5. Successively explores issues surrounding child abuse from the perspective of the perpetrator, the non-abusing parent, the abused child, the other siblings, extended family and friends, and from the position of the parents projected 20 years into the future to a time when they are grandparents.

As we proceed through this chapter, we will consider two different scenarios to more fully demonstrate how the similar-but-different process can be used. One scenario relates to a case involving an injured 4-month-old baby, the other relates to a sexual abuse case. We will use transcript material to follow the use of the similar-but-different process in both cases. Social services workers are unlikely to have the time to undertake this sort of extensive similar-but-different process. To connect this hypothetical process to the work of social services, two case examples will be presented at the end of this chapter from frontline practitioners who have utilized similar-but-different ideas in modified form in denial situations with which they were faced.

Preparing the couple for the similar-but-different role-play

At the initial briefing meeting with the parents, where we first introduce them to the resolutions approach, we describe the similar-but-different process as a 'slightly strange' role-play process in which the parents will take on the role of another couple who face 'similar-but-slightly-different' circumstances to their own. This initial introduction usually means the parents are well aware the hypothetical stage is coming up in the second half of the resolutions process. Most parents we have worked with carry a slightly nervous sense of 'what is this all about?' and recall from the briefing session that they are going to be asked to undertake some sort of role-play.

In reintroducing the similar-but-different process, we emphasize that it is designed primarily to enable the couple to safely undertake conversations about the seriousness and dynamics surrounding abuse that the court and social services would expect them to have before the family can be reunited and the case closed. We underline that the similar-but-different process is a safe context since social services and the court cannot gather incriminating evidence against them on the basis of a made-up, role-play scenario. When parents remain cautious about the hypothetical process, we encourage them to take legal advice.

On one occasion, Andrew was unsuccessfully trying to reintroduce and re-explain the similar-but-different process with a couple in the company of their lawyer, who was sitting in on some of the sessions. As Andrew's explanations floundered, the lawyer stepped in to help. She explained to her clients that she had used the same sort of approach to a problem she faced in trying to help her sister and 9-year-old niece. When the lawyer and her sister tried to talk to the 9-year-old girl about the fact her sister's ex-husband (the girl's father) had left them and why he didn't have contact with his daughter, both the sisters and daughter found the situation was impossible to talk about. So the lawyer helped her sister and her niece to create a pretend Barbie-doll family where a father had left his family. In this context, mother and daughter could talk about the situation; the daughter could say what she wanted and so could the mother. This explanation worked well for the couple and it is an explanation we have often used subsequently. This example was another demonstration for us of legal representatives also being very supportive of the resolutions process when they realize that it does not place their clients at risk of prosecution.

Wherever possible, we undertake this preparatory stage at the end of the session in which the words and pictures were presented to the family network. In this way we can involve the children in the introduction, which tends to make the preparation work more playful and mitigates some of the nervousness the parents might be feeling about the process. We will often ask the children something like: 'In the next session just your Mum and Dad will come and they are going to pretend to be a Mum and Dad in a different family. Will you help us create the pretend family, because kids are usually better at doing this sort of thing than adults?' At this point, we bring a number of empty chairs and place them in a circle close to where we are sitting (one chair for each anticipated member of the hypothetical family). To the children we then explain:

> Mummy and Daddy are going to look at the worries the social workers and the judge have about safety in your family. Mummy and Daddy have told the social workers and the court there is nothing to worry about but the social workers and the judge say they must be sure. So Mummy and Daddy will look at the difficulties in this pretend family and talk about how they would make sure everyone is safe in future in that family so social services and the court will know Mummy and Daddy understand the worries even though they disagree with them.

We then ask the parents to give names to the hypothetical adults they will role-play, always ensuring that they don't know any people close to them with those names. We will then explain that this family has one more or one less child than their family and we need to create names for these children and give them ages similar to but not the same as theirs. We usually involve the children in giving names to the hypothetical youngsters. As this is done, we write all the names and ages up on a whiteboard or flip chart for everyone to see. We then might ask the children if they would be willing to choose some soft toys from toys that we have available to represent these pretend children in the circle of chairs.

Working between the whiteboard and the chairs assigned to the mother and father of the hypothetical family, we then ask the parents to begin to create more of the identity of the similar-but-different adults. Whether the children are present in this preparatory stage or not, we continue to make this role-creation process as playful as possible. One of the key ways we do this is by asking each parent to imagine this hypothetical adult as the person they always wanted to be; for example, that this person has the job, car, money, friends, home and lifestyle they always dreamed of. In this way, we encourage a couple who may be disadvantaged or feel powerless in some way to create roles for themselves as influential and powerful people. In our experience, this role-creation process often seems very important for the possible non-abusing parent and seems to create a small shift in the dynamics between the couple. We have many times witnessed this partner grow in stature as we encourage them to explore and take on a role involving life options that enable them to be more powerful and in an egalitarian position with their partner. Susie will always remember one such instance involving a husband who frequently treated his wife disdainfully. This man seemed to see his wife of many years through new eyes, as she created for herself the role of an independently wealthy, internationally famous concert violinist.

Exploring parental perspectives in a sexual abuse hypothetical

At the following session, we set out two clusters of chairs – one for the couple and the other for the role-play family. To begin the session we recall with the couple the names and identities of the hypothetical family and write these details on a whiteboard or flip chart. We quickly summarize again the purpose of the process and let the parents know that in this first similar-but-different session we will be once again focusing primarily on the experience of the parents and that in a subsequent session we will focus on other perspectives and the experience of the victim. We look to keep this introduction brief, to re-set the scenes and to be able to move into the role-play as quickly as possible.

The first similar-but-different scenario we will consider involves a couple we will call Julia and Gerry. Julia and Gerry were undertaking the resolutions process because a pre-school girl from the Sunday school Gerry helped lead had alleged that Gerry had sexually abused her. The matter was not taken to court, but social services had substantiated the allegations based on the detail of the girl's report. As a result of this, social services were concerned for the safety of Julia and Gerry's 3-year-old daughter. Julia and Gerry undertook a similar-but-different process in which they role-played the parents in the following hypothetical family:

Andrew: Do you feel ready to start the role-play?
Julia: I'm not sure.
Andrew: Well, it's always a bit of a step to get this started, but what about if I get you to change seats and we see how we go. (*The couple shift into the role-play seats and Andrew shifts his own seat to face the hypothetical parents.*) So Warren and Caroline, I noticed you arrived here today in a Porsche sports car, whose car is that? (*In the preparatory stage Julia*

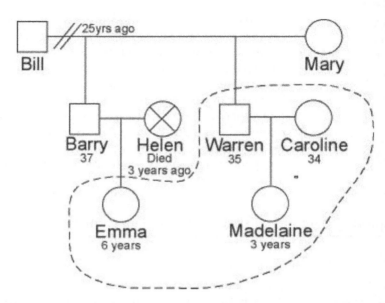

had chosen a Porsche sports car for her hypothetical character.)

Figure 8.1

Caroline: It's mine!

Andrew: Okay, nice car! How long have you had that?

Caroline: A few months.

Andrew: So Caroline, what do you do?

Caroline: I'm an architect, we live here but I work all round the country.

Andrew: Okay, and Warren what do you do?

Warren: I own a car dealership selling specialist imported cars. Caroline likes to change cars a lot to impress her clients.

Andrew: (*Laughing*) So is that why you set up the car yard?

Warren: No, I've been running the business for years but it sure helps to keep Caroline in the sorts of cars she likes.

Andrew: Okay, so am I right in thinking that you've put a manager in the car yard for the past two and half years so you had the time to look after Emma and Madelaine?

Warren: Yeah that's right.

Andrew: What I'd like to do now is just read the notes I have here from social services so you know what I know about your situation. Is that okay?

Caroline: Yeah (*Warren nods*).

At this point, we read the couple a story of the family (which we have prepared before the session) that fills out the hypothetical details we want them to think through and wrestle with in the similar-but-different process.

> Andrew (*reading*): In this family, Warren's father Bill abandoned the family 25 years ago and has had no contact with Mary or his sons since then. (*The therapist draws the extra people on the family map on the whiteboard.*) This made life hard for the family but was also a relief, as Bill had been very violent and abusive towards the boys but particularly towards Mary.
>
> Warren and Caroline have been married for 10 years. Warren owns a car sales yard, and has been very successful. He is very proud of what he has achieved. Warren owns a yacht and loves going sailing with his friends, who are mostly other local businessmen. Caroline is passionate about her work, she is an award-winning architect, who heads up her own architectural firm. Caroline loves going shopping, to the theatre, films and eating out. Caroline is very close to one of her sisters and has a number of close girlfriends who she does these things with.
>
> Caroline and Warren have a daughter, Madelaine, who is 3 years old. From the beginning of their marriage, Warren always wanted to have children, though Caroline was unsure. The issue wasn't really a problem because for many years they'd been unable to conceive. Warren's family thought it a shame because everyone always said he was 'so good with children'.
>
> Almost four years ago, Warren's sister-in-law Helen died. Helen was married to Warren's big brother, Barry (*Andrew points to the genogram on the flip chart*). Barry had always worked in oil exploration and usually worked away for six weeks in any two-month period. After Helen died in a traffic accident, Barry made it clear that he could not care for their $2\frac{1}{2}$ -year-old daughter Emma, saying he would pay for everything and visit her but that's all he could do. Barry arranged for Emma to move in with Mary and wanted Mary to take on the long-term care of Emma. Mary didn't really want to take on this role, particularly as she was often in poor health, but she felt obliged and very sorry for Emma. While all this was happening, Warren had excitedly suggested to Caroline that they should take Emma. Caroline had said she wasn't sure, that she would think about it and they could talk more about it. The next day Warren told his family they would take Emma, and he moved Emma into the family home. Warren told Caroline they had to do it and that he would appoint a

manager for the car yard and he would do most of the care.

Things seemed to go well, Mary would always say how good Warren was with Emma and congratulate Caroline for being so caring. At almost the same time Emma moved in, Caroline, to her own amazement, found herself pregnant. Warren told Caroline that they had got pregnant because they had been generous and done the right thing for Emma. Caroline had convinced herself it was all a good thing, and when Madelaine was born she thought it would be good that the two girls could be like sisters.

   Six months ago, Emma told her after-school babysitter that Uncle Warren had touched her. The babysitter felt panicked and told Caroline what Emma had said. Caroline in turn told their family doctor and he talked to Caroline and Emma about this. Caroline told Emma she could tell the truth, and Emma said Warren touched her between the legs and showed her his penis and got her to rub it. The doctor, who knew the family over many years, decided he needed to talk to Warren about this, and Warren admitted to the doctor that he'd done some of these things. (*Although an allegation of sexual abuse is very unlikely to be dealt with this way, we usually build the perpetrator's admission around someone like a doctor in the hypothetical scenario because we have found that parents often cannot imagine that they would have made a first admission to social services.*) After this, the police and social services got involved, Emma was placed in foster care and social services told Caroline and Warren that Warren would have to move out or they would remove Madelaine too. Warren immediately moved out. In court, Warren pleaded guilty to indecent assault and was given a two-year suspended sentence. He also had to attend sexual abuse treatment and counselling.

Andrew: That's a big thing, Warren, to admit you abused Emma, most people don't in your situation. Was that hard for you to do?

Warren: Well, I'd been feeling really bad about it and then talking with our doctor I knew the best thing was to face it. That's why I started going to counselling straight after I talked to the doctor too.

Andrew: So how has all this affected you? I bet you didn't get much sleep for quite a while.

Warren: Um, that's true, it's been hard, but look the children are the victims here, not me.

Andrew: Okay, so you can see that the children are the ones affected the worst by this, that's impressive and important. I want to come back to that later, right now I was wondering what was Caroline's reaction when you admitted sexually abusing Emma?

Warren: I don't know. Well, she was really angry that first day but she hasn't said much since. I've told her I want to get back together with her.

Andrew: Do you think she wants that?

Warren: I don't know, she hasn't said anything. I'm getting the cold silence treatment now. But I'm going to counselling about it, I know it'll take a long time to sort all this out, but I really want to know whether she's willing to commit to work on it.

Andrew: Right, do you think she's ready to decide yet?

Warren: I don't know what she's thinking, but I need to know if Caroline is willing to work on it. If she isn't, then I think I'll just go off and start a new life, probably go off on the boat ...

Andrew: Okay, it sounds like you've thought about this a lot and you're really ready to talk about what you're thinking, that's great.

After reading the prepared story, we always proceed by interviewing the hypothetical abusing parent and always compliment them on their admission and any other comments they make that show depth of thinking about the situation. Our aim here is to encourage the parent acting this role because the more we can engage them in the role and the more responses they provide, the richer the exploration of the scenario can be.

Andrew: Before we talk about what might happen in the future I'd like to find out what Caroline is thinking. I'm really wondering how you're coping. It doesn't get much worse for a mother to have to deal with something like this.

Caroline: Its been absolutely horrible, the worst thing that's ever happened to me.

Andrew: How have you been coping?

Caroline: My friends and my sister have been fantastic, helping out and we talk a lot.

Andrew: Has that been hard to do, talk to them? A lot of women in your situation might find it hard to talk about things like this.

Caroline: Well sometimes I feel ashamed and embarrassed, but I can't stop thinking about what happened to, ah (*looks at genogram*) ah, Emma.

Andrew: Okay, do your friends and sister mostly listen or do they say what they think too?

Caroline: They say what they think, especially my sister.

Andrew: So what are they telling you should happen?

Caroline: They all think I should dump him.

Andrew: Okay, that's pretty clear, what do you think about that?

Caroline: They're probably right, I don't know yet ...

Andrew: Can I ask what's the worst thing about all this for you?

Caroline: Um, the worst thing, well it's like, I can hardly believe he'd do this, that he'd be like this, after all we've shared.

Andrew: What do you want to say to him now?

Caroline: How could he have done this, why the hell did he do it?

Andrew: Warren, do you have any answer you can give to Caroline about that?

Warren: (*Pauses a long time*) I don't know ...

Andrew: Okay good, that's what most men say when they are asked that question. The research tells us most child sex abusers first of all deny the allegations, then if they do admit to it they minimize what happened. Often they blame someone else, the mother or the child. It is rare that the abuser accepts responsibility, they are often very aware of the consequences of doing that. So they rarely talk about the 'why' of it.

In almost every case of alleged sexual abuse we have worked with, where we ask the hypothetical mother is there anything she wants to say or ask the perpetrator, she immediately asks 'why did you do it?' (sometimes quite angrily). The role-play scenario creates the context in which the similar-but-different mother can speak what might well be unspeakable for the real mother, and the resolutions practitioner can then affirm the hypothetical non-abusing parent for her strength in facing and thinking hard about the issue. At the same time, as demonstrated in the therapist's last statement, the similar-but-different scenario creates numerous opportunities for the resolutions practitioner to weave professional knowledge about the dynamics of abuse and perpetrators into the conversation.

Andrew: Okay, is there anything else you want to ask him or tell him?

Caroline: Just that the situation he's put me in now is impossible. Madelaine's in care all the time, she's unhappy, I'm miserable, I have to work, and I'm not getting anything done properly. I don't understand how he could have done this at all.

Andrew: (*Pauses*) What do you think Madelaine's made of all this, it's not surprising she's unhappy, it's a lot of changes for her?

Caroline: She asks about Emma all the time, Emma was always playing with her. She wants to know when she'll come home.

Andrew: Have you thought about having Emma back or in your care at least?

Caroline: I'm not ready to take that on. They've just started seeing each other again.

Andrew: That must be important for both of them.

Caroline: Yeah, they both need that.

Andrew: Okay, Warren just said he wants to talk about what you're going to do, are you ready to make decisions like that yet? What do think about getting back together with him?

Caroline: Right now I want to go slowly, Madelaine is the priority, she has to be safe.

Andrew: Have you any ideas about what it would take for you to begin to trust him again?

Caroline: I really don't know, it would take years, I can't even begin to think ...

Andrew: It's a hard question. Is it like what Warren's done has shaken everything up, it's an enormous shock and it's hard to know where life goes to now?

Caroline: Yeah, you bet.

Andrew: So I'll come back to Warren for a while. You raised the issue of getting back together with Caroline, what do you think it would take to start to re-establish Caroline's trust in you?

Warren: Well, I have to keep going to counselling.

Andrew: Okay, so what difference do you think counselling will make?

Warren: Well, (*pauses*) the counsellor makes me face things and I'll talk to Caroline about that.

Andrew: Uh, huh, do you think the counsellor will ever be able to say that he's sure you are safe?

Warren: Um, I don't know.

Andrew: Do you think you could ever be sure that you won't be sexually attracted to young children again?

Warren: No, I'm always going to have to be careful.

Andrew: Wow, you know there's not many guys in your situation who will say that. Certainly from my experience and all the research I've read, I would never assume that someone who had sexually abused children would stop feeling that attraction. So I'd completely agree with what you've said. So you're clear that you're always going to have to be careful around children?

Warren: (*head bowed*) Uh huh.

There is a lot going on in a hypothetical role-play. Performance anxiety is always present and to our eyes the couple often seem also to be wondering what the hypothetical conversations they are having mean for them in real life. Our view is that we, and they, can never be certain. We do not try and interpret or analyse the roles the couple adopts; rather, we simply focus on utilizing those roles to strengthen the thinking of the likely non-abusing parent. In this instance, Gerry is playing Warren as a sensitive, I'm-working-hard, this-is-serious abuser, but it is important to emphasize that we are not looking for any particular right type of role-play performance from him. However the hypothetical perpetrator chooses to respond, we affirm and compliment their responses to encourage the actor in their role.

Our next step is to then utilize the hypothetical perpetrator's responses to deepen the exploration into the dynamics surrounding child abuse. Our primary strategy in doing this is to compliment the hypothetical abuser for their ideas and invite the role-playing safe parent to reflect on those positions and responses. Rather than seeking to interpret the couple's responses, our aim is as much as possible to expand the role-play, continually building upon the interactions and thinking of the couple. Though we can never be certain, we often have the sense that the couple are expressing ideas and sentiments they could not previously have entertained.

Andrew: Caroline, what do you think about this? It is impressive that Warren's clear that he will need to be cautious forever. He seems to be working hard on this, doesn't he?

Caroline: I don't know, perhaps it's just show?

Andrew: Oh, you think it might just be a show? You mean maybe he's just doing this to impress you and social services? (*Caroline nods*.) So you are not taking anything at face value. Do you think social services know you are being cautious and sceptical?

Caroline: I don't think so.

Andrew: I think they would be impressed if they knew. Warren is sounding impressive, but I can see you would want evidence. Did you know he would have the ability to face up to the problem in this way, given how horrified everyone is?

Caroline: (*Pauses*) I'm not sure because I don't know whether it helps me or not.

Andrew: That's what a lot of women in your situation experience; almost however the abuser responds, they have to struggle to figure out what's best. But it still seems brave of Warren to admit what he did. Do you think it was better for Emma that he took responsibility?

Caroline: (*Slowly*) Yes, that was important for her. But I'm still struggling with the fact he did it at all. I'm not sure I want him back.

Andrew: So you're weighing this up really carefully? (*Caroline nods.*) That's really important because it just is hard to figure it all out. As I said before, I'm sure social services will think that's impressive.

Throughout the similar-but-different scenario, we will always affirm and support caution on the part of the hypothetical safe parent regarding what would constitute meaningful evidence that abuse would not happen again. There is a sort of constant 'double dialogue' happening in the hypothetical conversations; the more cautious, critical and sceptical the role-playing safe parent is, the better the real couple are performing in demonstrating that they can think robustly about the consequences of the abuse. Hence we are constantly seeking to support both sides in the role-play and to thereby deepen the couple's own hypothetical exploration of the issues.

Andrew: Caroline, when you heard Warren saying he's started seeing a counsellor, were you impressed he has taken responsibility for getting help with this?

Caroline: Umm, maybe I guess, I'm not sure he will keep at it.

Andrew: So you're not sure, you wonder if he will keep going? (*Caroline nods.*) I like your caution, you seem to be wanting to take this slowly and make sure all the time it's for real, I think that's great! (*Turning to Warren*) I guess this must be hard for you that Caroline is sceptical of you (*Warren nods but also looks cautious*). I was thinking, though, that Caroline being cautious like this is probably good if you're going to get back together. I doubt social services and the court would be impressed if Caroline just accepted everything you say, would they?

Warren: (*Obviously thinking hard*) Well, she has to think about the children and what's best for them, that's what she has to do.

Andrew: Wow, so you can see that?

Warren: (*Somewhat angrily*) Of course I can! If I've done this to Madelaine, she, um (*looking up at the genogram*) Caroline has to think like that.

Andrew: Warren, really, that's great that you can see so clearly that Caroline has to be sceptical and cautious. (*Turning to Caroline*) What are the things that would make you think, yes I'll have him back, and what are the things that make you think no it won't work?

Caroline: (*Thinking*) I don't know, that's so hard to figure out (*pauses again*). I do know one thing, though, whatever counselling he has had I wouldn't ever leave him in the house on his own with the children.

Andrew: So you are taking this very seriously. I guess that would help show that the children would be safe, but would it also help Warren so that there can be no misunderstandings or allegations in the future?

Caroline: I think it would help Warren so he doesn't have to go through this again, I might trust him when the children are bigger, I don't know. Will social services be worried when they are bigger?

Andrew: Warren, what do you think?

Warren: I think Caroline's right, it would be best if I wasn't left on my own.

Andrew: Caroline, did you realize he thinks what you said will be helpful?

The similar-but-different conversations often provide the opportunity to focus on future safety and can serve as a prelude to the later safety planning stage of the resolutions process. The conversation just described also creates a context in which the hypothetical safe parent's views are privileged and she has the chance to put forward her own ideas about what is needed if the couple are to reunify. This is a process we want to encourage as we will be seeking to locate the likely non-abusing parent centre stage in the safety plan for the real family.

Andrew: Caroline, what else would you want to see Warren do to convince you he is serious?

Caroline: Well, I think he shouldn't whisper to Emma all the time. I never liked it. I used to worry what he was saying to her. She used to go all silly and run away. After that, I couldn't calm her down and he had to do it. If he comes back, I want us to parent her more together.

Andrew: That's great, so you want things to be open and to share any difficult bits together?

Caroline: Yes, I guess.

Warren: But I was just messing about, having fun.

Andrew: Hmmm, okay. I'm not sure whether Emma will be coming back to live with you if you reunite, but if you did the same whispering thing with Madelaine do you think the social worker would be impressed or worried?

Warren: I don't know.

Andrew: What do you think, Caroline, if you did get back together and Warren was always whispering things to Madelaine and she was getting wound up, would that be something that social services would worry about?

Caroline: I think they'd be worried, and it'd worry me, in fact he had started doing it with her and I hated it. If we're going to be altogether again, I think Emma and Madelaine should talk to us both about their worries. I need to be close to them both too. I wasn't very close to Emma.

Andrew: Caroline, that's great, social services will like the idea that Emma and Madelaine can talk to both of you. One of the things we know about people who sexually abuse children is that they always set things up in the family so they are the only one who is close to the child they want to abuse. Do you think it would be important that there are other people the girls are close to if you all get back together?

Caroline: Yes, that would be important too probably.

Andrew: Great. Is there anything else you can think of that you'd want to be confident it was okay to get back together?

Caroline: Not really right now, I've run out of ideas.

Andrew: Warren, have you got any ideas?

Warren: No, nothing else, what Caroline has said is pretty good.

Andrew: Okay, I want you to stand up, walk around Warren and Caroline's chairs twice and then sit down in your own chairs over there as Gerry and Julia. (*The couple do this.*)

Following each similar-but-different session, we review the session with the couple, as themselves out of role, in their own seats. We ask them what the experience was like and invite them to reflect on what they learned. In a situation such as the one we've just described, it is not uncommon for the couple to be quite distressed, so it's important to give the couple time to debrief from the process. One mother who was feeling distressed after a hypothetical session said: 'I never imagined I'd be in this sort of situation and be faced with these issues. You can say that family was different but this is us, that's our family.'

Our experience of facilitating hypothetical discussions is that there are always times when the conversations are stilted, but there are also always times when the process comes alive and is clearly significant for the couple. At some stage in the similar-but-different process the conversations also inevitably take surprising turns. In situations such as the scenario just described, we have found ourselves surprised when a man who is strenuously denying sexually abusing a child suddenly, as the hypothetical character, takes on the role of an apologetic, almost too-good-to-be-true, seemingly reformed sexual abuser. Whatever stance the person takes who role-plays the abusive parent, what is most important for us is to use that stance to help strengthen the likely non-abusing partner and help them consider different possibilities regarding the abuse. As intimated above, one of the key lessons we have learned in working in this way is to resist the urge to try and analyse the reasons behind developments in the roles people take and the issues they raise. Rather, the similar-but-different work is more productive when we find ways to deepen the conversations by asking as many questions as we can think of. The more questions we ask, the more we are increasing the possibilities for the role-playing couple to look at the issues surrounding child abuse in new ways.

Some of the typical questions we utilize in exploring the perspectives of the abusive and non-abusive parent include the following.

Perpetrator's perspective

What would you most like to say to your wife/partner?
I'm wondering what you think your wife would make of what you've just said?
If your wife and her friend were talking it over, what might they be thinking about your saying you couldn't help yourself?
What impact do you think this might have on your intimate relationship with your partner now and in the future?
How has what happened changed the way you think about yourself?
Does your mother know you have faced up to this and have had the courage to look at it in a direct way?
What would your mother make of your determination not to let anything like this happen again?
What do your wife's family think about what has happened?
What are your friends at church thinking about what has happened? Who is most concerned?
What do you think the women's group at the mosque is saying to your wife?
What do you think the child protection agencies are thinking?
What would you like to say to your children?
How might life need to be different in the future?
What help do you think you might need, now and in five years' time?
Who would you want to be most supportive of you?

Non-abusing parent's perspective

What will need to happen for you to trust your partner again?
Given what he has done, what do you want to say to him?
What might this mean for the future?
What have your own family said to you?
What has your partner's family said to you about what's happened?
What do your children want you to do?
What are you thinking about your partner?
What are you thinking about yourself?
How would your friends at Kingdom Hall notice your new independence?

What will be different about your future together now?

How will it be different from the future it would have been if your partner hadn't said anything?

What do you want from your partner now?

What does your partner want from you now?

Given what your partner has said, can you imagine other circumstances where he nearly lost it but managed to keep his temper?

What do you do that helps your partner control his temper?

What does your partner think helps him keep control?

Does the present situation offer you opportunities for making positive changes?

The similar-but-different parental role-play in an injured infant case

In cases of alleged sexual abuse, a likely abuser is usually clearly identified. In ACADE cases in which a baby has suffered serious injuries, it is usually far less certain who might have caused the injuries. For this reason, in injured infant cases, we often undertake two similar-but-different scenarios, one where the father accepts responsibility and the other where the mother identifies herself as injuring the baby. In this way, it is possible to present the two scenarios slightly differently, for example one hypothetical abusive parent can be constructed as drinking too much and losing control in the face of a crying baby. In the second scenario, the alternative abuser can be constructed as deeply depressed. The point is for the resolutions practitioner to use their imagination and weave details into the scenario that they think are most relevant for the couple they are working with.

In the situation we will consider, a first session had already been conducted where the father role-played the person admitting to injuring the baby under the influence of alcohol. In the second session, which we will look at below, the mother was cast in the role of the abusive parent. In this hypothetical family, the parents were called Paula and Henry and the children were Jeff, a 10-year-old boy, and Kylie, the baby. In cases of alleged child abuse involving a seriously injured baby, our experience, as well as the literature (e.g. Dale et al. 2005), suggests that the gender of the abused child is often a highly significant characteristic of these cases. Thus, in creating the similar-but-different injured infant scenarios we ensure that the gender of the hypothetical infant remains the same as the family's real child who was injured.

In this second session, we read the following briefing scenario to the parents:

Susie: (*Reading and looking at Paula*) So, as I understand things, it was a hard pregnancy and birth for you Paula? (*Paula nods.*) Jeff had been a really easy baby, he'd fed easily, hardly cried at all, looking after Jeff was hard work but compared to Kylie he was pretty easy. You were pretty shocked to find that Kylie was a really hard baby. Even at the hospital you noticed it, and once you got her home it only got worse. It seemed like Kylie was always crying. She wasn't easy to feed, with the breast or the bottle. She would only sleep for short periods and was always waking up. She'd wake up crying and you couldn't figure out what was wrong or what to do to make her happy. There were some times when you'd cuddle her, and she'd smile and you were both happy, but not very often.

You tried to talk to Henry about it, but he never seemed to listen, he'd just say things like: 'You can do it, you're such a good mum. You've done it all before, it's only a baby and anyway Kylie's fine.' Then he'd be off to work, or just go off with his mates drinking and fishing. It made you feel really angry, you wanted to yell at Henry, but he just didn't seem to get it. You started to wonder if it was all your fault?

Things got worse and worse, you hated Kylie's screaming, it was so bad you didn't want to go into her in the night at all, and you were tired out of your head all the time. You even found yourself thinking once or twice: 'She's wrecked my life', and you started to feel like you were a failure. You started to think that there was no way you'd be able to go back to your job as a lawyer when you felt like you couldn't even look after Kylie.

One night Henry came home and Jeff told him 'Mum and Kylie had a fight and I think Kylie's hurt'. Henry found Kylie in the cot with bruising around her eyes and she was limp. Henry you yelled at Paula: 'What happened, how the hell did this happen?' But Paula, you didn't say much, you were on the couch pretty out of it. Henry bundled everyone in the car and took everyone to the hospital. The doctors said Kylie had two rib fractures, a wrist and cheek fracture, and bruising and bleeding behind the eyes. They said the injuries were consistent with Kylie being shaken hard and thrown against the wall or onto the floor. The social worker and police reports say that, Paula, you told them 'it must have been me' and that you were crying a lot when they interviewed you.

Using this scenario, we will present excerpts of typical conversations from this sort of session.

Susie:	So Henry, did Paula tell you herself that she must have done it?
Henry:	About a week later she said it, because I'd been asking her what happened.
Susie:	Do you remember that Paula, saying to Henry it must have been me?
Paula:	Yeah, it was about a week later.
Susie:	Do you remember much else in that first week or was it all a bit of a blur?
Paula:	Well ... um ... no not really ...
Susie:	Henry, what did you say when she said 'It must have been me'
Henry:	I asked her how did it happen, but she didn't have any answers.
Susie:	Looking back on it, how do you think it happened? What might have caused it?
Henry:	Well ... she wasn't at work, she was worried about not having enough money for our loans and she was depressed and that.
Susie:	Paula, looking back on it, what do you think now, how do you think it happened?
Paula:	(*Very woodenly*) Well Paula must have been depressed, she must have been worried about ...
Susie:	Can you say it as 'I was worried about'?
Paula:	Ah, she was worried about the loans.
Susie:	Instead of saying 'Paula was worried about?' Can you say it as Paula herself and say 'I'm worried about'?
Paula:	Ah, yeah ... yeah um, I was worried, no I don't know, well it just happened all ... everything just happened all too fast.
Susie:	Paula, it looks to me like it's really hard for you to think and talk about this stuff. Is that right?
Paula:	Yeah (*a long silence*) ... Paula's in space land ...
Susie:	Okay, Paula's in space land. Does that mean Paula is still in shock from everything that's happened?
Paula:	Yeah, there you go, exactly!
Susie:	Okay, so, can you say more about what you mean by you're in space land, Paula?
Paula:	It's racking my brain all the time.
Susie:	What is, what's racking your brain?
Paula:	Thinking about what happened, how it happened to Kylie. How I could have done that?
Susie:	So, how Kylie got hurt, you don't understand how Kylie got hurt?

Paula: Yeah, I can't handle it, what's happened to Kylie, it really hurts, that's a big pain, a big pain.

Susie: Is that what keeps you in space land, that big pain, and racking your brain all the time, thinking how did this happen?

Paula: Yes! Thinking about 'how did this happen?' all the time.

Susie: How could we help you get out of space land?

Paula: I don't know, I don't know, do you know how you get out of space land?

Susie: Well, let's ask Henry. Henry, what are your ideas about getting Paula out of space land when her brains are always being racked by thoughts of how did this happen and how could I have done that?

Henry: Well ... she'd have to talk, you know when she's ready, no one can make her, when she's ready we'll talk.

Susie: Okay, so what do you think she needs to talk about?

Henry: Well that's hard, um, she has to say really, but what she's thinking of, what's on her mind.

Susie: Do you mean talk about how did this happen and how could I have done it? (*Henry nods.*) So are you willing to hear her talk about those things?

Henry: For sure, when she's ready.

Susie: Okay, so what else do you think, what else do you think would help Paula get out of space land?

Henry: Ah, (*pauses*) if we could get her to forgive herself, that would be good.

Susie: Really? Okay, so you think it'd be good if she could forgive herself? (*Henry nods.*) Any ideas how we could help Paula forgive herself?

Henry: Um, (*speaking carefully*) one step at a time, one step at a time, when she's ready.

Susie: Paula, any ideas, have you got any ideas about what would help you forgive yourself?

Paula: I don't think I can forgive myself.

Susie: You don't think it's possible?

Paula: No!

Henry: That's the hardest thing to think of forgiveness.

Susie: So do you think forgiveness can happen, even a little bit?

Paula: I need to understand why it happened.

Susie: Oh okay, you need to understand why it happened.

Paula: Yeah, but could we have a break?

We make a habit at the beginning of the hypothetical sessions of offering families the opportunity to ask for a break at any time. This is one small but simple way in which family members can feel they can maintain control over the process if they are feeling emotional. It is also common for us to suggest a break if we feel the situation is becoming too difficult to manage for ourselves or the couple, or if we need to think through how the session is proceeding and where we would like to take the conversations.

Susie: Okay, I was thinking about what you said, Paula, it seems like you're saying to even begin to forgive yourself, you'd have to understand why it happened. (*Paula nods.*) Do you think that's going to be possible, to understand everything about why and how it happened?

Paula: Umm, I don't know.

Susie: I guess my experience is that people, mums and dads I've worked with in your situation, haven't often ever felt like they've been able to fully understand how something so terrible could have happened.

Paula: Yeah, but if I can't understand, how can anybody else?

Susie: Yeah good question, I was wondering in the break, do you think it's possible to forgive yourself for what you've done even if you don't fully understand how it happened?

Paula: Umm, what do you mean?

Susie: Well, I guess I just don't know whether anyone could fully understand how and why something like Kylie being so badly hurt could have happened.

Paula: Yeah, okay . . . I don't know myself.

Susie: I think the idea of forgiving yourself as much as you can is really important and I think it was really good that Henry raised the issue for us. But it's a hard one, so let's see if we can come at it from a slightly different tack. (*Turning to Henry.*) What do you think, if Kylie was to come home now, do you think Paula feels she can trust herself that what happened to Kylie before won't happen again?

Henry: Well, yes, but it still needs time.

Susie: Time, okay, so how would you know she could trust herself with Kylie again?

Henry: Well it'd have to happen step by step.

Susie: Okay, so that means going slowly is important? (*Henry nods.*) How would you know that things were getting better and Paula was feeling like she could trust herself again?

Henry: She'd be happy, well happier anyway.

Susie: Okay, Paula, what do you think, do you think you could trust yourself if Kylie came home?

Paula: Um, I don't know how to answer, like Henry said, it'd have to go slow, step by step.

Susie: Okay, so what would be the first steps in building the trust in yourself a little?

Paula: Well, you know, bonding, bonding with Kylie again.

Susie: Okay, what would that look like, if you were bonded to Kylie again?

Paula: Well, I don't really know her any more, you know I haven't been with her for ages, ah, ah (*looking at whiteboard to check how long since Kylie was removed*) you know for almost six months, she's changed so much and the bonding's gone.

Susie: Okay, what needs to happen to rebuild the bonding?

Paula: Well, it's hard isn't it, you guys have got to let me have her more and then I'll see. At the moment I hardly see her.

Susie: Okay, that's a fair comment, I can see that. If you have more contact, how will you know the bonding is there again?

Paula: Well, I need to see her more and get to know her again, and try and rebuild things. Then we'll see. Like I said, step by step.

Susie: Okay.

In our experience, similar-but-different scenarios where babies have suffered serious injuries are somewhat different from sexual abuse hypotheticals. While sexual abuse hypotheticals will often see the parent role-playing the non-abuser expressing anger and the perpetrator defensiveness, in injured baby scenarios it is more common that issues of grief arise and the subject of forgiveness is not unusual. It is likely that the parents have previously been unable to give voice to these sentiments, so this in itself is a valuable process. By alternating the role of the hypothetical abusive parent it, often also seems fairly apparent that one of the parents did cause the injuries because of the intense distress they display when their turn comes to take this role. When this occurs, it is important for the therapist not to see or use this as an opportunity to 'get a confession'. However the parents present themselves in the role-play, the purpose of the resolutions approach and the hypothetical process is not to get a confession but rather to enable the couple to explore the issues surrounding the abuse more deeply, to make it more likely they can move forward.

In our experience, there is considerable value in spreading out three to five similar-but-different sessions over five to ten weeks, since this contributes to deepening the process. When the similar-but-different sessions are held weekly, there can be a sense for the couple that 'if we just hold our breaths this will all be over with', whereas taking time over the process tends to diffuse this impulse. Between sessions the resolutions practitioner can also reflect on the issues that have been covered and the standpoint the parents have brought to the conversations. It is also important for the therapist to consult with the child protection worker about whether the hypothetical conversations are covering the sort of territory and issues the worker expected. In this way the therapist can draw into the similar-but-different conversations the issues that the worker identifies need to be addressed.

The child's perspective

Most professionals involved in child abuse cases regard the parents' capacity to have understanding and empathy for the experience of the victim as a crucial element in rebuilding safety for the children and in the journey towards reuniting the family. In ACADE cases, professionals frequently believe that the parents lack empathy for the victim or that this empathy is compromised. The similar-but-different process offers a very powerful mechanism for exploring the abuse from the perspective of the child.

We usually undertake the exploration of the child's perspective in the second or third session of the similar-but-different process. We begin the session by explaining to the couple that this session is focused on the child's experience of the abuse, concentrating particularly on what the child thinks about themselves since the abuse, what they think about their parents and what they want to happen. We emphasize that in situations where they believe the parents have abused their children, professionals typically worry that caregivers are overlooking the experience of the child. We explain that this session is therefore all about giving the parents the opportunity to demonstrate that they are able to understand the child's experience. We explain that to do this, in their hypothetical roles, we will ask them to think about what it has been like for the child and to speak from the child's perspective as much as they possibly can. Once the parents are sitting in their role-play seats, a briefing narrative is read to them in similar manner to the earlier sessions. This narrative describes the child's experience of the events leading up to and following the abuse.

The similar-but-different process focused on the child's experience is often very distressing for the parents. For this reason, we read the narratives at the beginning of the role-play with a minimum of emotion and in a very neutral, flat manner. Our aim is to get across the information conveyed in the narrative without emotionally overwhelming the parents by what we are reading.

The child's perspective in a situation of an injured baby

In an injured baby scenario like the one we have been following in the hypothetical family of Henry, Paula, Jeff and Kylie, we would often use two scenarios, one relating to Jeff's experience and the other to Kylie's experience. Presented below are two narratives relating to each of these children and some dialogue that is fairly typical of the sort of conversations that this process can generate.

Jeff's experience

Jeff has had a pretty good life until recently. He has lots of friends and he plays football and cricket pretty well. There's always something to do and his mum and dad love having friends over and they love going fishing. But they haven't been doing any fishing lately or anything else as a family that's much fun.

It all started when Kylie came home from hospital – Jeff would sometimes think he really didn't love Kylie. All Kylie ever did was scream and cry and create problems for his family. Jeff even said that to his aunt one time but she told him he shouldn't think that way. Dad was looking after Kylie at home because Mum went back to work as a lawyer. He tried to help Dad look after Kylie but he really didn't know what to do to help. Dad would get angry and really yell at Kylie sometimes and he started to drink a lot, even during the day.

One day there was big football match on the television, and Dad invited a couple of his old friends over to watch the game and he got a whole lot of beer for all of them to drink. Kylie was really upset, she wouldn't take her bottle and was crying and screaming. Dad told his mates, she'd go off to sleep, saying there's nothing wrong. Well Kylie didn't go to sleep and she screamed so much Dad's mates left, saying they couldn't take it.

Dad was really angry then and Jeff ran off to his room. Dad was yelling and Jeff realized he was yelling at Kylie, screaming at her to shut up, yelling at her that she'd wrecked everything. Kylie was just screaming louder than ever. Jeff peeped out of his bedroom, he wondered whether he should do something but he didn't know what to do. Then suddenly he heard a thud and everything was completely quiet. Jeff came out after a while and saw Dad on the sofa looking bug-eyed and saying nothing. Jeff asked where Kylie was and then went into her bedroom, he looked at Kylie in her cot – she looked like she was dead.

Jeff felt really guilty then, like he should have done something, but he didn't know what. Jeff was really glad when his Mum came home just then, but she started yelling at Dad ... what the hell's happened? Mum got everyone in the car and took everyone to the hospital. Kylie wasn't dead but she was really hurt. Jeff had to go live with his Aunty for six weeks. He's been back home for eight weeks now but everything's pretty sad and they don't have much fun any more.

Paula:	That's a bit hard, it's too horrible. Would a boy feel like that?
Susie:	What do you think is horrible?
Paula:	I don't know, I don't know.
Susie:	What do you think Henry, does it make sense to you, how Jeff's feeling?
Henry:	I can understand, but Jeff shouldn't feel like it's his fault.
Susie:	No, he shouldn't but kids often do. Any ideas how you could help Jeff?
Henry:	Talk to Jeff and let him know it's not his fault.
Paula:	Reassure him.
Susie:	How?
Paula:	(*Softly*) Say sorry, apologize.
Susie:	Did you say apologize?
Paula:	Yes, obviously Henry did something to Kylie, he has to say something, make him understand.
Susie:	What can he say so he's not feeling it's his fault, so he'll listen?
Paula:	Say it was Henry, his fault and nothing to do with Jeff. That he was drunk as a skunk and doesn't remember what happened, reassure Jeff it's not his fault.
Susie:	Okay.

Kylie's experience

When I was born it was great, everyone seemed happy to see me, everyone smiling, I was warm and happy. But there was a problem, I had lots of pain in my tummy and the only way I could tell Mummy and Daddy I wasn't happy was to cry. We went home and I had my own room to sleep in. I didn't like that, I like being with Mummy and Daddy and Jeff and my Nana, when she comes. But they wanted me to be in my cot and my tummy always hurt and I was upset, so I cried and cried to tell them how much my tummy hurt and how lonely I was. After a while the only person I saw very much was Mummy. Mummy could be real nice, like sometimes when she fed me we cuddled lots and she smiled at me lots and it was the happiest I've ever been.

But one day I woke up and my tummy was really sore, I was crying and crying. Mummy tried to get me to have a bottle but I couldn't drink much and Mummy wasn't cuddling me, she was yelling at me. I don't know where Jeff or Daddy were. I cried and cried and Mummy's face got redder and redder ... and then she just lost it, I think she threw me and I think I hit something hard but I'm not sure, I don't remember much else.

I don't see Mummy and Daddy and Jeff very much now, I'm living with this strange woman, I don't know what went wrong … sometimes I feel confused and worried …

Susie: So how do you think Kylie is feeling?
Paula: She's still 6 months old?
Susie: Yeah.
Henry: Well she'd be confused she's with a strange lady.
Paula: She'd be thinking, what happened? What did I do, if she could speak she'd say, what happened?
Susie: Okay, so maybe it's like that'd be the feeling in her body, what happened? What do you think she's feeling about herself right now?
Paula: I really can't answer (*starting to cry*) probably say – why, what did I do?
Henry: Yeah just why?
Paula: Why, what, who, how?
Susie: Can you say more about what you mean by she'd be thinking why, what, who, how?
Paula: Well, she wouldn't even know who Mum and Dad are, she's with this strange lady. She wouldn't really know where she belongs or what happened.
Susie: Do you think she wants to be with her Mum and Dad?
Paula: Silly question, of course.
Henry: She may not want to …
Susie: I guess that's what I was thinking about, she may not want to.
Paula: Its hard to know, she's only a baby, given she was hurt like that though, she wouldn't want it to happen again.

The child's perspective in a situation of sexual abuse

The following is typical of the sort of scenario we would use in preparing parents to explore a hypothetical child's perspective in a situation of sexual abuse. As well as focusing on the child's experience, we use this scenario as a vehicle to more fully explore the grooming processes that typically surround the sexual abuse of children. This scenario again relates to the family of Warren, Caroline, Madelaine and Emma we considered earlier in the chapter. This particular child's perspective is designed to take the similar-but-different couple back to the time before Emma disclosed the abuse, as a way of focusing on the dynamics at play at that time.

Emma's experience

Emma is a 6-year-old girl who lived with her Uncle Warren and Aunt Caroline for three years. Emma is the daughter of Warren's brother Barry and his wife Helen. Emma came to live with Warren and Caroline just after her mother Helen died, because Barry was not able to look after her. Shortly after Emma moved in, Caroline surprisingly got pregnant with their daughter Madelaine, who is almost 3 years old now.

Warren provided most of the care for Emma and since she moved in, Warren has always played tickling and tumbling games with Emma. He especially played these games after baths, just before bedtime. Once Emma thought Warren's hand touched her between the legs but she couldn't be sure. When Emma had been there almost a year, the games became 'gymnastics lessons' and Warren would help her do handstands and head-over-heels. He often had to hold Emma's bottom to steady her. Emma began to think Warren looked strange when playing these games.

Then Warren said Emma was growing up and was his special girl. He told her he wanted her to know more about being a woman. Warren showed Emma his private parts and also told Emma this was 'a secret lesson', only for her because she was his special girl. Emma felt worried but did like being Warren's special girl and didn't want to upset him.

Warren began to take Emma to the gym club and helped her get into the tumbling tots gymnastics team. Late last year Emma became more worried when Warren not only showed Emma his penis but told her to touch it and rub it so that she would know what it felt like. Warren also started touching Emma's bottom between her legs. He told Emma she was still his special girl and this is what you did when you got bigger and thought someone was so special. Warren told Emma she liked it. Emma felt worried because her legs trembled. Emma thought a lot about telling Grandma Mary, but decided not to because Grandma had enough to worry about and everyone said she was getting sicker.

Emma likes feeling special and doesn't want to upset Warren but she is beginning to worry more and more and more. Emma is even more worried because of Madelaine, she has seen Warren playing tickling games with her and was talking about Madelaine joining the tiny tots gym club just like Emma.

Andrew: Warren, given that we are thinking about Emma's perspective before she disclosed the abuse, what do you think she is thinking and feeling now?

Warren: I'm not sure, confused, but maybe she likes to feel special too?

Caroline: She'd feel all in a mess, Warren's messed her head up.

Andrew: You're doing really well, this is just the sort of thing the research tells us children feel.

Caroline: She must be really worried she'll lose everyone.

Andrew: Yes, I guess so.

Warren: But maybe it isn't that serious. Like, if she was worried, why didn't she say no? Or tell someone?

Caroline: Yes, why didn't she come and talk with me?

Andrew: People often wonder that about children in Emma's position. Who do you think she could have told, what could she have said?

Caroline: She could have talked to me.

Andrew: What do you think she might have said?

Caroline: Um, well probably, well maybe have said that she didn't like the gym games with Warren?

Andrew: Okay, if she had said that, which might be hard for her, what would you have said?

Caroline: I would have said I needed to ask Warren, check with Warren.

Andrew: And Warren, what would you have said to Caroline?

Warren: Ah, well I guess I would have explained it was just a game.

Andrew: Exactly Warren, thanks for adding that, because that's probably exactly what a man in your situation would say.

Caroline: It'd be hard for her and for me too, to know what she was trying to say maybe.

Andrew: So Caroline, what could Emma have said to you to convince you there was a big problem?

Caroline: Now I don't know, it's not easy, she'd have had to say about the touching stuff, but I'm not sure she would be able to say what was worrying her.

Andrew: Yes, when you are young like that, what do you say? It's hard to even think of the words, let alone say them.

Typical questions we use in exploring the child's perspective include:

Does your child want you to stay together or split up?

If you stay together what does your child want to be different?

What do you think your child was thinking and feeling when they were abused?

How does your child feel about herself?

What do you think is the worst part of all this for him?

What does your child think about you as their father (mother)?

Who does she want to talk to, extended family, friends, teacher?

What does your child think is the best thing that could happen now?

What would your child see as an early sign that things are beginning to slip again?

What might your child be worried about in future?

Exploring consequences for the future

When child abuse has occurred in a family this has implications not just for the present but also for the future. To explore these issues, we involve parents in a final component of the similar-but-different process where we project them 20 to 25 years into the future, to a time when they have grandchildren. In the sexual abuse similar-but-different role-play we have been considering, the following future scenario could then be used:

> Madelaine is 26 years old and has two little girls, aged 4 and 18 months. Her husband James is a computer software designer. Tonight James and Madelaine, James' boss and his wife are taking the CEO of an international software firm to dinner, seeking to seal a huge deal. Madelaine had organized babysitting for the girls but at the last minute her arrangement has fallen through. James' parents are unavailable to help and James demands that he and Madelaine take the girls to her parents. Madelaine has never told James about Emma being sexually abused by Warren.
>
> Madelaine and James arrive at Madelaine's parents' home not knowing that Caroline is out for the night on a river cruise with her girlfriends. Warren listens to Madelaine and James' request and hesitates. Madelaine hasn't asked Warren to look after the girls on his own before but thinks to herself 'it'll be all right for one night'. Warren tries quietly to say no to Madelaine, but James pushes in on the conversation, saying 'we have to go we're late' and Madelaine says to her father, 'please just this once?'

Having presented the couple with this scenario, we can then explore with them the following sorts of questions:

What should Warren do?

Should James be told about Warren having sexually abused Emma? Who should tell him and what should they say?

What sort of plans should be in place so that it is certain any children Warren has contact with are safe and Warren is protected from anyone making allegations that he has molested a child?

How long should these plans stay in place for?

Is there a point when we can be certain Warren is no longer a risk to children?

Parents' comments

Although this has been a long chapter, there is considerably more we could write about using the similar-but-different process. We hope, however, that there is enough guidance and exemplifying material in the chapter to enable the reader to feel confident to begin to utilize the process. As we have emphasized throughout the chapter, it is never certain exactly where the hypothetical conversations will lead and how they will develop. We do know, however, that the similar-but-different process brings a very different and dynamic dimension to working with families caught up in a serious ACADE situation. This is also confirmed by Gumbleton (1997: 57). Parents who have undertaken the similar-but-different process provided the following comments:

- 'You could argue as if you weren't arguing, it was strange but good as well, it sorted things out, we learned to compromise.'
- 'It felt like us and someone else too, it was, it worked, it was like we could have the argument but not bring it home.'
- 'In the end you got so they (the hypothetical family) were part of you, it made you look into yourself more, solve problems, they even took us to being grandparents – it made you think.'
- 'Seeing it from the outside looking in made it easier to talk about the issues to each other.'
- 'We did ask each other difficult questions which at the time we wouldn't have asked at home.'

Using hypothetical scenarios in a social services context

To conclude the chapter, we want to offer two child protection casework examples in which investigative workers made use of hypothetical scenarios when facing problems of 'denial'. The workers involved had been exposed to the similar-but-different ideas we have presented in this chapter and subsequently adapted the ideas to fit their statutory investigative context.

Swedish example of using a hypothetical scenario to build safety

This example involves a father we will call Tomas, a mother, Karin, and their 12-year-old son, Kalle.

Kalle had got into trouble at school and his teacher told Kalle she would have to call his parents about the incident. Hearing this, Kalle began to cry and became very scared. As the teacher attempted to talk to him about this, Kalle said that he would be hit if the parents found out and that he was regularly beaten by them and was afraid of them. Following this, the school principal contacted social services.

Team leader Ann Gardeström took the phone call from the principal and they created a plan about how they would respond to the situation without making things worse for Kalle. Together they decided that social services workers Anna Svensson and Nina (Christina) Witt would interview Kalle and his teacher in the morning of the following day. While this interview was happening the principal would contact the parents to invite them to meet with Anna and Nina and the principal in the afternoon.

When Anna and Nina met with the parents, they denied they hit Kalle and seemed to be putting the blame onto the boy, saying he had very vivid fantasies. Kalle was involved at the beginning of the interview, he was very scared and began crying hysterically when he saw his parents. As the meeting progressed, the parents continued to deny that they hit Kalle but were willing to accept that Anna and Nina still held concerns. Tomas and Karin agreed they were willing to work with Nina and Anna, in Karin's words she said she wanted to 'show social services that Kalle is well and safe at home'. Anna and Nina used this statement as the focus for arranging further meetings with Kalle and his family.

The following day, Nina and Anna met with Kalle and he began to take back his story, saying that things weren't that bad and he had been exaggerating. Nina and Anna responded skilfully at this point, telling Kalle they understood what he was saying, but they couldn't just leave it at that. They explained that they heard what he had said yesterday and saw how afraid he was, so they had to follow through to satisfy themselves that he was safe. Anna and Nina also told Kalle that they were used to children in his position taking back their story, that this was understandable, because it's very difficult for the child having said something like this when they want to go on living with their parents.

Following this, Anna and Nina thought hard about how they could best work with the situation and support Kalle. They decided that in the subsequent meetings with the parents they would organize things so that Kalle would take a listening-only role. Anna and Nina would take the role of 'standing up' for Kalle's original story. Hoping to make progress with the case and still work with the parents' position that they had not hit Kalle, Anna and Nina decided they would explore the situation more hypothetically. To this end, in the next meeting they initiated a conversation focused around the following questions:

'Lets think about the next time Kalle does something he's not supposed to, that you feel is quite serious, how would you want to deal with that? What would you define as okay ways of disciplining and responding to Kalle in that situation?'

This lead into a conversation in which Karin stated she would talk to Kalle and give him chores to do as a punishment, such as washing the dishes. Karin also gave an example of a situation where Kalle had hit a friend and she responded by talking to him about it and why it was wrong. Anna and Nina made a point of complimenting Karin for how she had handled this situation. Both Tomas and the older brother stated that they would want Kalle to understand he'd done something wrong.

From here, Anna and Nina turned the conversation in a way that used the parents' position that they had not hit Kalle by asking them for their reasons for saying they wouldn't hit Kalle. In this process they created a long list of the parents' reasons that Anna and Nina wrote up on a sheet of paper. During this conversation Tomas stated, '*I am not mad enough to hit my son!*' Anna and Nina saw this as an opportunity to build a hypothetical focus around possible hitting and so they asked 'let's suppose for a minute you did get mad enough to hit Kalle, what should Kalle do then?' Tomas and Karin responded by saying that they as the parents are responsible for their behaviour and that it's not okay for either of them to hit Kalle even if has done something wrong. Anna and Nina took this further by asking 'So if it did happen, would it be okay with you if Kalle went for help or tells someone about it?' Tomas and Karin responded that it would be unlikely this would happen but if it did, Kalle should tell someone and he could go to his grandparents. At this point, Tomas surprised everyone by saying he wouldn't hit him unless he really had done something very bad. Anna and Nina felt that the atmosphere in the room thickened with a long silence as all the family members seemed to be holding their breath while looking at Tomas.

Anna and Nina felt a little thrown; reflecting later on what had happened, they thought that perhaps they should have made more of this opportunity of Tomas seeming to begin to acknowledge having hit Kalle. In our view, Anna and Nina had already done an enormous amount to create a conversation where Tomas would make this statement, to take that revelation further and try and get some sort of full acknowledgement would likely have only caused the father to retract what he had already said.

As the silence and tension of what Tomas had said eased, Anna and Nina focused further on safety for Kalle. They asked if Tomas did hit Kalle, what would Karin do, or if the situation was reversed, what would Tomas do? Both Karin and Tomas agreed that the other parent would step in between Kalle and the parent who wanted to hit him and tell the other one to take it easy. Anna and Nina explored in detail how they would do this. The elder brother also got involved in the conversation, saying that he could understand the parents had had a stressful day and became upset at Kalle but he would try to calm them down. Karin brought a lot of emotion and another silence to the conversation when she said that if one of them did hit Kalle, it would cause her pain in her heart. Following this session, the family met with the principal and teacher at the school to brief them about what they had discussed and explain the safety plans that they had decided on for Kalle.

Using the hypothetical conversation they created, Anna and Nina were able to have a very extended discussion of the issue of Kalle being hit and they felt pleased with the outcomes of their work. In a situation where previously they would have probably tried to get one of the parents to admit to hitting Kalle and in the process alienated themselves from the family, they felt they were able to have a very substantial and serious set of conversations about the possible abuse. They had also been able to make it clear to the parents that they held very serious concerns for Kalle's safety while at the same time respecting the parents' position, maintaining a relationship with them and minimizing the likelihood of backlash towards Kalle. In Anna and Nina's assessment, Kalle had been hit, but following their intervention they felt there was less likelihood it would happen again. They felt it was very important that Kalle had heard his parents saying explicitly that they did not think it was acceptable to hit him again and that he should speak out if it did happen. If Kalle was hit, Anna and Nina felt confident he would speak out about it in the family and at school.

This piece of work captures very well the benefits and

uncertainties of working in the hypothetical. On the one hand, it is very satisfying to be able to create conversations where families talk about a subject that has previously been a no-go zone. At the same time, there is always some sense of uncertainty regarding how much difference working in this way makes. What is clear, as in this case, is that working in this way creates a context where the professionals can talk seriously about the concerns with the family and still maintain a relationship with them. There are no easy answers in cases like this, and certainly no guarantees Kalle won't be hit in the future, but Anna and Nina rightly felt pleased with what they had achieved in opening up and building a very substantial safety plan in a situation that previously would have had them very stuck.

A social services worker using an 'as if' approach with a mother of an at-risk baby

Kath O'Leary, an English social services intake and assessment worker, used an 'as if' strategy in her assessment work involving a 23-year-old woman we will call Jean. Jean had just given birth to 'Kelly' and refused to acknowledge social services' concerns regarding her previous daughter and her half-sister. Jean, who had a history of mild learning difficulties, had been in and out of the care system during her childhood. As an adult, Jean lived with her own mother Sheila and Sheila's partner Jim.

Three years prior to Kelly's birth, social services had removed and then adopted out Sheila and Jim's 4-year-old daughter when that child had revealed sustained and severe sexual and physical abuse that involved Jim, Sheila and Jean. About a year after the removal of her half-sister, Jean had given birth after she was taken to hospital in late stages of labour following a pregnancy that she said she was completely unaware of. The health authorities also deemed Jean's pregnancy with Kelly to be a concealed pregnancy, since Jean had either not been aware of or not acknowledged her state to anyone and had made no preparations for the new arrival. Jean had also stated she had no idea who Kelly's father was, a fact that raised suspicions for social services, health and legal professionals that Jim was the father. While both Jean and Jim refused to undertake DNA tests to confirm or deny the hypothesis, this remained a significant issue for the professionals involved. Social services placed Kelly in foster care following her birth, and Kath was assigned the case to undertake an assessment and make recommendations regarding permanency for Kelly.

In the first meetings between Jean and Kath, Jean refused to speak to Kath, becoming angry, repeatedly swearing at Kath, and telling her she wasn't going to talk to her because social services never listened and had it in for her family. Jean was allowed weekly access visits with Kelly, and Kath decided to supervise some of these contacts to see if this created a context in which she could begin to talk to Jean. During the access visits, Kath observed that Jean was noticeably calmer and was responding well to the baby and, while Kath found it easier to talk with Jean during access visits, she felt she was still making very little headway in attempting to discuss the concerns and Kelly's future safety. Kath was determined to do everything she could to involve Jean in the assessment and decision-making process and during one of the access visits Kath almost by accident began to speak to Jean in an infant's voice 'as if' she was Kelly. To Kath's surprise, Jean began to respond as she asked in a high-pitched, shaky voice 'will I be safe if I come to live with you Mummy?'

Reflecting on the success she had had in engaging Jean in this way, Kath decided to arrange another meeting with Jean, this time without Kelly, and use this strategy of talking to Jean as if she was baby Kelly throughout the entire meeting. Kath focused the discussions around a hypothetical 24-hour period when Jean had sole care of baby Kelly, asking Jean how she would recognize and respond to Kelly's needs. At various points during this meeting, when Kath as Kelly was challenging Jean to think what she would do in various difficult situations, Jean became angry and walked out of the room. However, following each outburst Jean came back after she had calmed down and, several times, to Kath's surprise, apologized for getting angry and swearing.

Ultimately, Kelly was adopted, since the concerns held by the professionals continued to outweigh Jean's perceived capacity to care for and protect Kelly. However, Kath's persistence and use of the 'as if' strategy substantially changed the nature of Jean's relationship with social services and improved Jean's relationship with Kelly. This work also set the context in which Kelly's is an open adoption. For Kath, the 'as if' strategy was a breakthrough in enabling her to involve Jean in the decision-making process. As an intake and assessment social worker, Kath's involvement with Jean lasted for only about three months. However, Jean has continued to go out of her way to keep in contact with Kath. Kath's efforts in building a good working relationship with Jean meant that the process by which Jean's parental rights were terminated was much more collaborative than the process that followed the birth of Jean's first child. It is very likely Jean will have future contact with social services and certainly possible that she will become pregnant again, so as well as improving the context surrounding the planning and decision making for Kelly, Kath's persistence and creativity may well have laid a foundation for future contact between Jean and social services practitioners to be more constructive.

Chapter **Nine**

CREATING AND MONITORING THE FAMILY SAFETY PLAN

In this chapter we will look at how the resolutions practitioner works together with the family and network to translate the interim safety guidelines into the final safety plan. The process of creating the final safety plan begins in earnest when the family members who have been out of the home (whether the parent or children) return for the first overnight stay. This is a critical point in the reunification, and at this stage the planning focus shifts to making the safety rules applicable to the living arrangements in the home. We will begin the chapter by describing the process we usually follow in creating the final safety plan and then illustrate this by looking at two separate final safety plans.

Creating the final safety plan

Creating the final safety plan usually involves the following steps:

1. Preparing a first draft of the final safety plan

In situations of alleged sexual abuse the identity of the likely abuser is usually clear, so in these cases we invite the likely non-abusing parent to create a first draft of the safety plan with one or two support people. In cases where a teenager or older child has made allegations of sexual abuse and the goal of reunification remains alive, we involve the young person directly in the safety plan drafting process jointly with the likely non-abusing parent. So that this process of working first with the likely non-abusing parent is not a surprise for either partner, we make a point of underlining that the draft will be created in this way from the first briefing we provide to the parents about the resolutions programme. From that first briefing onwards, we explain the process in terms of social services expecting the likely non-abusing caregiver to take the role of principal safety person in the family. We ask the likely abuser to support their partner in taking the lead role in drafting the final plan as an additional means by which the couple can demonstrate to the statutory agency that they are committed to the safety-building process.

In SIDE-type cases we are not so prescriptive about the drafting process and often involve both caregivers in the process as well as support people.

The drafting of the final safety plan involves exploring in increasing detail what needs to happen in the living arrangements of the reunified family to demonstrate that the children will be safe and the possible abuser is protected from further allegations or misunderstandings. In this regard, the process of drafting the final safety plan is usually enriched by the work of the similar-but-different sessions. Working with the couple in the hypothetical sessions regarding possible antecedents to child abuse, such as stress, depression or grooming behaviours, creates opportunities for more grounded and specific discussions about the sort of safety plans that are needed to address those circumstances.

2. Begin overnight stays involving network people

Having steadily increased the network-supervised, social services-monitored contact arrangements over a period of two to three months, and having begun to draft the final safety plans, we are looking, with the statutory agency's approval, to initiate the family's first overnight stay. Typically, the first overnight stay occurs toward the end of the similar-but-different sessions, so we often take a break from the hypothetical work to conduct the first safety plan drafting session prior to the overnight stay. Usually we will ask that a support person sleep over in the house during the initial overnight stays, to support the family in the transition and supervise the implementation of the safety plan.

3. Involving the likely abusing parent in refining the draft plan

Once the safety plan has been drafted, it is presented to the likely abusive parent in a session involving both partners. This provides the opportunity for the likely abusive parent to make suggestions for refining the plan. During this stage of the drafting process, we usually undertake a home visit to explore with the parents how the plan will work 'on the ground' in the family home. Particularly in cases of alleged sexual abuse, this visit allows the resolutions practitioner to fully understand the layout of the home and to explore in detail with the parents the family's daily routine and how the parents can ensure that the alleged perpetrator will not be alone with children within the home environment.

4. Presenting the plan to the children

The final safety plan document is created in a similar fashion to the creation of the words and pictures document. The rules of the final safety plan are presented to the children and they help the resolutions practitioner create drawings for each rule to illustrate the final document.

5. Involving the children in active rehearsal

To be sure the children understand the aspects of the plan that actively involve them (for example, being able to contact a safety person at any time), we ask the children to rehearse their parts of the safety plan. We explain this to the children and their family as the equivalent of practising a fire drill at a school or workplace.

6. Presenting the final safety plan to the whole network

Mimicking again the words and pictures process, the parents invite as large a network of people as they can gather and then the safety plan is presented to this group.

7. Family reunification

Alongside the process of drafting, finalizing and then making the safety plan public, the number of weekly overnight stays increases successively, until the stage is set for full reunification. Throughout this process, the social services worker continues to monitor that the safety plan is being followed and the resolutions practitioner reviews any lessons or challenges that arise for the family and its network, to further bed down the use of the plan. When social services and the court are satisfied, reunification can take place. Once reunification has occurred, we ask social services to continue their monitoring for up to six months to further ensure the safety plan becomes part of daily family life. We generally also conduct follow-up sessions at three and twelve months after reunification, to review the family's implementation of the plan and if necessary make any amendments.

Final safety plan in an ACADE injured baby case

The following final safety plan relates to a composite family, with parents 'Will' and 'Sasha' and their children, 'Jenny', aged almost 3, and 'Harry', an 8-year-old. Jenny suffered serious, suspicious injuries at 4 months and social services placed her into the care of her grandparents following hospitalization. With each safety plan in this chapter we have included some of the pictures related to each rule. In this example, the pictures are drawn with the children, using Andrew's usual process. In the sexual abuse example that comes later in the chapter, the pictures were drawn by Susie to be finished off with the children.

In this case, the maternal grandparents, 'Bert' and 'Dorothy', who had been caring for Jenny for over two and half years, wanted to be involved in the safety planning process, because after being Jenny's primary carers for most of her life they felt very invested in making sure everything went well after reunification. Will's sister Moira had also been involved in the supervised contact and Andrew asked that she come to some of the safety planning sessions as a support person from Will's side of the family and to create an additional primary safety person within the family's network. The following dialogue is typical of the way we go about the initial drafting process of the final safety plan.

Andrew: I wanted to start by just saying thanks to all of you for coming in today. It really shows me, and more importantly, shows social services how committed you all are to doing everything you can for Jenny and to make this reunification go well. This is the business end of the resolutions work now, when we work out the final rules for the safety plan together so social services and the court are confident that Jenny will be safe at home with Sasha and Will. It's great Bert and Dorothy, and Moira, that you want to be so involved in this, I know that really makes Megan (social services worker) confident that everything will go well.

So today, what I want to do is start by brainstorming as many things as we can think of that should be in the final safety plan. We don't have to get all the exact words sorted out for every rule, but I'd like us to get as many categories and issues that we can think of, mapped out. We can draw on the safety guidelines you've been using during contact, that Moira you've been supervising at Sasha and Will's home and on outings and that have applied at Bert and Dorothy's home when Sasha and Will come over to help look after Jenny. (*The safety guideline arrangements had been set up so that Bert and Dorothy weren't supervising the contact at the family home, as Sasha and Will felt the grandparents would want to be too controlling of what they did*.) We have to think about it as well in terms of what Megan and social services want in the plan. The similar-but-different conversations Sasha, Will and I have been having in the past few months should help us to think it through as well.

So, what rules do you think we should have in this final safety plan? Have you all had a chance to look at the (anonymous) example of the safety plan I gave to Sasha and Will and Megan a few weeks ago?

Sasha: Well, I guess reading that (the safety plan example), I was wondering do Will and I get to look after Jenny on our own?

Andrew: That's a good question, you probably noticed in the safety plan example I gave you, that that child was younger than Jenny, just on 2. In that case, one of the grandparents moved in for eight weeks and then we agreed that the parents would do all the care together for a year. What were you thinking, Sasha? As well as satisfying social services, a big part of this is to create a safety plan that makes you and Will feel comfortable in bringing Jenny home full time, because I know you slowed the reunification down because you and Will felt you weren't ready.

Sasha: I don't know really.

Andrew: That's okay, let's just go slowly here because it's hard to figure out what's best. Will, what do you think, do think it's a good idea to have you both doing the care together, so for example you'd have to get up together during the night to Jenny if she needed something?

Will: Yeah, I think so, but it's hard too, I'm not sure how we can schedule all that.

Andrew: That's true, and we've got to keep this realistic. Other parents I've worked with in your situation have been worried about the scheduling issues too, but they have been able to work it out. My thought is that we can figure out more about the exact scheduling later, are you okay for now with us saying you'll do the care together? (*Will nods*.)

Sasha: Yeah, that's okay, but I guess I'd like some idea of how long we do that for?

Andrew: Can I ask what you think, what would make you feel comfortable? You've said before it'll take time to feel confident and relaxed in caring for Jenny after everything that's happened. Any thoughts about how long you think you need?

Sasha: (*Frowning a little and thinking*) Well I don't know, maybe six months or something (*turning toward Will*), is that too long honey?

Will: Umm, I think that's okay, but it's not just up to us, what do you think it should be Andrew?

Andrew: I've talked to Megan about exactly that, she and I went through the safety plan example I gave you and I asked her how long she'd want you doing the care together. After that Megan talked to her supervisor about it and their thinking is that because Jenny will be 3 by the time she's living with you full time again, they'd like to see that apply for six months too. So it seems like you're on the same wavelength as social services there. Now that's a scary thought!

Will: (*Laughing*) You can say that again! I think we've been spending way too much time with people like you.

Andrew: Okay, what else do you think needs to be in the safety plan?

Dorothy: I've told Sasha that I don't think there can be any drinking when they are looking after Jenny, I think there needs to be a rule in the plan saying that. I think that was part of the problem when Jenny got hurt.

Andrew: What do you think, Will and Sasha?

Sasha: Um, yeah, I think it has to be in there, but does that mean Will and I don't drink anything, ever?

Andrew: I'm not sure. That's what we've got to negotiate. I know in the similar-but-different scenario we worked with two weeks ago, that was a problem for the hypothetical couple too and you seemed to think that was significant in the role-play. With some families the rule has been that if someone wants to drink, they have to go out and usually sleep the night somewhere else and the parent left at home rings a support person to come over for the night. The other option, of course, is that if the couple wants to drink that they arrange for the children to stay with someone else. What do you think?

Dorothy: I think they should agree that they're just not going to drink at all.

Andrew: Okay, that's clear and thanks for making us think about

	this Dorothy. I guess my question is: is that a realistic rule? I don't want to set Will and Sasha up to fail around whether they drink or not. My concern is that we know Jenny is safe even if they decide to drink. Will, what do you think about this?
Will:	Well, I do want to be able to have a drink, with my mates and that sort of thing sometimes, and Sasha and I like to go to a party every now and then.
Andrew:	Well, right now what I'm hearing is that everybody agrees the drinking issue has to be part of the safety plan, and we've already had it as part of the safety guidelines that neither of you can look after Jenny if you've even had one drink. So is it okay with everyone if we put it down as one of the issues we have to make a final rule for? (*Everyone nods.*) Okay, could both of you (Will and Sasha) talk about this between now and next time and think about what you think might work for you? The other thing is we should hear what Megan thinks about this too, when she comes to the next session. Okay, what other issues do you think we need to address in the safety plan?
Moira:	I looked at the safety plan you gave us and it talks about a family safety object. I was wondering what that is.
Andrew:	Okay, thanks for asking about that, you don't have to have one but I really like doing this when there's older children like Harry in the family. The whole idea is that Harry would choose an object, it could be anything, a toy, a statue, something like that. Harry also gets to choose where it should be put, but it needs to be somewhere really obvious in the home, for example on a bookshelf or coffee table, a place where everyone sees it every day. The deal is that the object sits in that place in one particular position, and the only person who can move it is Harry. If it is shifted in any way that means Harry is worried for himself or about Jenny, and either Will or Sasha or one of the people in the safety network who come to the home regularly have to talk to him and check out what he's worried about.
	Having a safety object like this helps in lots of ways. It reminds everybody when they see that object that they all have to keep thinking about safety and it also reminds everyone, including Harry, that he is part of this too. Harry knows what happened to Jenny now after we did the words and pictures with him and we know he was confused after Jenny went to hospital and then went to live with Bert and Dorothy. So it's important he feels he can let people know if he's worried or unsure in the future

and knows he doesn't have to keep things to himself. The family safety object is one very clear way of letting him know that. I'll probably be suggesting that Will and Sasha have someone live with them at the beginning after Jenny moves back full time. If that happens, whoever that person is, it'll also be part of their job to talk to Harry if the object is moved as well. It doesn't matter how many people check in with Harry, the more the better really, and Harry is the only one who can put the object back in its right place. Does that make sense?

Moira: Yes, it does, and I think it sounds like a good idea for Harry.

Andrew: Will and Sasha, could you think about whether that would be okay to include a safety object in the plan? (*They both nod.*)

By evolving and carrying forward these sorts of conversations over two or three sessions, the final safety plan is negotiated and co-created with the family and the support people. In this case we would anticipate that the final safety plan would look something like the following:

Safety plan rule 1: Primary care responsibility

Figure 9.1

> For the first six months Mummy and Daddy will do all the care of Jenny together – for example, if Jenny is sick in the middle of the night they will both get up to look after her. For the first four weeks Auntie Moira and Mummy's best friend Mary will come to stay to help Mummy and Daddy. Auntie Moira or Mary will get up too if Jenny wakes in the night.

In some ACADE cases it becomes fairly evident through the ongoing involvement with the parents, which of them is more likely to have injured the child. In that circumstance, this first rule may then direct that the possible abusing parent will not be alone with the child. However, more often the first rule in these cases stipulates the parents undertake the care together. During the initial overnight stays and in the first weeks of the reunification, we always seek to have a network member staying with the family. This means the support person can help out in the home and also monitor how the parents are managing the stress of intensively caring for the child again. Involving a network person in this way leads to richer, more detailed review discussions with the social services worker and the resolutions practitioner can also draw upon the insights of that person to review how the parents are coping with the caring role.

The length of time that this joint care rule will apply depends on the age and development stage of the child when the family reunifies, but our aim is always for it to apply until the child is walking and articulate and is being seen regularly in pre-school or school.

Safety plan rule 2: Safety people to support Mummy and Daddy

> Nanny, Grandpa, Auntie Moira and Mary are the key 'safety people' to help Daddy and Mummy care for Jenny. So, for example, if Mummy and Daddy need help at any stage they will come immediately, even if they are called in the middle of the night. There is a rota of these 'safety people' so that someone is always there to come quickly and they have all agreed they will come and take the children with no questions asked if they are called.

Safety plan rule 3: Drinking

> Daddy and Mummy have said they won't drink when they are looking after Jenny. If one of them decides to have even one drink, then the drinker will leave the house. Because in the first six months this cuts across the joint care arrangement of rule one, whoever is left in charge will immediately ring one of the safety people to come and help.

Figure 9.2

Safety plan rule 4: Stress and communication

> Everyone will watch carefully to see if things are getting too difficult for Mummy and Daddy. Daddy and Mummy will talk to each other if they are worried and will get help if they can't fix the problem. Nanny, Grandpa, Auntie Moira and Mary will also talk to Mummy and Daddy if they are worried things are getting too much. After Mary and Moira finish staying overnight one of the safety people will visit every day for the next two months. There is a rota for visiting so that they can all take turns.

Safety plan rule 5: Looking after Jenny

> Jenny will continue to go to day care three days per week and Nanny and Grandpa will look after her two days per week until she goes to school. Mummy and Daddy will take her to the doctor regularly for a check-up.

Safety plan rule 6: Explaining what happened to Jenny

> Jenny has been told what happened to her as a baby and why she lived with Nanny and Grandpa for the first few years of her life. Mummy and Daddy and the safety people will go through the

Figure 9.3

words and pictures again with Jenny in the week after she turns 4, 5 and 6. Nanny will make the arrangements to get everyone together to do this each year.

Safety plan rule 7: Safety people for Jenny or Harry to talk to

If Jenny or Harry are worried, they can talk to Mummy and Daddy, Grandpa, Nanny or Auntie Moira.

Safety plan rule 8: Family safety object

Harry has chosen a rubber fish as the family safety object. It will be put on top of the fridge. If the fish is ever moved in any way Mummy, Daddy, Grandpa, Nanny or Auntie Moira have to talk immediately to Harry and ask him if there is anything he is worried about. Grandpa, Nanny or Auntie Moira will check when they visit each day and ask about the fish.

Safety plan rule 9: Safety plan on the pantry door

So everyone remembers the rules the safety plan will be put on the inside of the pantry door where everyone can easily see it every day.

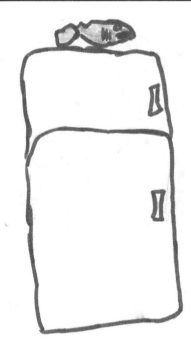

Figure 9.4

Safety plan rule 10: How long will the safety plan apply for?

> Mummy and Daddy have agreed with social services that they will keep following the rules of the safety plan until Jenny is 6 years old and begins school.

Celebration

> Mummy and Daddy want everyone to be happy. There will be an outing every year just before Christmas for everyone, Mummy, Daddy, Jenny and Harry, Nanny, Grandpa, and Auntie Moira, to celebrate all the hard work on safety. (Auntie Moira says she will take everybody to the circus this year.)

Final safety plan in a case of alleged sexual abuse

> In situations of sexual abuse, the perpetrator typically 'grooms' the environment to establish themselves in a close relationship with the

child they are seeking to abuse, while at the same time distancing the protective parent and other people the child may be able to draw upon for help (Conte et al. 1989; Smith 1995). In the similar-but-different sessions we endeavour to sensitize the likely non-abusing caregiver to these dynamics to enhance their commitment to demonstrably adopt the role of the primary caregiver in the centre of the child's life. Calder and Peake (2001) identify the most critical task in building safe care arrangements for children after disclosure of sexual abuse lies in re-establishing the likely non-abusing parent's control of the home environment. They describe that to do this requires detailed discussions about the minutiae of daily life: sleeping arrangements, bath and toilet routines, appropriate physical contact, day care and school arrangements and the like.

Rose and Savage (2000) echo this view, based on their experience leading what they call 'living with risk' groups, with mothers who choose to continue to live with alleged or convicted sexual abuse offenders. Rose and Savage describe an evolving process in which they and the women engaged together in a mutually challenging journey about how to create safety for children. The authors comment that, above all, the mothers they worked with wanted information and support that could inform their practical day-to-day decision-making.

The safety-building work we undertake in the resolutions process seeks in as many ways as possible to explore the day-to-day details of ensuring the children are demonstrably safe and to simultaneously benefit the alleged abuser by ensuring that no one can make allegations against them or misconstrue their actions in the future. The process of creating the safety plan is as important as the plan itself. The exploration of each issue that generates a particular rule enables the resolutions practitioner to further normalize the discussions and enactment of the safe living arrangements for the parents, network and children.

The following example is typical of the sort of safety plan we develop with reuniting families in situations of alleged sexual abuse. After presenting the safety plan, we will provide commentary on its content and creation. This plan relates to a family in which 'Milly' as a 5-year-old had made statements about her stepfather that indicated he had touched her vagina and shown her his penis, which the stepfather denied. Milly's brother 'Brendan' is two years older than her and social services had concerns that Brendan had perhaps seen, or at least was aware of, some of the abuse. These concerns could not be confirmed. The safety plan was developed two years after the initial disclosure, by which time Milly was 7 and Brendan was 9. Accompanying each rule of the plan, we have included a description of the pictures we intend to prepare with or for the children, related to each rule. This safety plan is presented below in a format we often provide to the parents in advance of presenting the safety plan to the children. To ensure there is a clear, mutual understanding between ourselves and the parents about the wording of the rules and the pictures we will create with the children, we often detail all of this in a document the parents can read through before the session with the children. Susie's drawings are used to illustrate four of the rules.

1. The most important rule

Daddy will not be left alone with Milly or Brendan or any other children. Someone else will always be with them.

Figure 9.5

Two pictures will be prepared for this rule. The first picture will show Daddy with Milly and Brendan on their own in the house. A second picture will show Daddy, Milly and Brendan together but this time with Mummy present. Milly and Brendan will be asked which drawing is right and to place a big tick beside it, and which drawing doesn't follow the rule and place a big cross beside or through that drawing.

2. Milly and Brendan's personal needs

Mummy is in charge of taking care of Milly and Brendan, so if either of them is sick or needs help with private things like washing or dressing, Mummy is the one that they should go to and Mummy will help them.

The picture for this rule will show Milly sick in bed, having just vomited by the bed. Mummy is looking after Milly and Daddy has brought a bucket and mop to clean up the vomit.

3. Pools and beach

Daddy will not go in the water with Milly and Brendan when they go swimming.

This picture will show Milly and Brendan in a swimming pool with Mummy and Daddy watching on the side of the pool.

4. Rooms

Milly and Brendan will always sleep in their own rooms.

This picture will show one of Milly and Brendan in their own bed in their own bedroom.

5. Bedtimes

At bedtimes Daddy will read Milly and Brendan a bedtime story in the living room, then Mummy will put Milly and Brendan to bed.

This picture will show Daddy reading a story to Milly and Brendan on the couch in the living room with Mummy watching.

6. Cuddles and kissing

Mummy and Daddy have agreed how people will kiss and cuddle Milly and Brendan. If people are going to cuddle Milly or Brendan they will sit beside them or Milly and Brendan will sit sideways on the adult's lap. If people are going to kiss Milly or Brendan, they can kiss them on the cheek or forehead. Mummy and Daddy will tell their friends and everyone in their families that this is what they've decided.

This picture will show Granny cuddling Milly or Brendan with the child sitting sideways on her lap.

Figure 9.6

7. Waking up at night

If Milly and Brendan wake up at night, they won't go into Mummy's and Daddy's room, they will call out for Mummy, who will hear them on her 'monitor' and come to see Milly or Brendan.

This picture will show one of Milly and Brendan in their own bed sitting up and Mummy coming in to see if they are okay.

8. Sex education

Mummy will be responsible to talk to Milly and Brendan about sex and how babies are created.

This picture will show Mummy in the kitchen with Daddy reading a Christmas book to Milly on the couch. Milly is asking Daddy 'how did the baby Jesus get inside Mary's tummy?' Daddy replies 'that's a good question, Milly, let's get Mum so we can all talk about it'.

9. If Mummy is sick

If Mummy is sick and can't get out of bed, Aunty Sally or Granny will come and stay and do Mummy's jobs until Mummy is well.

Figure 9.7

This picture will show Mummy sick in bed and either Aunty Sally or Granny helping out in the home.

10. Milly and Brendan will always have someone to talk to

If there are things that upset or worry Milly and Brendan they can talk to Nan, Grandpa and Mummy and Auntie Sally. Milly and Brendan each have a mobile phone with phone numbers of those people in the memory. Nan, Grandpa and Mummy and Auntie Sally will listen very carefully to whatever Milly or Brendan say. They will talk about the problem themselves and decide what to do and then tell Milly and Brendan what is going to happen.

This picture will show Milly and Brendan calling one of the safety people on the phone.

11. School

Daddy will not go into Milly and Brendan's school alone. The school principal will always know when and where Daddy is at the school and who he's with.

Figure 9.8

Two pictures will be prepared for this rule. The first picture will show Milly and Brendan going to school with Daddy on their own. A second picture will show Daddy, Milly and Brendan at the school with Granny. Milly and Brendan will be asked which drawing is the right one and to place a big tick beside it, and which drawing doesn't follow the rule and place a big cross beside or through that drawing.

12. Family safety object

Milly and Brendan have chosen a large river stone that they really like. They have put the stone on the coffee table where everybody can easily see it. If the stone is ever moved in any way Mummy, Granny, Eileen, Aunt Sally or Uncle Bob have to immediately talk to Milly and Brendan and ask them if there is anything they are worried about.

Exploring details

In drafting the details of the safety plan with the likely non-abusing parent and a support person and subsequently when we involve the likely abusive parent we are constantly exploring the distinction between behaviour that is clearly safe for the children and protects the alleged abuser and behaviour that is open to misinterpretation. In doing this, we are not seeking to locate ourselves as the expert who knows definitively where the boundary lies between these two types of behaviour, rather we constantly position ourselves to be able to ask the parents what would others (social services, grandmother, school teacher, best friend) think if they saw that particular behaviour? In working with the parents and their support people to mark out what is clearly safe and what can be misinterpreted, we are helping the couple make commitments to each other regarding how they will live in the future. These commitments can then be translated into the safety plan rules and made public with the children and the family's network.

In reviewing recordings of the safety planning work we do with parents, one of the most frequent questions we ask the couple is 'can I raise another issue?' By this stage in the resolutions journey, the couple and the support people have come to expect that the resolutions practitioner will continually raise difficult issues. We often also comment, usually quite playfully by this stage, something like 'Well here comes another issue that I can see. I know social services and the court expect me to talk about this but if you prefer we can leave it and let social services come knocking on your door about it some time later.'

Not every issue we raise with a couple finds its way into the safety plan as a specific rule. The final safety plan is designed to be a working document that the whole family, and particularly the children, can understand, so we are seeking to build in as much detail as possible without creating a plan that, while it might look comprehensive, actually overwhelms the family. However, even though a specific rule may not be drawn up regarding that subject, in the two or three drafting sessions we typically address additional issues such as:

- Nakedness in the bedroom and around the home.
- Privacy in the bathroom and the toilet.
- Areas in and around the home where the likely abusing parent might inadvertently find themselves alone with a child. (This is an important part of making a home visit.)
- Adults having secrets with the children.
- Transport arrangements.
- Sleepovers for children's friends.

To give an additional sense of how we negotiate these sorts of conversations, we will consider some typical dialogue from a session in which the likely non-abusing caregiver's draft of the safety plan is presented to the likely abusing caregiver. This dialogue relates to the plan we have just considered and in this example we will give the parents the names 'Frances' and 'Bill'.

Andrew: I wanted to start out this session by just saying how impressed Jon (social services worker) and I were that you, Bill, accepted that Frances, Eileen and Sally draft up the safety plan. I don't know whether you knew but Jon was convinced you wouldn't let that happen.

Bill: Well Jon doesn't know me does he? Maybe he might realize now that everything he thinks about me isn't necessarily true. But anyway it's the way he wanted the plan made so it's better we got on with it.

Andrew: Well it's impressed Jon enough that he even talked about the fact you did that with his supervisor too.

Bill: Yeah, well sometimes I get sick of having to worry about what they think of me.

Andrew: I bet, but hopefully we can make this plan work for you and your family and then you won't have to see so much of Jon. Shall we go through the draft safety plan now and we can talk about what we might need to be adapted from your perspective?

Bill: That's what we're here to do.

Andrew: What I'd like to do is go through all the draft rules of the plan and then we can go back through them one by one.

After having gone through the whole plan:

Andrew: So having gone through the whole thing, what do you think so far?

Bill: About what I expected really, from what we'd been doing on the overnights, but its pretty hard on Frances.

Andrew: It is, that's true. (*Turning to Frances.*) Frances, did you know Bill was worried that the plan's hard on you?

Frances: I hadn't thought about it really, to be honest. It's not going to be easy but it's the way it has to be if we're going to all be together again.

Andrew: Okay, so Bill are there rules you want to talk about?

Bill: Yeah, the bedtime and the cuddling and kissing ones. Is this bedtime one saying that I can't put Milly or Brendan to bed like I used to?

Andrew: Okay good. Thanks for raising what you're worried about, it's really important we talk about what you think. We always have to look at bedtimes, and how adults touch the children, social services expect us to do that. Let's take them one at a time. I guess the bedtime routine probably won't be like you used to do it, if you used to do that on your own. Did you used to put them to bed on your own?

Bill: Yeah.

Andrew: Well suppose Aunty Sally came around during the bedtime and realized you were putting one of the kids to bed on your own, or if Brendan told Jon or a teacher about that. Is that something those people could misconstrue or wonder about?

Bill: Yeah, but you people are always wondering and worrying about the worst things.

Andrew: It's true, and I know you get tired of that, but if I'm going to be able to help you get back together we have to talk about what those people worry about. So back to the bedtimes, what do you think, are you willing to give up on doing it on your own or do you want to argue for it?

Bill: Well I can't really, can I? I haven't been doing it on the overnight stays so it's pretty much the same as when I'm there overnight already.

Andrew: Okay, but there are different ways to approach it. Sometimes the couple do the goodnight bed thing together, sometimes they have some nights where the mother is nearby in the next room and the father keeps the door open and keeps the goodnight short. It depends how the house and the bedrooms are set up too. It's one of the things we could talk more about next week when I come out and look at the house, if you like. I can probably give you more idea what I think when I see where the bedrooms are too. What do you think, Frances?

Frances: Well, I just made the rule of me taking them to their room based on what we'd been doing on the overnight stays already. Whether Bill's there or not, we've got into the routine of Brendan going to his room at the same time as Milly's bedtime. He stays awake for another hour, but reads or listens to his music in his room. I thought we'd keep going with it that way.

Andrew: Okay, sounds like you have been thinking a lot about what will work Frances.

Frances: Well a mother has to, doesn't she, we can't just suddenly make everything up when Bill comes back with us, I need to get the kids used to a routine that'll work for all of us.

Andrew: I didn't know you'd thought through the bedtimes like that but I'm glad you told me. Is it okay if I tell Jon about

	this, I'm sure he'd like how you've been figuring this
	bedtime thing out.
Frances:	That's fine.
Bill:	You keep asking a lot of us, don't you?
Andrew:	I do, it's always my job, to keep raising all these hard
	issues. It's probably exactly like the going swimming rule

Frances: That's fine.

Bill: You keep asking a lot of us, don't you?

Andrew: I do, it's always my job, to keep raising all these hard issues. It's probably exactly like the going swimming rule we set up a couple of months back for the safety guidelines, I know you didn't like that either, but you seem to be making it work. Jon has told me that he's checked with the kids and your supervisors that you have been doing things that new way at the pool every time for the past two months.

Bill: Yeah, lots of new ways.

Involving people from other organizations

In situations of alleged sexual abuse we place particular emphasis on involving people from the organizations and institutions the family is involved with such as school, pre-school or place of worship. In the safety plan presented here this can be seen in the rule regarding the school in which the principal is actively involved. In suggesting this emphasis many professionals will wonder how is it possible to involve the likes of school professionals when the family may well feel involving them breaches their privacy. We build the leverage to do this in part by exploring what needs to be done to satisfy the court and social services but our primary approach is to engage the parents with the idea that it is in their own best interests to proactively involve people from these organizations.

Typically, we do this by exploring with the parents the problem that for families dealing with sex abuse allegations, it is inevitable that a wider group of people hear about the issue, sometimes legitimately but just as often through gossip. We emphasize again that the alleged perpetrator needs to protect themselves from future allegations or misunderstandings and the family also needs to protect the involvement of the children in the organization, particularly when it is the child's school. We ask the parents to consider what would happen if for example someone in the school community who had heard about the allegations or convictions against the likely abusive parent went to the school principal asking why that person was able to come into the school with no supervision or restrictions.

We are not always successful in being able to gain the permission of parents to involve members of organizations central to the children's life, but even if this does not eventuate, it remains a valuable process to engage the parents and network people in these sorts of discussions. Each parent usually carries their own unspoken concerns about what would happen if 'the secret' of the allegations or convictions became more widely known and these sorts of discussions can also serve as a means of getting these worries out in the open. While it is always an uncomfortable process to open up the possibility of involving others in the parents' problems, we consider it an additional valuable means of demonstrating to the family and network our determination to build as widely as possible the informed safety network around the children. We have learnt that to extend the safety network around the children, whether it be from extended family or organizations the family is involved with, requires conviction and tenacity on our part to raise and sustain discussion about involving others in the safety plan even when the subject is uncomfortable. We are regularly surprised at how frequently parents are willing to include members of organizations and groups that are involved in their family life.

Once the parents accept the idea of involving people from organizations or groups the family is involved with, the issue remains how to approach these individuals. Depending on what the parents want, we will often make the initial approach for the parents and have at times been surprised to find that though the individuals are often aware of the allegations or convictions they may not have thought about the consequences for their organization. At times, for example, we have contacted a principal to ask for their involvement in the safety planning process, to find that the they don't see the issue as something they should be involved with. When we invite a principal to consider what would happen if others in the school community became aware that an alleged or convicted child abuser was coming on to the school property with no restrictions, this inevitably engages a principal's mind. Following this sort of discussion the principal will usually readily agree to be involved in the safety planning and frequently also want to include a legal representative in the process.

In involving the likes of school professionals, we will often organize a meeting at the school since it will always be easier to involve the staff in this way. We always begin this sort of meeting by presenting the words and pictures document, which ensures the school personnel understand the seriousness of the problem and know what the child knows. We also always come to this meeting with a simple proposal regarding the safety rule that we have worked out ahead of time with the parents so that the meeting can remain focused on what needs to be done rather than become bogged down in focusing on the past. In this sort of manner, we are usually able to involve organizations and groups in the safety planning process.

Involving a young person in the safety planning

As discussed earlier in the book, cases in which young people have made sexual abuse allegations against one of their caregivers are a dynamic and demanding proposition and the process of creating the safety guidelines and final safety plan inevitably bring the reunification issues to a head. The most important aspect of working with these situations is to slow down the process and create as many opportunities as possible for the parents, young person, their support person and network to openly consider the different perspectives and possibilities. This may add considerable time to the safety planning but the slower and more considered the process, the more likely it is that the decisions that are taken will be sustainable.

The final plans we create with families involving older children and teenagers look essentially the same as that described above, but it is crucial to involve the young person in the safety planning process with the likely non-abusing parent. To do this will often require that time and effort is put into rebuilding the trust and communication in this relationship. Our experience is that the resolutions process with these cases leads as often to reunifying the family as it does to long-term arrangements being established for the young person to live apart from their family. In either circumstance, it is empowering for the young person to be actively involved in the creation of the safety guidelines and plan. Wherever the young person lives, at the very least guidelines will need to be created to cater for ongoing contact for the teenager with the family.

Our experience is that the young person derives considerable benefit from the resolutions process and the safety planning process since they can see that we are taking the allegations they made seriously and are actively engaging all of their family in making meaningful changes based on those allegations. The process, however, is always complex territory. In one case Susie worked with, the teenager was so actively engaged in the safety planning it led a statutory professional to comment that it seemed the teenager had become 'over-empowered' in terms of influencing the new living arrangements within the reunifying family. The safety plan the teenager had been so central in shaping, alongside her mother, went ahead unchanged, since the mother and stepfather believed it to be the best set of arrangements to satisfy the court and keep social services out of their lives.

Framing difficulties as opportunities

The whole safety planning process is about creating as many ways as possible to explore the challenges of creating and implementing a meaningful safety plan in relationship to the seriousness of the allegations. This is never easy since there is no way of proving definitively that the children in question will be safe with absolute certainty. To pose and try and answer meaningfully the question how can the parents demonstrate to social services and the court that a vulnerable child will be safe is therefore a journey into uncertainty for the professionals and the family. To negotiate this territory collaboratively with the family and their network, it is vital for the resolutions practitioner to adopt a mentality where it is absolutely fine for the parents and their support people to be confused, uncertain, angry and have difficulties in not only thinking about but also implementing a meaningful safety plan for their situation. To adopt this stance the practitioner needs to avoid framing any of these responses as evidence of resistance or dysfunction. This enables the practitioner to approach family uncertainties and difficulties with good grace and even humour and to utilize these instances as opportunities to deepen the exploration of how to create and implement a meaningful safety plan.

By way of example we will consider a short piece of dialogue based on a case Susie once worked with where 14-year-old 'Katie' had made sexual abuse allegations against her stepfather 'Bill'. This family had only recently reunified and Bill was angry about some aspects of the safety plan focused particularly around the issue of Katie's tennis lessons. The conversations went something like this:

Bill: This plan's impossible! Katie's hating it too! She can't go to tennis and she loves tennis. I can't be alone with any of the children so I can't stay home and look after the little ones while Sarah takes Katie to tennis and of course I can't take her myself either. So no tennis for Katie, you're punishing her now. This plan is impossible!

Susie: Wow it sounds like you've been working really hard to make the plan work, so much so that even though you were frustrated you realized you couldn't follow the rules of the plan and get Katie to tennis, so you called off the tennis. That's impressive! But I get that you're angry about it too!

What message would you most like social services and the court to get, that you think its impossible and want to give up on the plan or that you're working really hard to make it work even though you feel frustrated with it at times? What do you think, Sarah?

> Sarah: It is hard, Bill's right, but I don't want social services to think we're giving it up. Bill used to like taking Katie to tennis but he just can't do it anymore even though he thinks it's not fair.
>
> Susie: Is that it Bill, you don't like the way the plan has changed things for you?
>
> Bill: Yeah, pretty much.

As this short dialogue highlights, when parents or the network are struggling, angry or frustrated with any aspect of the safety plan this demonstrates they are engaged with the task and taking the process seriously. Challenges and difficulties almost always provide rich opportunities to explore the details of how the family is making sense of and implementing the plan. In our view, the more difficulties and frustrations people express with the plan the greater confidence we have that they are working at implementing it. In our experience, adopting a mindset that opportunities reside behind a family's struggles with the safety plan significantly enhances out capacity to work with the family on their implementation of that plan.

Final steps toward reunification

It is obvious but important at this point to re-emphasize that the statutory authorities control the reunification process. It is vital therefore that during the concluding stages of the programme that the resolutions practitioner maintains an ongoing dialogue with the social services worker to ensure that statutory agency continues to support and endorse each new step in the process. The resolutions practitioner cannot afford to be in a position where they are advancing the resolutions process with the family toward reunification without statutory endorsement. This sort of eventuality would rightly anger the parents and also be distressing and confusing for the children. To ensure that we are 'on the same page' as social services regarding the reunification process, we maintain regular, usually weekly, contact with the statutory worker during the period the safety plan is being drafted and finalized. During this same period, we would also expect the social services worker is undertaking weekly monitoring of the family's implementation of the plan in its current form.

Once the plan is fully drafted and social services endorse the plan as the basis on which reunification can proceed, the plan can then be presented to the children and then to an extended network. As with the words and pictures explanation the safety plan rules are always prepared in language that the youngest child can understand. This is essential so that the children can fully understand the new family arrangements. To maximize the childrens' understanding, we also actively engage them in creating the drawings for the final safety plan document.

With the plan having been fully explained to the children in this way, it is then possible to have them practise and trial aspects of the plan in which they have an active role. The plans we create always have safety people available for the children who they can contact if they have worries about life in their family. To bring this process to life for the children and the adults we always ask the children to 'test out' their safety people. We typically ask the children to do this by ringing one of their safety people late at night (perhaps they may need to use an alarm to wake themselves up) or at a time when we anticipate problems may occur. It is then possible to see if the safety person does in fact respond and come to see the child immediately as they have promised to do. We always advise the children's safety people that we will be asking the children to test them out and check they are okay with this, though we generally don't tell them details of what we will ask the child to do. The children inevitably enjoy the sense of fun and influence this trial run gives them but more importantly it underlines for everyone involved that there are adults available for the children outside of their immediate family. To follow up on the children's tests of the safety people, the social services worker can also be enlisted to check in with the children, the parents and safety person to review how they experienced the test.

The use of a family safety object provides another means of actively engaging the children in the safety planning and offers another opportunity for trialing whether the adults are paying attention to the children. The use of the safety object can readily be adapted. It is possible for each child to have their own safety object or all the children in a family can share the same object. The person who is to respond to the object being moved can be one of the parents or someone from outside the family who comes to the house regularly, or both. It is also possible to set up an arrangement whereby if the child moves the object twice in a certain period of time that means the parents must call a meeting with a particular member of the safety network. However it is used, the family object serves as a tangible, in-home reminder to everyone that they have to be continually conscious of demonstrating that the children are always safe.

As the last step before the full reunification we ask the parents to call together as large a network of friends and kin as possible to the final session where the plan is presented by the parents to the network. We always endeavour to have at least 6 to 8 people additional to the immediate family attending this meeting, but it is not uncommon in our final sessions to have up to 15 people in attendance. Once the 'hard work' of presenting the plan to the network is dealt with, this gathering can serve as a celebration of all the hard work the family and their support people have put in to enable to family to reunite.

By this stage, we usually have prepared a final report for social services and the court regarding the family's participation in the resolutions process. This report focuses in detail on the signs of safety created within the family through the resolutions process and is written not only as a professional document but also with the parents in mind as a primary audience. As such, we always prepare the document in common rather than professionalized language and in this way the report can function as a valuable means of reiterating and capturing the significance of the work the family has engaged in.

Follow-up

Once the family has reunified, follow-up is undertaken by:

- Asking the social services worker to continue to monitor the situation with particular emphasis on meeting with the children as well as the adults. We generally ask that social services continue this monitoring role for at least three to six months after reunification. As part of the final work we always establish an agreement between social services regarding the length of time social services require successful implementation of the safety plan before they will close the case.
- Scheduling two home visits with the family, which we usually undertake three and twelve months after reunification. The purpose of these visits is to review the family's implementation of the safety plan and here again any difficulties the family is having are framed positively and seen as a mechanism for further refining the rules. In these visits it is also possible to consider any amendments to the plan that might be required because of family or network changes and the need to adapt the rules as children grow older.

Conclusion

The research by Gumbleton (1997) and Hiles (2002) shows that the majority of parents continue to follow the safety plan created during the resolutions process. In Gumbleton's study 21 of the 27 respondents stated that the safety plan continued to be an important part of their family life. These studies also found that even two years later, the kin and friendship safety networks were still fully supporting the plan in large part because they did not want the children or parents to go through similar problems ever again. These findings also seem to be confirmed by the low re-abuse rate following the resolutions programme, reported earlier. It is important to note that though most parents described following the plan, this did not mean that all of these parents liked the process. One father commented, 'I could see the sense in it but I also resented being told what to do' (Gumbleton 1997: 53). Both Hiles and Gumbleton's research suggests that parents are also motivated by the need to protect themselves. This is reflected in the following comments: 'It really safeguards the children and safeguards me as well, it was a useful thing' (Gumbleton 1997: 53). 'It's not just about protecting the child, it's protecting yourself. There's a lot of vulnerability there. As much as we want to protect our child, what we are doing different is protecting ourselves as well' (Hiles 2002: 27).

In our view the most important aspect of the safety planning we undertake is that the plan is co-created with the family and an informed safety network. In this way the safety plan is operationalized, monitored and refined carefully over time and the commitments involved in the plan are made interactionally by the parents in front of their own children, kin and friends.

Chapter **Ten**

JOURNEYING WITH
COMPLEXITY

Navigating problems in intimate relationships is never easy. When these problems involve alleged child abuse and a 'denial' dispute with statutory child protection authorities, the difficulties in the relational terrain become immense. We began the book by quoting poet, potter and educator M.C. Richards (1996: 119) when she said, 'The world will change when we can imagine it differently, and, like artists, do the work of creating new social forms.' We believe the professional imagination of the child protection field frequently fails in the face of 'denial' cases and gives way to the sort of pessimism that then asserts that these cases are impossible or untreatable.

This book describes our efforts to try and re-imagine professional responses within this conflicted territory, since it seems apparent that our best professional imagination is needed if practitioners are to sustain hope when working with serious ACADE cases. While the resolutions model is in some senses a new social form, it is also built on long-standing knowledges about what works in struggling with complex human problems. At its core, this model is about professionals, caregivers, children, friends and kin journeying together into disputed territory and jointly facing the seriousness of the alleged abuse and the dilemmas involved in building future safety in relation to allegations that are always, in some measure, in doubt.

The resolutions approach is grounded not on the premise that there is a definitive truth 'out there' but rather on the principle that a process of 'truth telling' among the community of family, friends and professionals involved in the dilemma has the potential to transform ACADE-type situations. Late in the process of preparing this book, we discovered Stanley Cohen's book *States of Denial: Knowing about*

Atrocities and Suffering published in 2001. We recommend this work for anyone interested in journeying further into the dilemmas and complexity of working with situations of 'denial'. One of Cohen's central images throughout his book is the idea that denial is as much 'a collective turning away' as it is an individual response to atrocity.

Cohen's writing in turn led us to the work of 'Truth Commissions' that have been utilized in Africa, Latin America and Asia over the past two decades to create societal transformation after a period of human rights abuse and atrocity. Our understanding of these commissions is that they first and foremost are about a collective opening up and exploration of atrocity – truth as a process more than an entity. However, the opening up and facing of the stories of grief and horror is not simply about catharsis. The value of the truth commission is not located in the extent to which it can ascribe blame. Rather, the truth commission's ultimate value resides in its capacity to create a more open, robust society that can better ensure similar atrocities do not happen again in the future. Lawrence Weschler (1997) writes on Harvard Law School's human rights' website: 'We must not forget, but we must remember in a living way. Truth commissions must be future oriented; they must make space for living' (http://www.law.harvard.edu/programs/hrp/Publications/truth1.html#N4T).

In like manner, while the resolutions approach is energized by its capacity to open up the problem of the disputed allegations within and around the family, the ultimate value of the approach lies in its capacity to strengthen the family and its network so that the chances of the alleged child abuse arising in the future are significantly diminished. In drawing a connection between our approach to disputed serious child abuse and the work of international truth commissions, we are seeking to raise the fundamental issue of how human beings respond collectively when faced with situations in which people from the communities they belong to may have treated each other brutally. A family grappling with the problem of 'denied' child abuse has not only to come to terms with what they can talk about regarding what might have happened, but they also have to grapple with the very real possibility that the past they believed they had as a family might be a fiction. Think here of a mother trying to grapple with the possibility that her husband has sexually abused her daughter. On a micro scale, this is a grappling with 'truth' that closely parallels a society that is trying to make sense of a tragic history of human rights abuse.

In exploring this territory, Weschler invokes a poem by W.S. Merwin, called 'Unchopping a Tree', to interpret the work of the truth commission that for us echoes the resolutions work with families dealing with disputed child abuse. Weschler writes:

> Merwin describes the step-by-step process of how one would put
> back together a tree that has fallen after its leaves, twigs, nests

and so on have all broken off. All *'must be gathered and attached once again to their respective places across an endless painstaking process. At last the scaffolding for reconstruction must be removed. Finally, the moment arrives when the last sustaining piece is removed and the tree stands again on its own ... You cannot believe it will hold. How long will it stand there now? ... You are afraid the motion of the clouds will be enough to push it over. What more can you do? There is nothing more you can do. Others are waiting. Everything is going to have to be put back'.*

This poem captures very eloquently the uncertainty, even precariousness, we often feel about the resolutions work we undertake. When we finish each resolutions case, we are never satisfied; there is always more we wish we could do. But like Merwin we wonder 'what more can you do?' We often wonder, have we done enough? Our own answer to ourselves is that it is probably not enough, but it is something, and it is all and the best, of what we have been able to imagine, in our ongoing journey with the complexity of ACADE cases.

Throughout this book, drawing upon examples of social services workers who have utilized resolutions ideas and practices, we have tried to demonstrate that the thinking and elements of the model can be adapted to most cases where child abuse is alleged but the explanations are disputed. The full treatment approach also has wider applicability than just the alleged sexual abuse and injured infant cases we have primarily focused on to explain the model. We have, for example, used the full resolutions approach in other ACADE situations, including 'facticious illness' cases and situations involving domestic violence between partners where social services are concerned the children are affected, but the couple refute that view. We have not canvassed this work because we felt there was not space herein to do justice to additional types of case scenarios. Our point here is that the reader should feel free to adapt and develop the approach to their particular context and their cases. The approach is an evolving one, not something that is set in stone.

Our best hope is that this book might stimulate the imagination of professionals whose daily fare involves journeying into the complex territory of serious alleged child abuse when professionals and family members dispute the explanations. If this book energizes these practitioners and increases their hope of making a difference for the vulnerable children caught in these situations, we will be happy.

REFERENCES

Aderman, J. and Russell, T. (1990) A constructivist approach to working with abusive and neglectful parents. *Family Systems Medicine,* 8(3): 241–50.

Aldgate, J. and Statham, J. (2001) *The Children Act Now: Messages from Research.* London: The Stationery Office.

Alexander, R., Crabbe, L., Sato, Y., Smith, W. and Bennett, T. (1990) Serial abuse in children who are shaken. *American Journal of Disease of Children,* 144: 58–60.

Allan, J. (2004) Mother blaming: a covert practice in therapeutic intervention. *Australian Social Work,* 57(1): 5–70.

Anderson, H. and Goolishan, H. (1988) Human systems as linguistic systems: preliminary and evolving ideas about the implications for clinical theory. *Family Process,* 27(4): 371–93.

Bagley, C. (1997) *Children, Sex and Social Policy: Humanistic Solutions for Problems of Child Sexual Abuse.* Aldershot: Avebury.

Baistow, K., Cooper, A., Hetherington, R., Pitts, J. and Spriggs, A. (1995) *Positive Child Protection.* Dorset: Russell House Publishing.

Baldry, S. and Kemmis, J. (1998) The quality of child care in one local authority: A user study. *Adoption and Fostering,* 22(3): 34–41.

Bentovim, A. (2003) Is it possible to work with parental denial?, in P. Reder, S. Duncan and C. Lucey (eds), *Studies in the Assessment of Parenting.* Hove: Brunner-Routledge.

Bentovim, A., Elton, A., Hildebrand, J., Tranter, M. and Vizard, E. (eds) (1988) *Child Sexual Abuse within the Family: Assessment and Treatment.* London: Butterworth.

Berg, I.K., and Kelly, S. (2000) *Building Solutions in Child Protective Services.* New York: Norton.

Berliner, L. (1991) Interviewing families, in S.K. Murray and D. Gough (eds), *Intervening in Child Sexual Abuse.* Edinburgh: Scottish Academic Press.

Birchall, E. and Hallett, C. (1995) *Working Together in Child Protection.* HMSO: London.

Boffa, J. and Podestra, H. (2004) Partnership and risk assessment in child protection practice. *Protecting Children,* 19(2): 36–48.

Bools, C.N., Neale, B.A. and Meadow, S.R. (1993) Follow up of victims of fabricated illness (Munchausen syndrome by proxy). *Archives of Disease in Childhood,* 69: 625–30.

Boscolo, L., Checcin, G., Hoffman, L. and Penn, P. (1987) *Milan Systemic Family Therapy.* New York: Basic Books.

Bouchel, M. (1994) The protective environment of children: toward a framework for anti-oppressive, cross-cultural and cross-national practice. *British Journal of Social Work,* 24: 173–90.

Browne, D.H. (1986) The role of stress in the commission of subsequent acts of child abuse and neglect. *Journal of Family Violence,* 1: 289–97.

Burford, G. and Hudson, J. (2001) *Family Group Decision Making: New Directions in Community-Centered Child and Family Practice.* New York: Aldine de Gruyter.

Butler, I. and Williamson, H. (1994) *Children Speak: Children, Trauma and Social Work.* Essex: NSPCC-Longman.

Calder, M. and Peake, A. (2001) Evaluating risks and needs: A framework, in M. Calder, A. Peake, and K. Rose (eds) *Mothers of Sexually Abused Children: A Framework for Assessment, Understanding and Support.* Dorset: Russell House Publishing.

Cashmore, J. (2002) Promoting the participation of children and young people in care. *Child Abuse and Neglect,* 26: 837–47.

Cashmore, J. and Paxman, M. (1996) *Wards Leaving Care: A Longitudinal Study.* Sydney: New South Wales Department of Community Services.

Checcin, G., Lane, G. and Ray, W. (1992) *Irreverence: A Strategy for Therapists' Survival.* London: Karnac Books.

Clark, C. (2000) *Social Work Ethics: Politics, Principles and Practice.* London: Macmillan.

Cleaver, H. and Freeman, P. (1995) *Parental Perspectives in Cases of Suspected Child Abuse.* London: HSMO.

Cohen, S. (2001) *States of Denial: Knowing about Atrocities and Suffering.* Cambridge: Polity.

Cohn, A. and Daro, D. (1987) Is treatment too late? What ten years of evaluative research tells us. *Child Abuse and Neglect,* 11: 433–42.

Conte, J., Wolf, S. and Smith, T. (1989) What sexual offenders tell us about prevention strategies. *Child Abuse and Neglect,* 31: 293–301.

Corby, B. (1987) *Working with Child Abuse.* Milton Keynes: Open University Press.

Cousins, C. (2003) Where the explanation doesn't fit the injury: child protection and infant harm. *Child Abuse Prevention Newsletter,* 11(2): 4–13.

Dale, P. (2004) 'Like a fish in bowl': parents' perception of child protection services. *Child Abuse Review* 13: 137–157.

Dale, P., Davies, M., Morrison, T. and Waters, J. (1986) *Dangerous Families: Assessment and Treatment of Child Abuse.* London: Routledge.

Dale, P., Green, R. and Fellows, R. (2002) What really happened? Child protection case management of infants with serious injuries and discrepant parental explanations. *Child Abuse Review,* 11: 296–312.

Dale, P., Green, R. and Fellows, R. (2005) *Child Protection Assessment Following Serious Injuries to Infants: Fine Judgments.* Chichester: John Wiley and Sons.

Dalgleish, L. (1998) *Issues in Risk Assessment: A Motley Assemblage.* Paper presented to the Risk Round Table at the 1998 ISPCAN Congress, Auckland, New Zealand.

Davies, L. and Krane, J. (1996) Shaking the legacy of mother blaming: no easy task for child welfare. *Journal of Progressive Human Services,* 7(2): 3–22.

DePanfilis, D. (2000) How do I develop a helping alliance with the family?, in H. Dubowitz and D. DePanfilis (eds) *Handbook of Child Protection Practice.* Thousand Oaks, CA: Sage.

DePanfilis, D. and Zuravis, S. (1999) Epidemiology of child maltreatment recurrences. *Social Services Review,* 73(2): 218–30.

Department of Health (1995) *Child Protection: Messages from Research.* London: HSMO.

Department of Health (2002) *Learning from Past Experiences – A Review of Serious Case Reviews.* London: The Stationery Office.

de Shazer, S. (1984) The death of resistance. *Family Process,* 14: 79–93.

de Shazer, S. (1991) *Putting Difference to Work.* New York: W.W. Norton.

de Shazer, S. and Berg, I.K. (1995) The brief therapy tradition, in J. Weakland and W. Ray (eds) *Propagations: Thirty Years of Influence from the Mental Research Institute.* New York: Harworth Press.

DHS (Department of Human Services) (1999) *Victorian Risk Framework: A Guided Professional Judgment Approach to Risk Assessment in Child Protection (Version 2.0).* Melbourne: Protection and Care Branch.

Dietz, C. and Craft, J. (1980) Family dynamics of incest: A new perspective. *Social Casework,* 61(10): 602–609.

Dingwall, R., Eekelaar, J. and Murray, T. (1983) *The Protection of Children: State Intervention and Family Life.* Oxford: Blackwell.

Dobash, R.E. and Dobash, R.P. (1992) *Women, Violence and Social Change.* London: Routledge.

Dolan, Y. (1985) *A Path with a Heart: Ericksonian Utilization with Resistant and Chronic Clients.* New York: Brunner Mazel.

Egan, G. (1994) *The Skilled Helper,* 5th edn. Pacific Grove, CA: Brooks/Cole.

Elbow, M. and Mayfield, J. (1991) Mothers of incest victims: villains, victims or protectors? *Journal of Contemporary Human Services,* 72(2): 78–86.

Ellaway, B., Payne, E., Rolfe, K., Dunstan, F., Kemp, A., Butler, I. and Sibert, J. (2004) Are abused babies protected from further abuse? *Archives of Disease in Childhood,* 89: 845–6.

English, D., Marshall, D., Brummel, S. and Orme, M. (1999) Characteristics of repeated referrals to child protective services in Washington State. *Child Maltreatment,* 4(4): 297–307.

Epston, D. (1983) Internalizing discourses versus externalizing discourses, in S. Gilligan and R. Price (eds) *Therapeutic Conversations.* New York: Norton.

Essex, S. and Gumbleton, J. (1999) Similar but different conversations: working with denial in cases of severe child abuse. *Australian and New Zealand Journal of Family Therapy,* 20(3): 139–48.

Essex, S., Gumbleton, J. and Luger, C. (1996) Resolutions: Working with families where responsibility for abuse is denied. *Child Abuse Review,* 5: 191–202.

Essex, S., Gumbleton, J. and Luger, C. (1999) Determining probable abusing carer/ non-abusing carer. *The Incest Survivors' Association Journal,* Autumn: 1–20.

Essex, S., Gumbleton, J., Luger, C. and Luske, A. (1997) A suitable case for treatment. *Community Care,* February: 20–6.

Faller, K.C. (1988) The myth of the 'collusive mother'. *Journal of Interpersonal Violence,* 3(2): 190–6.

Faller, K.C. (1991) What happens to sexually abused children? *Children and Youth Services Review*, 13: 101–11.

Farmer, E. and Owen, M. (1995) *Child Protection Practice: Private Risks and Public Remedies*. London: HMSO.

Farmer, E. and Parker, R. (1991) *Trials and Tribulations: Returning Children from Local Authority Care to their Families*. London: HMSO.

Farmer, E. and Pollock, S. (1998) *Substitute Care for Sexually Abused and Abusing Children*. Chichester: Wiley.

Featherstone, B. (1999) Taking mothering seriously: the implications for child protection. *Child and Family Social Work*, 6: 1–12.

Ferguson, H. (2005) *Protecting Children in Time: Child Abuse, Child Protection and the Consequences of Modernity*. London: Palgrave.

Fisch, R., Weakland, J. and Segal, L. (1982) *Tactics of Change*. San Francisco, CA: Jossey Bass.

Fluke, J., Edwards, M., Bussey, M., Wells, S. and Johnson, W. (2001) Reducing recurrence in child protective services: Impact of a targeted safety protocol. *Child Maltreatment*, 6(3): 207–18.

Fluke, J. and Hollinshead, D. (2003) *Child Abuse Recurrence: A Leadership Initiative of the National Resource Center on Child Maltreatment*. Duluth: National Resource Center on Child Maltreatment. Available at: www.nrccps.org/PDF/MaltreatmentRecurrence.pd

Foucault, M. (1986) The history of sexuality, Vol. 3 (trans. R. Hurley). Harmondsworth: Penguin.

Freud, A. (1966) *The Ego and the Mechanisms of Defense*. London: Hogarth Press.

Fromm, A. (1968) *The Revolution of Hope: Toward a Humanized Technology*. New York: Harper and Row.

Furniss, T. (1991) *The Multi-Professional Handbook of Child Sexual Abuse: Integrated Management, Therapy and Legal Intervention*. London: Routledge.

Gelles, R.J. (2000) Treatment resistant families, in R.M. Reece (ed.) *The Treatment of Child Abuse*. Baltimore, MD: John Hopkins University Press.

Giaretto, H. (1982) *Integrated Treatment of Child Sexual Abuse*. Palo Alto, CA: Science and Behaviour Books.

Gibbons, J., Gallager, B., Bell, C. and Gordon, D. (1995) *Development After Physical Abuse in Childhood*. London: HMSO.

Gilligan, R. (2000) The importance of listening to the child in foster care, in G. Kelly and R. Gilligan (eds) *Issues in Foster Care: Policy, Practice and Research*. London: Jessica Kingsley.

Gumbleton, J. (1997) *Untreatable Families? Working with Denial in Cases of Severe Child Abuse*. Unpublished MSc thesis, University of Bristol.

Gumbleton, J. and Lusk, A. (1999) Child abuse: Rehabilitation without admission – a new way forward. *Family Law*, 29: 822–5.

Gunderson, K. (1998) Pre-conference preparation: an investment in success. *Protecting Children*, 14(4): 11–12.

Haapasalo, J. and Aaltonen, T. (1999) Child abuse potential: how persistent? *Journal of Interpersonal Violence*, 14(6): 571–85.

Haley, J. (1980) *Leaving Home: The Therapy of Disturbed Young People*. New York: McGraw-Hill.

Hammond, K. (1996) *Human Judgment and Social Policy: Irreducible Uncertainty, Inevitable Error, Unavoidable Injustice*. Oxford: Oxford University Press.

Healy, K. (2000) *Social Work Practices: Contemporary Perspectives on Change.* London: Sage.

Hiles, M. (2002) *How Do Parents Explain the Contribution of the Resolutions Programme to their Task in the Parenting and Protection of their Children?* Unpublished Master's thesis, University of Bristol.

Hiles, M., Luger, C. and Rivett, M. (in press) A reflection upon two pieces of qualitative research into the Resolutions approach, which aims to engage with parental denial in child protection cases. *Journal of Systemic Therapy.*

Hill, S. (2005) Partners for protection: A future direction for child protection? *Child Abuse Review,* 14: 347–64.

Hooper, C. (1992) *Mothers Surviving Child Sexual Abuse.* London: Routledge.

Hooper, C. and Humphreys, C. (1998) Women whose children have been abused. *British Journal of Social Work,* 28(4): 565–80.

Hubble, M.A., Duncan, B.L. and Miller, S.D. (1999) *The Heart and Soul of Change.* Washington, DC: American Psychological Association.

Humphreys, C. (1992) Disclosure of child sexual assault: Implications for mothers. *Australian Social Work,* 45(2): 27–35.

Hyde, C., Bentovim, A. and Monck, E. (1995) Some clinical and methodological implications of a treatment outcome study of sexually abused children. *Child Abuse and Neglect,* 19: 1387–99.

Jeffreys, H. and Stevenson, M. (1997) *Statutory Social Work in a Child Protection Agency: Guide for Practice.* Whyalla: University of South Australia.

Jones, D. (1987) The untreatable family. *Child Abuse and Neglect,* 11: 409–20.

Kalichman, S., Craig, M. and Follingstad, D. (1990) Professionals' adherence to mandatory reporting laws: effects of responsibility attribution, confidence ratings and situational factors. *Child Abuse and Neglect,* 14(1): 69–77.

Kelley, S. (1990) Responsibility and management strategies in child sexual abuse: A comparison of child protective workers, nurses and police officers. *Child Welfare,* 56(1): 43–51.

Kempe, R. and Kempe, H. (1978) *Child Abuse.* London: Fontana.

Levy, H. B., Markovic, J., Chaudhry, U., Ahart, S. and Torres, H. (1995) Reabuse rates in a sample of children followed for 5 years after discharge from a child abuse inpatient assessment program. *Child Abuse and Neglect,* 19: 1363–77.

Lipchik, E. (1993) Both/and solutions, in S. Friedman (ed.) *The New Language of Change: Constructive Collaboration in Psychotherapy.* New York: Guildford Press.

Lohrbach, S. (2003) Family group decision making: Partnership-based practice. *Protecting Children,* 18(1 and 2): 12–15.

Lohrbach, S. and Sawyer, R. (2004) Creating a constructive practice: Family and professional partnership in high-risk child protection case conferences. *Protecting Children,* 19(2): 26–35.

Luger, C. (2003) *The Hopes and Expectations of Referrers at the Point of Referral to the Child Protection Consultancy for Work Using the Resolutions Approach.* Unpublished MSc dissertation, Bristol University.

Lupton, C. and Nixon, P. (1999) *Empowering Practice? A Critical Appraisal of the Family Group Conference Approach.* Bristol: The Policy Press.

MacKinnon, L. (1998) *Trust and Betrayal in the Treatment of Child Abuse.* New York: Guildford Press.

MacKinnon, L. and James, K. (1992) Working with 'the welfare' in child at-risk cases, *Australian and New Zealand Journal of Family Therapy,* 13(1): 1–15.

MacKinnon, L. and Miller, D. (1988) The new epistemology and the Milan approach. *Journal of Marriage and Family Therapy*, 13: 139–55.

MacLeod, M. (1996) *Talking with Children about Child Abuse*. London: ChildLine.

Masson, H. and O'Byrne, P. (1990) The family systems approach: A help or hindrance?, in Violence against Children Study Group, *Taking Child Abuse Seriously*. London: Unwin Hyman.

McCullum, S. (1995) *Safe Families: A Model of Child Protection Intervention Based on Parental Voice and Wisdom*, unpublished PhD thesis, Ontario, Canada, Wilfrid Laurier University.

McGee, C. and Westcott, H.L. (1996) System abuse: Towards greater understanding from the perspectives of children and parents. *Child and Family Social Work*, 1(3): 169–80.

Monck, E., Sharland, E., Bentovim, A., Goodall, G., Hyde, C. and Lwin, R. (1996) *Sexually Abused Children: A Descriptive and Treatment Outcome Study*. London: HMSO.

Morrison, T. (1996) Partnership and collaboration: rhetoric and reality. *Child Abuse and Neglect*, 20(2): 127–140.

Munro, E. (1998) Improving social workers' knowledge base in child protection work. *British Journal of Social Work*, 28: 89–105.

Munro, E. (2002) *Effective Child Protection*. London: Sage.

Murphy, J., Bishop, S., Jellinek, M. and Quinn, D. (1992) What happens after the care and protection petition?: Re-abuse in a court sample. *Child Abuse and Neglect*, 11: 433–42.

Parton, N. (1998) Risk, advanced liberalism and child welfare: The need to rediscover uncertainty and ambiguity. *British Journal of Social Work*, 28: 5–27.

Parton, N. (2004) From Maria Colwell to Victoria Climbie: Reflections on public inquiries into child abuse a generation apart. *Child Abuse Review*, 13: 80–94.

Parton, N. (2005) *Safeguarding Childhood in a Late Modern Society: Early Intervention, Surveillance and Individualisation*. London: Palgrave.

Parton, N. and O'Byrne, P. (2000) *Constructive Social Work: Toward a New Practice*. London: MacMillan.

Procter, H. (1981) Family construct psychology: An approach to understanding and treating families, in S. Walrond-Skinner (ed.), *Developments in Family Therapy*. London: Routledge and Kegan Paul.

Proctor, H. and Walker, G. (1988) Brief therapy, in E. Street and W. Dryden (eds) *Family Therapy in Britain*. Milton Keynes: Open University Press.

Putnam, H. (1981) *Reason, Truth and History*. Cambridge: Cambridge University Press.

Reder, P., Duncan, S. and Gray, M. (1993) *Beyond Blame – Child Abuse Tragedies Revisited*. London: Routledge.

Reder, P. and Duncan, S. (2004) Making the most of the Victoria Climbie inquiry report. *Child Abuse Report*, 13: 95–114.

Richards, M.C. (1996) *Opening Our Moral Eye: Essays, Talks, and Poems Embracing Creativity and Community*. New York: Lindisfarne.

Rooney, R.H. (2000) How can I use authority effectively and engage family members?' in H. Dubowitz and D. DePanfilis (eds) *Handbook of Child Protection Practice*. Thousand Oaks, CA: Sage.

Rose, K. and Savage, A. (2000) Living with risk, in A. Wheal (ed.) *Working with Parents: Learning from Other People's Experience*. Dorset: Russell House Publishing.

Rossi, E.L. (1980) *The Collected Papers of Milton Erickson, Vol. 1.* New York: Irvington.

Scott, W. (1993) Group psychotherapy for male sex offenders: Strategic interventions. *Journal of Family Psychotherapy,* 5: 1–20.

Scourfield, J. (2001) Constructing women in child protection work. *Child and Family Social Work,* 6(1): 77–87.

Scourfield, J. (2003) *Gender and Child Protection.* Basingstoke: Palgrave.

Sgroi, S., Blick, L. and Porter, F. (1985) A conceptual framework for child sexual abuse, in S. Sgroi (ed.) *Handbook of Clinical Intervention in Child Sexual Abuse.* Lexington, MA: Lexington Books.

Sharland, E., Jones, D., Aldgate, J., Seal, H. and Croucher, M. (1995) *Professional Intervention in Child Sexual Abuse.* London: HMSO.

Smith, G. (1989) *After Abuse.* London: BAAF.

Smith, G. (1995) Assessing protectiveness in cases of child sexual abuse, in P. Reder and C. Lucey (eds) *Assessment of Parenting: Psychiatric and Psychological Contributions.* London: Routledge.

Teoh, A.H., Laffer, J., Parton, N. and Turnell, A. (2003) Trafficking in meaning: constructive social work in child protection practice, in C. Hall, K. Juhila, N. Parton and T. Pösö (eds) *Client Practice.* London: Jessica Kingsley.

Thoburn, J., Lewis, A. and Shemmings, D. (1995) *Paternalism or Partnership? Family Involvement in the Child Protection Process.* London: HMSO.

Thomas, G. (1995) *Travels in the Trench Between Child Welfare Theory and Practice.* New York: Harworth Press.

Tinling, L. (1990) Perpetuation of incest by significant others: Mothers who do not want to see. *Individual Psychology,* 46(3): 280–97.

Todd, N. and Wade, A. (2004) Coming to terms with violence and resistance: From a language of effects to a language of responses, in D. Pare and T. Strong (eds) *Furthering Talk: Advances in the Discursive Therapies.* New York: Plenum Publishers.

Trotter, C. (1999) *Working with Involuntary Clients.* Sydney: Allen and Unwin.

Trotter, C. (2002) Worker skill and client outcome in child protection. *Child Abuse Review,* 11: 38–50.

Trotter, C. (2004) *Helping Abused Children and their Families.* London: Sage.

Turnell, A. (2004) Relationship-grounded, safety-organised child protection practice: Dreamtime or real-time option for child welfare? *Protecting Children,* 19(2): 14–25.

Turnell, A. (in press) Constructive child protection practice: An oxymoron or news of difference? *Journal of Systemic Therapy.*

Turnell, A. and Edwards, S. (1997) Aspiring to partnership: The signs of safety approach to child protection. *Child Abuse Review,* 6: 179–90.

Turnell, A. and Edwards, S. (1999) *Signs of Safety: A Safety and Solution Oriented Approach to Child Protection Casework.* New York: W.W. Norton.

Turnell A. and Lipchik, E. (1999) Empathy in brief therapy: The essential but overlooked aspect. *Australian and New Zealand Journal of Family Therapy,* 20(4): 177–182.

Walsh, F. (1998) *Strengthening Family Resilience.* New York: Guildford.

Watzlawick, P., Weakland, J.H. and Fisch, R. (1974) *Change: Principles of Problem Formation and Problem Resolution.* New York: Norton.

Welfare, A. (1999) Response to Essex and Gumbleton. *Australian and New Zealand Journal of Family Therapy,* 20(3): 149–51.

Weschler, L. (1997) Basic purposes and justifications, in R. Rotberg and H.J. Steiner (eds) *Truth Commissions: A Comparative Assessment.* Harvard Law School's human rights program: http://www.law.harvard.edu/programs/hrp/Publications/truth1.html#N4T

Westcott, H. (1995) Perceptions of child protection casework: Views from children, parents and practitioners, in C. Cloke and M. Davies (eds) *Participation and Empowerment in Child Protection.* Longman: London.

Westcott, H. and Davies, G.M. (1996) Sexually abused children's and young people's perspectives on investigative interviews. *British Journal of Social Work,* 26: 451–74.

White, J., Essex, S. and O'Reilly, P. (1993) Family therapy systemic thinking and child protection, in J. Carpenter and A. Treacher (eds) *Using Family Therapy in the 90s.* Oxford: Blackwell.

White, M. (1989) *Narrative Means to Therapeutic Ends.* New York: Norton.

Winn, M.E. (1996) The strategic and systemic management of denial in the cognitive/behavioural treatment of sexual offenders. *Sexual Abuse: A Journal of Research and Treatment,* 8(1): 25–36.

INDEX

Page numbers for figures have suffix **f,** those for examples have suffix **e.**